Euroscepticism and the Rising Threat from the Left and Right

Euroscepticism and the Rising Threat from the Left and Right

The Concept of Millennial Fascism

Prebble Q. Ramswell

LEXINGTON BOOKS
Lanham • Boulder • New York • London

Published by Lexington Books
An imprint of The Rowman & Littlefield Publishing Group, Inc.
4501 Forbes Boulevard, Suite 200, Lanham, Maryland 20706
www.rowman.com

Unit A, Whitacre Mews, 26-34 Stannary Street, London SE11 4AB

British Library Cataloguing in Publication Information Available

Library of Congress Cataloging-in-Publication Data Available

ISBN 978-1-4985-4603-4 (cloth : alk. paper)
ISBN 978-1-4985-4604-1 (electronic)

∞™ The paper used in this publication meets the minimum requirements of American National Standard for Information Sciences—Permanence of Paper for Printed Library Materials, ANSI/NISO Z39.48-1992.

Printed in the United States of America

Contents

Acknowledgments vii

1 New Threat, New Era 1

2 The Evolution of Fascism 7

3 Euroscepticism and Its Instrumental Role 15

4 The Case for Millennial Fascism 25

5 Examination of the Threat: Qualification and Determination of Millennial Fascist Groups (MFGs) 39

6 The Rise of MFGs: Theoretical Justification and Selection of Causal Conditions 97

7 The Rise of MFGs: Analysis of Causal Conditions 105

8 The Elements Leading to the Rise of MFGs: Analysis and Discussion of Results 143

9 The Rising Threat of Millennial Fascism and the Ensuing Implications 153

Bibliography 161

Index 191

About the Author 199

Acknowledgments

This book is dedicated to my motherchange, Al-Rue McLaughlin, who always told me I could do anything I wanted to do; and my father, Joe McLaughlin, who gave me his gift (and curse) of not being able to read or write a single sentence without correcting it, as well as his intrigue for fascism. One of my greatest sadnesses is that you are no longer here to share these moments with me. I love you and miss you terribly, though your guidance and support remain with me always.

Briar: Thank you for understanding mommy was doing lots and lots of "homework." You heard too many "in a little while" responses as I tried to squeeze in every spare minute possible to write and research. The good news is—you've got me back!

Tony: I know you often lost me for days at a time when I sequestered myself from life in order to have chunks of time in which I could write. Your support has not only made everything possible, but has also served as a reminder of how much I love you.

Source: Created by the author.

Chapter 1

New Threat, New Era

It was Marcellus who famously remarked to Horatio in Shakespeare's *Hamlet*, "Something is rotten in the state of Denmark." Such sentiment captures the thoughts echoing in the minds of many Europeans as they bear witness to the rise of euroscepticism[1] within member states across the European Union (EU) and the greatly altered European political landscape emerging as a result.

In 1998, scholar Robert Paxton noted fascism's "politics in a new key," evident through much of Europe at the turn of the nineteenth century. This transition was reflected in a changing political environment that emerged as "an assembly of all nationalists who hated the Left and found the Right inadequate." His observations led to this thought-provoking idea:

> We must be able to examine this phenomenon as a system. It is not enough to treat each national case individually, as if each one constitutes a category in itself. If we cannot examine fascism synthetically, we risk being unable to understand this century, or the next. We must have a word, and for lack of a better one, we must employ the word that Mussolini borrowed from the vocabulary of the Italian Left in 1919, before his movement had assumed its mature form. Obliged to use the word fascism, we ought to use it well. (Paxton 1998, 9)

Paxton was clearly on to something. Even to an untrained eye, the sense of great change throughout Europe in the new millennium is palpable and no longer able to be ignored. There is, undoubtedly, a certain "something" occurring in Europe, a certain something that has allowed for the emergence of non-traditional, often right-wing, "fascist," parties in large numbers, with manifestations evident at both the national and international levels.

Speculation abounds. Why is this happening? Why now? Will it last? Scholars, historians, theorists, and politicians alike all have widely varying ideas as to the cause and explanation of the emergence and subsequent success of previously dismissed fascist groups. There is one common thread that can be clearly identified and established: the pervasive presence of nationalism within Eurosceptic groups.

In and of itself, nationalism can be a tremendously positive source of unity, patriotism and, pride, serving to bring people and communities together. However, taken to the extreme, nationalism can be a tool of division and method of exclusion. In 1960, noted British historian Elie Kedourie observed that nationalism was often associated with the radical right and criticized as "an irrational doctrine with a fanatical vision and a propensity towards violence." Other scholars of nationalism such as Tom Nairn underscored the historical link between nationalism and right-wing extremism, highlighting traditional Italian fascism, National Socialism (Nazism), and Japanese militarism.

The negative connotation associated with far-right political parties remains, despite efforts from many groups to distance themselves from violence and repeated denials from others wrongfully accused of perpetrating acts of violence and hate. One example: in 2006, a young member of a family of known Flemish Block[2] militants who shot a child and two women from ethnic minority backgrounds was alleged to have been motivated by racist beliefs; however, Flemish Interest denied any direct or indirect connection to the shootings (Ramalingam 2012).

Throughout Europe, the vast majority of radical right political parties profess to be non-violent. However, there are exceptions, including former British National Party (BNP) member David Copeland, known as the "British nail-bomber," and former BNP candidate Robert Cottage, who was arrested in 2006 for stockpiling weapons (Ramalingam 2012, 2–3).

Yet, many of these nationalist, right-wing groups have been successful in extricating themselves from the pejorative press and public, so much so that they are no longer considered to be "extremist." The uncommon has become common, the disturbing becoming acceptable. Case in point: many of these groups rising in unprecedented numbers and with unprecedented success embrace elements of traditional fascism while avoiding the more damning aspects that would repel the majority of the people they seek to attract.

Historically, fascism has been viewed in many different lights from radical to patriotic, though the pejorative connotation has proven most enduring. Interestingly, the term is considered by many scholars to have been overused to the point of losing its sting. George Orwell wrote in 1944 of how trite the term had become, opining that "the word 'Fascism' is almost entirely meaningless … almost any English person would accept 'bully' as a synonym for 'Fascist.'" Indeed, the new millennium finds society several generations removed from the visceral reaction evoked by World War II era fascism.

The turn-of-the-century wave of fascism, the anti-EU sentiment known as "euroscepticism," and nationalism have strongly resounded with the masses, changing the face of right-wing extremism and rendering it palatable to those who previously deemed it radical and even perverse. Eurosceptic groups have become widely accepted legitimate groups and political parties now making an indelible mark on the political landscape throughout Europe.

What led Europe to this historical shift, moving the populace from a region embracing unity and a European rather than national identity to a public growing evermore wary and disillusioned with the reality of membership in the EU? Instead of a battle of ideas, Leonard et al. (2013) opined that "the EU has been marred by a vicious circle between anti-EU populism and technocratic agreements between member states whom are afraid of their citizens." Regardless of reason, a deeply divisive strand of discontent has led to increasing criticism of the EU and opposition to the process of political European integration, extending throughout the political spectrum. Those citizens and politicians who identify themselves as "skeptical" and critical of the EU have become known as "Eurosceptics" and contend that the EU usurps power from national governments and poses a threat to national sovereignty (EurActiv.com 2013).

This Eurosceptic attitude has steadily increased since the late 1990s, culminating in the emergence and success of numerous Eurosceptic and anti-establishment parties at both the national and international level. Though considered fascist and extremist by many people witnessing their rise, these groups have succeeded in achieving national recognition and mainstream support as their once untraditional ideas have become the norm. Which begs the question: How is it possible that these groups—some of whom do employ traits reminiscent of traditional fascism—have become acceptable?

If historical trajectories of fascism were applied, the current resurgence of right-wing nationalist parties with provocative similarities in traits to traditional fascism would be short-lived, would fail to represent popular belief, and would be incapable of reaching the masses—much less resonating with them. However, we are witnessing a new reality, a world in which these groups have endurance, mainstream popularity, and growing positions of power in Europe. Groups bearing traits of traditional fascism have softened their stance and methods to appeal to larger audiences. The restructured platforms have become palatable when couched within the larger vision of protecting sovereignty and embracing nationalism. These changes resounded with the masses who latched on to the big picture of regaining national pride and protecting citizens. As a result, many of these groups have become successful political parties winning seats in their national elections and in

European Parliament despite their both overt and covert undertones of some traditionally fascist ways of thinking.

Such success has been increasingly underscored, perhaps most notably following the European Parliamentary elections in May 2014. This massive political shake-up was the result of Eurosceptic and anti-establishment parties capturing nearly one-third of the vote. The most remarkable victories occurred in France, with the far-right Front National (FN) taking 25% of the votes, as well as in Britain, where the United Kingdom Independence Party (UKIP) garnered 26.8% (Wagner and Nagy, 2015). The momentum was so strong that an August 2014 poll indicated that FN leader Marine Le Pen would have won the French presidential election had it been held at that time (Hallett, 2014).

The success is not limited to England and France. The anti-immigrant Danish People's Party won in Denmark; the far-right Jobbik came in second in Hungary; and Germany saw its first neo-Nazi member elected to parliament (*Economist* May 2014). Al Jazeera noted that "Golden Dawn, a former neo-Nazi organisation whose leader and members are to face trial for criminal acts including murder, arson and extortion, will send three representatives to the European parliament … Austria's far-right Freedom Party advanced to take 20 percent of the vote with an anti-immigrant campaign that called for halving Vienna's EU contributions and demanded a referendum on the EU's crucial bailout fund" (Al Jazeera May 26, 2014).

The startling results from the European Parliament 2014 elections clearly demonstrated Europe's swing to the right and led to an affirmation by socialist French prime minister Manuel Valls that the situation was equivalent to "a political earthquake." In an interview with the British newspaper the *Guardian*, UKIP leader Nigel Farage said the result justified the description of an earthquake because "never before in the history of British politics has a party, seen to be an insurgent party, ever topped the polls in a national election" and voters had "delivered about the most extraordinary result that has been seen in British politics for 100 years" (Wintour and Watt 2014). The election was a clear indicator of the loss of trust in the EU and its institutions and the impact of the rise of the Eurosceptics.

Concern had begun mounting several years prior, and preventative measures began being discussed. In 2008, Eurosceptic momentum had prompted the EU assembly's political establishment to pursue changes that would have altered the rules allowing Members of European Parliament (MEP) to form political groupings (Waterfield 2008). The attempt was foiled only months later when voters solidly rejected the ratification of the Treaty of Lisbon, the international agreement forming the constitutional basis of the EU. In a foreshadowing of things to come, by November 2014, it was reported that as many as 200 Conservative Members of Parliament (MP)[3] were prepared to call for Britain to leave the EU in an escalation of pressure on David Cameron over Europe and immigration (Merrick 2015).

The impact of these groups is undeniable and has led to a number of scholarly attempts seeking to properly define, describe, and categorize the ideas they embrace. Among the labels scholars have proposed for these groups in the past several years are neo-populism, radical right-wing populism, ethno-nationalism, and populist nationalism. Each of these terms is certainly applicable, but a greater takeaway is what the various potential classifications tell us: that the anomaly we are experiencing is a combination of multiple ideologies. As such, it proves the point that there is a need for one new term to properly identify these groups, recognizing that they are distinct from others, yet with roots within these others. Identification as solely "radical right-wing populism" or "neo-populism" would be erroneous. Thus, in the new millennium, the EU, once held as a harbinger of hope and source of a European unity and identity, has now become a despised enemy—the source of stolen nationalism, culture, and tradition. Peripheral groups of the far right and left have now emerged as the voices of moderation, attempting to forge a path to a Europe reflective of the union they had envisioned, a Europe that at once embraces national and European identity without a loss of economic and political sovereignty. These groups are resilient, competent, rational, and, above all, successful. They epitomize a new form of extremism and fascism—fascism not in a strict, traditional sense in the vein of Benito Mussolini or Adolf Hitler, but rather in the sense of a central authority advocating nationalism and identifying specific intolerances that threaten that nationalism. It is an evolved fascism, fascism in the modern era, fascism through the lens of euroscepticism; it is *Millennial Fascism*: the reinterpretation and new iteration of the ideology that propelled Mussolini and Hitler to infamy.

NOTES

1. It should be noted that "euroscepticism" and its various derivatives can alternatively be spelled using a "k" instead of a "c" as in "euroskepticism." Factors such as location and language contribute to the variance.

2. The Flemish Block is known in Belgium as the Vlaams Blok or VB. They were a Belgian far-right and secessionist political party with an anti-immigration platform. The group was strongly nationalist and sought the independence of northern Belgium, known as Flanders. In November 2004, the group instituted several changes to address charges of racism and changed its name to Vlaams Belang, or Flemish Interest.

3. By definition, MEPs are Members of European Parliament and MPs are members of the British Parliament.

Chapter 2

The Evolution of Fascism

The concept of fascism as evolutionary is by no means new or novel, yet defining the word is a far more difficult task than one would imagine. In 1944, writer George Orwell posed a compelling and enduring question: "Of all the unanswered questions of our time, perhaps the most important is: 'What is Fascism?'" It is a question that continues to perplex scholars and historians alike as deeper analysis generates more questions than answers. Also playing a role is the competing perception of fascism as an artifact of the twentieth century and the idea of its continued presence in a distilled form. Observed prominent fascism scholar Roger Griffin (2003): "Every attempt made by a non-Marxist scholar since the 1920s to offer a way out of the conceptual labyrinth posed by fascism seemed only to have enlarged and complicated it further, with the result that historians attempting to study aspects of the generic phenomenon 'ideographically' were generally at a loss as to which 'expert' to turn for a working definition."

Fascism has consistently been viewed by scholars through a traditional lens. This view neatly packages fascist groups within one of three categories: fascist, neo-fascist, and neo-Nazist. This is the perspective that continues to overshadow the idea that fascism could exist in an evolved form. It is important to consider that no matter the ideology, there are variances and offshoots existing within in it. As only one example, consider the differences in the Republican Party from its original inception to its current iteration. The differences are profound. Viewing fascism through the singular scope of Mussolini or Hitler would be a mistake. It, too, has evolved, its nature and composition has changed, necessitating—it is argued—a new conceptual perspective.

TRADITIONAL LENS

Fascism has long been studied but the literature tends to focus on classifying groups within its existing categories. In an effort to sidestep the problem of answering the question "what is fascism," scholars have attempted to develop a consensus definition. The concept of "generic fascism" developed from a need to identify and concisely define the shared essential elements of fascism. Attempting brevity, Nolte (1968) proposed the concept of a "fascist minimum"—a succinct, concise definition of fascism. This led to what would become Griffin's infamous three-word definition, "palingenetic populist ultra-nationalism." In efforts to establish a singular, comprehensive definition, scholars in the field have tended to take one of two paths: one focusing on cause and viewed through a political and institutional lens (Sternhell, Gentile, Paxton); or the path referred to as the "new consensus" which often takes a more culturalist and ideological approach (Griffin, Iordachi, Payne, Kallis, Eatwell). Other scholars, such as Renton (1999), tweak the two perspectives such that there is a distinction between those who view fascism primarily in terms of its ideas, such as Griffin, Payne, and Sternhell, and those who define fascism through the actual practice of Mussolini's Italy or Hitler's Germany. Still, others utilize a dividing line based on Marxist versus non-Marxist perspectives.

Paxton (1998) noted that Pierre Milza (1987) presented a four-stage model of fascism; Philippe Burrin (1986) traced the itineraries by which Jacques Doriot, Marcel De´at, and Gaston Bergery, steering between blockages and opportunities, shifted from the left to fascism. Indeed, Paxton (1998) observed that most recent authors seek some "fascist essence." Rejecting any mono-causal or reductionist theory, Payne (1995) presented the "elements of a retrodictive theory of fascism" that applied to movements and regimes; Laqueuer (1997) found fascism similar to pornography in that "it is difficult—perhaps impossible—to define in an operational, legally valid way," yet still presented "the essence of fascism."

All of these studies have systematically laid the foundation and provided evidence indicating that fascism has various types and is of varying degrees. Fascism in and of itself cannot be singularly defined; as such, it behooves us to identify those characteristics within it that remain consistent.

As we turn to the idea of this twenty-first-century iteration of fascism, consider the theory posed by Paxton. In 1998, Paxton maintained that "fascism is the most original political novelty of the twentieth century, no less. It successfully gathered, against all expectations, in certain modern nations, such as Germany and Italy, which had seemed firmly planted on a path to gradually expanding democracy, a popular following around hard, violent, anti-liberal and antisocialist nationalist dictatorships." Further, it then "spread its 'politics in a new key' through much of Europe, assembling all nationalists who hated the Left and found the Right inadequate" (Paxton 1998). His thoughts, though originally directed at turn of the nineteenth-century issues were eerily prescient of circumstances at the end of the twentieth century.

The seminal works in the field of fascism have stemmed from three primary scholars: Stanley G. Payne, Griffin, and Paxton. As the foundational theorists in the field of fascism, these authors are a necessary component of any work done in the field. Of course, there are many other authors who have contributed engaging and provocative work and who will also be explored. A central tenet of the concept of Millennial Fascism is that fascism has evolved. To determine its evolution, it is necessary to explore all aspects of it as a solid basis is built for the necessity of a new form of fascism.

In 1995, Payne created a lengthy itemized list of characteristics to identify fascism. This typology is regularly cited as the standard descriptor of fascism and is built upon ideas he presented in *Fascism: Comparison and Definition* (1980). Payne presented these elements as "a wide-spectrum description" comprised of three main components that embody the idea of fascism (Table 2.1).

Payne posited that the fascist "style" included such traits as its emphasis on violence, its exaltation of men above women and its positive evaluation of the young against the old (Renton 1999, 20). He also espoused the intellectual caliber of fascist thought with focus on the psychological and sociological aspects, as did historian Zeev Sternhell (1980, 1995). Sternhell (1995) argued that fascism first emerged in France during the 1880s and 1890s as a concept borne of intellectuals and artists such as Drumont, Peguy, Barrès, and Maurras. This first incarnation of fascism began as a rejection of the idea that reason could be used to understand society and resulted in the formation of a "new generation of intellectuals [which] rose violently against the rationalist individualism of liberal society" (Sternhell, 1995).

Building on Payne's typology, Dimitri Kitsikis (1988) offered a typology of fascism comprised of 13 categories in which fascist ideologies, movements, and establishments could be analyzed and contrasted with others. Kitsikis (1988) echoed Payne's observations but created a shorter list of values he felt were most relevant:

- The idea of class and the importance of agrarianism;
- Private ownership, the circulation of money, the regulation of the economy by the state, the idea of ethnic bourgeois class, economic self-sufficiency;
- The nation and the difference between nation and state;
- The attitude toward democracy and political parties;
- The importance of political heroes, that is, the charismatic leader;
- The attitude toward tradition;
- The attitude toward the individual and society;

Table 2.1 Payne's Typology of Fascism

The Fascist Goals (Ideology and Goals):	• Espousal of an idealist, vitalist, and voluntaristic philosophy, normally involving the attempt to realize a new modern, self-determined, and secular culture; • Creation of a new nationalist authoritarian state not based on traditional principles or models; • Organization of a new highly regulated, multiclass, integrated national economic structure, whether called national corporatist, national socialist, or national syndicalist; • Positive evaluation and use of, or willingness to use violence and war; and • The goal of empire, expansion, or a radical change in the nation's relationship with other powers.
The Fascist Negations:	• Anti-liberalism; • Anticommunism; and • Anticonservatism (though with the understanding that fascist groups were willing to undertake temporary alliances with other sectors, more commonly with the right).
The Fascist Style (Style and Organization):	• Specific tendency toward an authoritarian, charismatic, personal style of command, whether or not the command is to some degree initially elective; • Attempted mass mobilization with militarization of political relationships and style and with the goal of a mass single-party militia; • Emphasis on aesthetic structure of meetings, symbols, and political liturgy, stressing emotional and mystical aspects; • Extreme stress on the masculine principle and male dominance, while espousing a strongly organic view of society; • Exaltation of youth above other phases of life, emphasizing the conflict of the generations, at least in effecting the initial political transformation.

Note: From Payne, Stanley. *A History of Fascism 1914–45;* London: University College London Press, 1995; and Payne, Stanley. *Fascism: Comparison and Definition*, University of Wisconsin Press; p. 7; 1980.

- The attitude toward equality and hierarchy;
- The attitude toward women;
- The attitude toward religion;
- The attitude toward rationalism;
- The attitude toward intellectualism and elitism; and
- The attitude toward the Third World. (Kitsikis 1988).

Arguably the most seminal work in the field of fascism comes from Griffin (1991), who posited that fascism was best understood as a series of propositions or "myths." In 1991, Griffin began what he called an "odyssey" to unveil what he termed the "fascist minimum." He conceded to "the realization that there is no mysterious essence waiting to be discovered which will constitute the 'fascist minimum,'" and contended that "the 'fascist minimum' had to be invented 'not discovered 'through a process of 'idealizing abstraction,'" (Griffin 2003).

Griffin is perhaps best known for his theory of "palingenetic ultranationalism" which holds that fascism is defined by its core myth, namely that of national rebirth, or *palingenesis*. He believed fascism was anti-liberal, anti-conservative, charismatic, anti-rational, socialist, totalitarian, racist, and eclectic. He also suggested that fascism emerged when a nation perceived itself to be in crisis. Dave Renton (1999) observed that Griffin, however, moved beyond Payne, arguing that there was one single thread which linked this common "mythic core": nationalism.

Paxton (1998) contended that there were five major difficulties undermining any effort to define fascism: a problem of timing; the problematic role of mimicry in defining fascism; the problem with defining fascism posed by the dauntingly wide disparity among individual cases in space and in time; the ambiguous relationship between doctrine and action in fascism; and the overuse/misuse of the word. Indeed, Paxton believed that the word "fascist" had become the most banal of epithets (1998).

Paxton is widely recognized for isolating five stages of fascism, each utilizing very different sociopolitical processes: (1) the initial creation of fascist movements, (2) their rooting as parties in a political system, (3) the acquisition of power, (4) the exercise of power, and (5) radicalization or entropy (Paxton 1998). Quite logically, he asserted that since different kinds of historical processes are involved in each stage, different scholarly strategies must be utilized in the analysis of each (Paxton 1998). Such perspective has far-reaching significance, particularly in conjunction with euroscepticism.

In his 1995 essay "Ur Fascism," philosopher Umberto Eco used the term "Ur-fascism" (or eternal fascism) as a generic description of different historical forms of fascism. Eco also enumerated 14 general properties of fascist ideology, arguing the impossibility of organizing these elements into a coherent system (1995). However, he also contended that it was "enough that one of them be present to allow fascism to coagulate around it" (Eco 1995). Observed Eco:

> Fascism became an all-purpose term because one can eliminate from a fascist regime one or more features, and it will still be recognizable as fascist. Take away imperialism from fascism and you still have Franco and Salazar. Take away colonialism and you still have the Balkan fascism of the Ustashes. Add to the Italian fascism a radical anti-capitalism (which never much fascinated Mussolini) and you have Ezra Pound. Add a cult of Celtic mythology and the Grail mysticism (completely alien to official fascism) and you have one of the most respected fascist gurus, Julius Evola. (Eco 1995)

In 1963, German historian and scholar Ernst Nolte published what many scholars consider to be the magnum opus of fascism. Released in English in 1965 as *The Three Faces of Fascism*, Nolte argued that fascism arose as a form of resistance to and a reaction against modernity. Further, he asserted that fascism functioned at three levels: in the world of politics as a form of opposition to Marxism, at the sociological level in opposition to bourgeois values, and in the "metapolitical" world as "resistance to transcendence" (Nolte 1965, 537). Scholars, such as Griffin (1998), acknowledged Nolte's work as "a seminal contribution to the creation of a theory of generic fascism based on a history of ideas, as opposed to the previous class-based analyses that had characterized both Marxist and liberal interpretations of fascism."

Renton (1999) posited that the interpretations offered by scholars in the field of fascism clearly diverged. Indeed, Griffin (1995) argued that fascism and Nazism are different from one another, though at the same time linked, through a common mythic core. However, Sternhell (1995) maintained that National Socialist German chancellor Adolf Hitler "was not fascist" and that, despite such differences, there were far more significant areas in which the historians agreed. For example, Roger Eatwell, Griffin, Sternhell, and Payne all adhere to the concept of an "ideal type," derived from Max Weber. Renton (1999) observed that they generated an "ideal" fascist by presenting a list of carefully selected ideas of fascism from which they then constructed a "fascist minimum." If a group or individual adhered to the greater number of these fascist ideas, then the adherent himself was fascist (Renton 1999, 22).

Much literature rightly focuses on the negative connotation of the word "fascism." Sakai (2002) observed that some people still believe fascism is simply extreme white racism. One recurrent theme was the idea that in order to be racist, one had to be white. Indeed, Sakai noted the insanity of the concept that fascism was a unique idea that could only lodge in the brain of members of a single race. Other scholars echoed the 1920s European belief that fascism was "a tool of the ruling class … violent thugs in comic opera uniforms doing repression for their capitalist masters" (Sakai 2002). More often than not, both views overlap and are held simultaneously. As a result, Sakai opined that we "know" fascism, but in reality we don't know it yet. Indeed, "once reclothed, not spouting old fascist European political philosophy, fascism walks right by us and we don't recognize it at first" (Sakai 2002). Such views serve to highlight the reasons why fascism needs to be viewed in a "new light."

MODERN LENS: NEW POLITICS, NEW SCHOOL OF THOUGHT

Scholars have focused on various aspects within the existing paradoxical confines and breadth of fascism, often with significant overlap or no logical placement whatsoever—a significant reason in itself to propose and refine parameters for a modern form of fascism. Groups and parties of the twenty-first century have a very different world in which to operate with multiple tools in their proverbial toolboxes to facilitate their operation.

In 1993, Emilio Gentile published a highly regarded book on fascism underscoring his conviction that "Italian fascism was more than just the use of force, that it achieved a form of consensus." Gentile combined the idea of myth and consensus as a single concept with "the fascist stress on externalities, both on a lower (in the realm of 'culturalist' studies) and on a higher (the masses as the aesthetic, active element in the creation of consensus) level, with an analysis of the cultic character of Italian fascist mass society … he sees fascism as action, as theater" (Nelis 2006). In 2000, Gentile discussed the fall of fascism and how the world was witness to a "de-totalitarization" of fascism that was "reduced, in totalitarian theories, to a kind of authoritarian regime or even to a personal dictatorship, a 'mussolinism.'" Gentile observed that during the 1990s, a new side of the problem of fascist totalitarianism had risen via an "expanding range of research on fascism to areas long remained unexplored by historians, such as ideology, the party, the regime, the system of rites and symbols of fascism intended as a political religion" (Gentile 2000, 6).

In 1999, Erol Kaymak argued for an alternative classification for the rising number of right-wing populist parties. He observed that some neo-populist parties had been successful at exploiting resentment among a growing number of unaligned voters. What differentiated neo-populist parties from their supposed forerunners, Kaymak argued, was their distinct ability to mobilize the voters' resentment (Kaymak 1999). Unlike neo-fascist parties, he argued, successful neo-populist parties appealed to heterogeneous groups; a populist style, including scapegoating common enemies, real or imaginary, helped keep the disparate coalitions together (Kaymak 1999). The organizational attributes of successful neo-populist parties, centralized authority, and charismatic leadership, not only distinguished neo-populist parties as a unique party type, but also accounted for their success and appeal (Kaymak 1999). Kaymak's findings implied that growing disenchantment with institutions of authority actually served to increase the support of neo-populist parties. Such findings are relevant to this examination of fascism in that they indicate the significance of discontent and institutions (structural integrity), particularly in France, Germany, Italy, and Norway. Like Paxton, Kaymak noted an atmosphere of impending change. Indeed, the growth and success of neo-populist parties and right-wing nationalist groups such as England's UKIP, France's Front National, and Hungary's Jobbik has increased exponentially.

As discussed briefly above, Paxton observed fascism's "politics in a new key" throughout Europe in the late nineteenth century (1998). He theorized that this "new form of politics" was the creation of the "first popular movements dedicated to reasserting the priority of the nation against all forms of internationalism or cosmopolitanism." He observed that the 1880s—with its simultaneous economic depression and broadened democratic practice—was a crucial threshold (Paxton 1998). Undeniably, the world was about to enter into a significant time of change, an era that would see world war and fascism at an unprecedented level. Paxton's identification of a new form of politics riding on the heels of depression and expanded liberalism is not only highly perceptive, it is wholly applicable to the changes in Europe's political landscape in the twenty-first century as a result of the rise of euroscepticism.

Chapter 3

Euroscepticism and its Instrumental Role

Defining the word "Eurosceptic" is almost as problematic as finding a universally accepted definition of fascism. Perhaps the most simplistic definition of Eurosceptic would be someone who is skeptical of the EU. However, not only would that be an inadequate definition, in some cases it could be erroneous.

Many scholars who study euroscepticism have focused their research on categorizing the degree of euroscepticism, developing typologies based on a variety of factors. It is my opinion that, for purposes of classification and consideration as a Millennial Fascist Group (MFG), no further distinction is necessary. It was Paxton who, in 2005, pointed to the "latent (but misleading) Darwinian convention that if we study the origins of something, we grasp its inner blueprint" (2005). This observation leads to an acknowledgment of a need for a macro-level study into a theoretical explanation for euroscepticism. Indeed, the aspects of euroscepticism utilized to further deconstruct parties, such as exit strategy, primary source of euroscepticism and goals, do not detract from the core tenet held by them all—a growing intolerance for and dissatisfaction with the EU and a desire to change many of the policies they have enacted.

In fact, the degrees of euroscepticism presented by various scholars (*hard, soft, reject, phobe, enthusiast*) are found comparable to factions within existing parties. For example, in the United States, members of the Republican Party often hold very divisive views depending on their stance as a conservative, moderate or libertarian. These perspectives and ideals have changed significantly since its inception in the mid-1800s. Further, members hold a variety of perspectives on the same issues. As a result, members are often subcategorized based on foundational leanings, such as fiscally conservative or socially conservative. The bottom line remains—each party member still identifies with and considers himself a Republican, despite often significant differences in beliefs. In fact, recent analyses of the Conservative Party in England have "identified a spectrum of Eurosceptic views ranging from outright withdrawal to those who accept the status quo but object to further integration" (Lynch and Whitaker 2012).

The genesis of euroscepticism is firmly entrenched within the EU during the late 1980s and early 1990s. However, determining whether this skepticism originated within and/or as a direct result of the European Parliament, the Economic and Monetary Union (EMU), the establishment of the Schengen area, or from any other of a myriad of possibilities is a source of ongoing debate often resulting in the answer "It depends."

It is no secret that as the EU grew increasingly authoritative, it also became more contentious (Albert, 1992; Crouch and Streeck, 1997; Hooghe and Marks, 1999; Rhodes and Van Apeldoorn, 1997). Eichenberg and Dalton (2007) noted that the signing of the Treaty of Maastricht in 1993[1] evoked concerns regarding the proper parameters of integration (Hooghe and Marks 2007). Indeed, scholars have noted that "social movements, along with political parties and the public began to pay serious attention. A new political front of contestation was opened between those seeking to protect their communities from the disruptive forces of globalization and European integration and those supporting integration" (Hooghe and Marks 2007). Asserted Walsh (2014), founded in the wake of World War II, "the EU was a self-conscious rejection of nationalism."

Though the modern iteration of the EU was borne from the Maastricht Treaty, the EU traces its roots to the aftermath of World War II. Observed Sliwinski (2015):

> With the continent in ruins, several representatives from leading nations attempted to finally find some way to unify the region and put an end to the seemingly endless fighting that had just led to the most destructive war the world has ever known. The process started with the European Coal and Steel Community in 1951, with six founding members whom agreed to merge their coal and steel production: West Germany, France, Italy, Belgium, Luxembourg, and the Netherlands. The foundation was further solidified with the Treaty of Rome in 1957, which created the European Economic Community (EEC). In 1967, the European Parliament was created and had its first direct elections in 1979; in 1993, the European Union was codified through the Treaty of Maastrich. (Sliwinski 2015)

European Parliament (EP) has a unique composition. An MEP is elected via national vote. Once elected, MEPs either join one of the existing cross-national political groups (eight as of March 2016) or choose to be unattached and identify as a "Non-Inscrit" (NI). These groups differ from national parties in that they consist of members from several different parties from different member states. MEPs are able to (and often do) switch groups during their term. EP was founded on June 23, 1953, as the Christian-Democratic Group in the Common Assembly of the European Coal and Steel Community (ECSC) (CVCE 2015). The ECSC established several supranational institutions, including the High Authority, the Council of Ministers, the Assembly, and the Court of Justice. The six founding countries (the Federal Republic of Germany, France, Italy, Belgium, Luxembourg, and the Netherlands) formally decided to sit together in the assembly according to political affiliation, rather than in national delegations (Fontaine 2010). This tradition carried on as the assembly evolved into its modern iteration as European Parliament comprised of 27 European countries with 500 million inhabitants.

Since 1979, members have been directly elected by the citizens of the member states. This first election resulted in seven groups and several non-attached members. Following the second enlargement of the EU and national developments leading to the realignment of political groups within EP, the number of groups peaked at 10 in 1989. Subsequent elections saw this number start to fall, returning to its 1979 level in 2004 (European Parliament 2015). According to European Communities (2009), since 2004, several enlargements of the EU and increasing fragmentation of national partisan systems during European elections—particularly in France, the UK, and Italy—have caused a threefold increase in the number of national parties with elected representatives. In 2008, 185 parties were represented in the European Parliament, however, despite one or two fluctuations, the number of groups has remained constant (European Communities 2009). Consequently, the ratio of groups to parties has steadily risen over the years to stand at 26.4:1 in 2008, compared with 7.7:1 in 1979 (European Communities 2009). The 8th EP, elected in 2014, resulted in the highest number of Eurosceptic MEPs in history.

Though Paxton's observation of a "new form of politics" was made in connection to the political atmosphere at the turn of the nineteenth century, it is equally applicable a century later in conjunction with the burgeoning euroscepticism that has changed the political environment in Europe. The European Parliamentary elections in May 2014 resulted in an influx of far-right and far-left Eurosceptic and Euroreject parties, which now form approximately 27% of the assembly. Observed Siddi (2014) in *EU-Watch*, "Overall, populist, right-wing and far-right parties are much more strongly represented in the new European Parliament: the Europe of Freedom and Direct Democracy (EFD) group has 48 seats (17 more than in 2009), while the number of non-attached members—who are almost exclusively representatives of the xenophobic far right—rose from 33 to 52." Following the 2014 EP elections, the *Economist* reported: "Anti-establishment parties [now] control nearly one-third of the parliament. Beyond the victories of the

Eurosceptics in France and Britain, the anti-immigrant Danish People's Party won in Denmark, the far-right Jobbik came second in Hungary and Germany has its first neo-Nazi MEP" (5/31/2014).

However, the formation of the Europe of Nations and Freedom (ENF) in 2015, led to significant shuffle. As of March 2016, EFD lost three members, dropping to 45; the Non-Inscrits (NI) dropped to 15; and the newly formed Eurosceptic ENF grew to 38 members (European Parliament 2016).

In 2016, nationalists and Eurosceptics accounted for approximately one-third of MEPs in the 751-seat European Parliament. Prior to the creation of EFD, most sat as NIs, or joined one of the existing political groupings, which provides extended funding options and allocated time allotments for speaking (Wagner-Nagy 2015). The largest cluster of Eurosceptics was previously found in the EFD group. This 48-member (45 in 2016) Eurosceptic group is led by Nigel Farage of UKIP and is dominated by UKIP and the Italian Five Star Movement. The other nations in the alliance, Czech Republic, France, Lithuania, Poland, and Sweden, contribute only one or two representatives each (Wagner-Nagy 2015).

The next largest grouping of Eurosceptics had been found in the "far more eurocritical than eurosceptical" European United Left–Nordic Green Left (GUE–NGL—52 seats) and the European Conservatives and Reformists (ECR—70 seats), respectively left and right of the political spectrum (Poli and Rosselli 2014). The 21 French Front National MEPs and the handful of Hungarian Jobbik and Greek Golden Dawn MEPs are NIs.

Several anti-establishment parties won their first seats in parliament, including Beppe Grillo's Five Star Movement (Italian) and Germany's Alternative für Deutschland (AfD). Bruneau (2014) observed that, following the elections, there were 65 newly elected members who joined a political group, and 41 others declared as NIs; therefore, there are "more than 100 MEPs and 14% of European Parliament who can influence the direction of new policy over the next five years. It is certain to be a very vocal minority."

It did not take long for the "very vocal minority" to form its own group. Reported the *New Observer*, "The Europe of Nations and Freedom was launched on June 15, 2015, after extended negotiations between the French National Front (FN), the Dutch Party for Freedom (PVV), the Italian Lega Nord (LN), the Freedom Party of Austria (FPÖ), Belgium's Vlaams Belang (VB), and the Polish Congress of the New Right (KNP) … the 36-strong group gained two additional members when former UK Independence Party member Janice Atkinson, and former Conservative Party of Romania (Partidul Conservator, PC) member Laurentiu Rebega, joined in their private capacities" (2016). As a result, EP now consists of eight political groups: European People's Party–European Democrats (EPP–ED); Party of European Socialists (PES); Alliance of Liberals and Democrats for Europe (ALDE);

Union for Europe of the Nations (UEN); The Greens–European Free Alliance (Greens–EFA); European United Left–Nordic Green Left (GUE–NGL); Independence/Democracy (IND/DEM); Europe of Nations and Freedom (ENF); and the Non-Inscrits (NI).

At the local level, results are even more impressive. The March 2015 French elections gave the French extreme-right party Front National the highest percentage of votes it had ever achieved in a local election (Pezard 2015). With 26% of the votes, the Front National staunchly confirmed that it is in the ascendant and its leader, Marine Le Pen, stands well-positioned as a strong contender in France's presidential elections in 2017 (Pezard 2015).

Interestingly, England's UKIP fell surprisingly short in the April 2015 UK local elections. Predicted to take upwards of 18 seats, the party succeeded in only earning two. Did the "loss" signify a loss in popularity and the beginning of a downward spiral? Quite the opposite. The voting results were indicative of UKIP's widespread appeal in the UK, and highlight the important fact that their popularity is not limited to a few districts. They won 14% of the vote in England (and 12.6% across the UK); they finished second in more than 120 seats and won 20% in at least 45 seats; and, in total, the party accrued approximately four million votes—as many votes as the Scottish National Party, Plaid Cymru, and the Liberal Democrats combined (Black 2015).

In May 2014, the *Economist* emphatically declared that "the blunt reality is that Europe's political fault-line is shifting: from left versus right, to pro-Europeans against anti-Europeans. This election night belongs to the likes of Marine Le Pen, who has polished the Front National [National Front] in France and trounced both the centre-right UMP party and the Socialist Party of President François Hollande. Further, they acknowledge that the Euroskeptics now have political momentum." Indeed, governments in Britain and France face an acute dilemma regarding how they should respond, and the likelihood is that they will harden their stance on a host of issues, particularly immigration and EU enlargement; pressure will rise for EU powers to be repatriated (*Economist* May 2014). Further muddying of the waters in the UK was the July 2014 appointment of outspoken Eurosceptic Phillip Hammond as foreign secretary in what many observers called "a major cabinet reshuffle."

But euroscepticism was not a construct of the 2014 Parliamentary elections. The 2005 referenda defeats in France and Holland for the proposed treaty establishing a European Constitution were widely interpreted in EU studies as signaling a major dislocation between political elites and the wider population of citizens (Fossum and Trenz 2006). Wellings (2014) reported that the "Future of England" surveys, published by the Institute for Public Policy Research (IPPR) in 2012 and 2013, were the first to note a link between "Englishness and Euroscepticism":

> The first point they discovered was that Englishness had become politicised, mostly since 2007, and was a vehicle for a variety of political grievances. The second point was that the British were not Eurosceptic, but that the English were. In other words, among those who identified as "British not English," 45% thought that UK membership of the EU was a good thing, but this figure dropped to 14% for those who identified as "English not British."

Scholars offer a variety of causes as explanation for the surge in Eurosceptic parties. Many cite economic causes and soaring unemployment (Sliwinski 2015; Eichenberg and Dalton 1993; Gabel 1998; Marks and Steenbergen 2004; Brown 2015; McLaren 2002); others point to a loss of nationalism and identity (Hooghe, Huo, and Marks 2007; Halikiopoulou et. al. 2012; Brown 2015; McLaren 2002; Lochocki 2014); still others cite socio-economic, socio-cultural, and political factors, pointing to the relationship between low education and euroscepticism (Hooghe and Marks 2005; Loveless and Rohrschneider 2008; Lubbers and Jaspers 2011; Lochocki 2014).

Studies have sought an explanation for the success of some far-right groups and not others, when conditions appear similar. Golder (2003, 433) observed that empirical studies investigating the variation in the success of these parties have quite often produced inconsistent results. For example, Golder noted that some studies find that immigration matters (Anderson 1996; Knigge 1998; Martin 1996), others find that it does not (Mayer and Perrineau 1989). Others have found that it only matters in some countries (Givens 2000). Further, as Golder acknowledged in 2003, the same inconsistent results can be found for unemployment and electoral institutions. Jackman and Volpert (1996) argued that electoral thresholds influenced the support for extreme-right parties, whereas Swank and Betz (1996) provided evidence to the contrary. Knigge (1998) claimed that unemployment reduced support for extreme-right parties, though Jackman and Volpert (1996) concluded the opposite. Lewis-Beck and Mitchell (1993) stated that the effect of unemployment depended on the level of immigration (Golder 2003), yet Sliwinski (2015) argued that what has led to this rise is how economic problems are perceived as being compounded by immigration. Sliwinski noted, in particular, that in the EU the youth unemployment rate as a whole was 23%; in Greece it had risen as high as 60%. Thus, studies reveal contradictory information and mixed results.

In 2008, White cited "cleavage theory," a common analytical perspective in the EU literature, as the causal factor of euroscepticism. Lochocki (2014) observed that "studies have identified two components that make right-populists' programs appealing to voters: they offer an agenda of neo-nationalism, combined with an opportunity to cast a protest vote expressing general dissatisfaction with the political establishment … their programs combine 'neo-nationalism' with 'anti-elitism': for the nation, against the political establishment." In doing so, he believed, they blame the established, moderate parties for any *alleged* social change—primarily caused by globalization—brought upon the *alleged* homogenous community of the nation (Lochocki 2014). Indeed, Lochocki (2014) posited that prime threats were generally symbolized by immigration and multiculturalism as much as the influence of the EU on daily life (Ivarsflaten 2008; Arzheimer 2009; Ellinas 2010; Yilmaz 2012).

Analyses of citizens' attitudes toward the EU have consistently identified a mass-elites divide or an "elite-mass opinion incongruence," one Bertoncini and Koenig (2014) believed lent itself to the idea that so-called "populist" discourses usually reject European integration.

In an effort to better explain the many dimensions of euroscepticism, many scholars have chosen to focus on the differences between Eurosceptic groups. The subsequent research led to a flurry of manuscripts heavily focused on typologies. Taggart and Szczerbiak (2001) presented the concept of hard versus soft euroscepticism, with hard euroscepticism defined as the opposition to membership of, or the existence of, the EU as a matter of principle. Szczerbiak (2008) selected the EFD group, typified by such parties as the United Kingdom Independence Party, as an example of hard euroscepticism. Soft euroscepticism, on the other hand, was what he described as support for the existence of, and membership of, a form of EU, but with opposition to specific EU policies, and opposition to a federal Europe. Blurred lines and further research led the pair to redefine hard euroscepticism as "principled opposition to the project of European integration as embodied in the EU" and soft euroscepticism as "not a principled objection to the European integration project of transferring powers to a supranational body such as the EU, but … opposition to the EU's current or future planned trajectory based on the further extension of competencies that the EU is planning to make" (Szczerbiak and Taggart 2008a). Thus, soft euroscepticism can best be described as "qualified" opposition, while hard euroscepticism is viewed as "outright" opposition. There is a debate among scholars concerning the tipping point when soft euroscepticism transitions into hard. Kopecky and Mudde (2002), and Vasilopoulou (2009), have noted the flaws in such a distinction. As Vasilopoulou (2009) queried, "If a party opposes three or more EU policies, is its euroscepticism still soft or has it crossed the boundaries and has become hard? Would this depend on the number of policies or their substance? Or somehow on both?"

Pursuant to Szczerbiak and Taggert's distinction of hard and soft euroscepticism, scholars began to immerse themselves in study and debate to further delineate euroscepticism. In 2007, Flood and Usherwood presented a six-point scale ranging from EU-reject to EU-maximalist, while Rovny (2004) focused on differentiating between the motivation and the magnitude of opposition to the EU. Krouwel and Abts (2007) developed a two-dimensional conceptualization by combining both the targets and the degree of popular discontent toward "Europe" (Brack and Startin 2015).

Using qualifiers such as pro- or anti-integration, and pro- or anti-EU, many scholars began to reclassify Eurosceptic groups using terms such as Europhobe, Euroreject, Euroenthusiast, Eurorealist, and Eurosceptic (Vasilopoulou 2011; Sorenson 2008; Kopecky and Mudde 2002). Heinisch and Lansberger (2011) note that, according to the typology proposed by Kopecky and Mudde (2002), "so-called 'Euroenthusiasts' support the general idea of European integration as well as its current manifestation as embodied by the EU, 'Eurorejects' are opposed to both. By contrast, 'Europragmatists' do not support the general idea of European integration but accept the EU for pragmatic reasons. Finally, the term 'Eurosceptic' is left for those supporting the general idea of European integration while rejecting the current gestalt of the EU."

Factors such as exit strategy and basis, national influence, vision, and ideology often serve as variables. Interestingly, some terms have been incorporated by groups in EP; on its website, the European Conservatives and Reformists Group (ECR) presents itself as "eurorealist" and calls for an EU of openness, transparency, and eurorealism (ecrgroup.eu 2015).

Another area of focus in Eurosceptic research has led to what some scholars refer to as the North Carolina/Sussex debate. Mudde (2011) highlighted the respective impacts of ideology and strategy in euroscepticism and elaborated the concept of two schools of thought in euroscepticism studies: the Sussex School and the North Carolina School. The foundation of the North Carolina School was the 1999 work of Leonard Ray, research from Hooghe and Marks (2007), and, in particular, Hooghe's 2007 essay "What Drives Euroscepticism?" (Mudde 2011). The North Carolina School emphasizes party-based euroscepticism and argues that party positions on European integration are a reflection of a new cleavage in European politics (Mudde 2011).

The Sussex School is based on the works of Szczerbiak and Taggart (1998, 2001, 2008) and was the first attempt to comparatively and systematically research party-based Euroscepticism. This approach focuses on characteristics inherent to the nation as a whole, such as party competition and objectives, electoral systems, and institutional structures.

Vasilopoulou (2013) observed that this segment of literature portrays "Euroscepticism as a new and marginal phenomenon, located at the periphery of society and the party system and to focus mostly on its nature and its sources" (Brack and Startin 2015). Serricchio, et al. (2013) concurred, observing how Euroscepticism's increasing shift from the periphery of society "to the mainstream and the Eurozone crisis triggered fundamental changes in the attitudes of both citizens and elites vis-á-vis the EU but also towards national institutions" (Brack and Startin 2015).

It is precisely the change in attitude and perspective described by Vasilopoulou that warrants examination of euroscepticism on a macro level. Further, though the emergence and success of euroscepticism and, subsequently, Eurosceptic groups, is a relatively new phenomenon, the underlying tenets are not. The similarity to fascism should not and cannot be ignored.

Griffin (2003) believed that fascism (like euroscepticism) was influenced by both left and right, conservative and anti-conservative, national and supranational, rational and anti-rational. Additionally, nationalism, considered the foundation of fascism, is also a primary component of euroscepticism. Another compelling aspect is the fascist view of the nation as "a single organic entity which binds people together by their ancestry and is a natural unifying force of people" (Zimmer 2003). Yet perhaps the most persuasive example of a parallel between fascism and euroscepticism is recognition that fascism seeks to solve economic, political, and social problems by achieving a national rebirth (Paxton 2005; Griffin 1991; Laqueuer 1998; Passmore 2002).

To date, research in the areas of fascism and euroscepticism has focused on each field independently, failing to unite the two. Scholars routinely focus on the right-wing, populist, and nationalistic aspects of each and often label many of the emergent groups as "fascist." The similarities go far beyond labeling and name-calling. As a result, I link these two areas of study together, proposing a new conception of fascism in the twenty-first century: Millennial Fascism (MF). In the next chapter, the concept of MF will be discussed and dissected at length. This will lead to the creation of a working definition, characteristics of MF, parameters, and necessary components for a group/party to be recognized as an MFG.

NOTE

1. The Treaty on European Union (TEU) was signed in Maastricht on February 7, 1992 and entered into force on November 1, 1993. The signing of the Maastricht Treaty created the European Union, which consists of three pillars: the European Communities, Common foreign and Security Policy and Police and Judicial Cooperation in Criminal Matters. The Maastricht Treaty brought the three Communities (European Atomic Energy Community (Euratom), European Coal and Steel Community (ECSC), European Economic Community (EEC)) under one umbrella—the EU—and institutionalized cooperation in the fields of foreign policy, defense, police, and justice. The EEC was renamed, becoming the European Community (EC) (Europa.eu).

Chapter 4

The Case for Millennial Fascism

> The modern bourgeois society that has sprouted from the ruins of feudal society has not done away with class antagonisms. It has but established new classes, new conditions of oppression, new forms of struggle in place of the old ones
>
> –Karl Marx, 1848. (Marx and Engels 1969)

In 1995, Tarrow indicated that two scholarly specialisms—European integration and the study of social movements—needed to come together to help understand how a European conflict structure is emerging (Tarrow 1995). This prescient comment captures the essence of *Millennial Fascism*—the idea behind euroscepticism as fascism of the twenty-first century.

Many people have a visceral response to the word "fascism." Its history is emotionally charged and enduringly embedded as part of society's evolution. But its evolution continues, rendering it at once similar to and distinct from its original form and what is generally referred to as traditional fascism.

Renowned scholar of fascism, Roger Griffin (2003) acknowledged the dynamic nature of fascism, stating: "Fascism is thus to be seen ideologically as a constantly evolving constellation of fascisms rather than a static, monolithic whole." Similarly, as Pierre-André Taguieff, a French expert on contemporary racism, observed: "Neither 'fascism' or 'racism' will do us the favour of returning in such a way that we can recognize them easily" (Taguieff 1993–4).

Millennial Fascism (MF) is absolutely not traditional fascism. As such, characteristics and actions that may be true of traditional fascism are not necessarily true of MF. Hence, the use of "millennial" as a descriptor, indicating the distinction from mere traditional fascism.

Just as traditional fascism was founded by Benito Mussolini in response to an ineffective Italian parliament being unable to provide for its people, MF has emerged in response to a lack of faith in and growing intolerance of the European Parliament. Further, it must be recognized that nationalism, reform, and the identification of a common enemy—the fundamental elements of fascism—are also the primary elements of MF. But beyond these highly significant points (which I believe make the case for MF on their own), it is important to take a look at what other scholars and experts have observed, particularly in light of enduring belief that fascism would emerge again, albeit in a different form.

The *Encyclopedia of Marxism* (2008) defines fascism as "right-wing, fiercely nationalist, subjectivist in philosophy, and totalitarian in practice," and identifies it as "an extreme reactionary form of capitalist government." It enumerates nine fundamental characteristics of fascism: right wing, nationalism, hierarchy, anti-equality, religious, capitalist, war, voluntarist ideology, and anti-modern (*The Encyclopedia of Marxism* 2008).

Dr Evan Smith, adjunct fellow in the School of History and International Relations at Flinders University in South Australia, observed: "One of the fundamental principles of the Marxist interpretation of fascism is that fascism is not an ideology buried in the historical past, but a living phenomenon that has re-emerged in times of economic and political turmoil" (Smith 2012). Indeed, throughout Europe and in other former colonies around the world including the United States, Canada, Australia, New Zealand, and South Africa, there has been a "revival of fascist groups" at different times (Smith 2012). Smith also asserted that in the immediate post-war period, "these groups were often remnants of the inter-war fascist parties, but the social mobilization of groups of 'classical fascism' were replaced by new groups who took inspiration from the groups of the 1930s and 1940s, but with new and younger personnel, often including figureheads from the inter-war period" (Smith 2012).

Neocleous (1997, xi) presented a similar observation, recognizing that fascism viewed through a singular lens "as a historical phenomenon that ended in 1945 or thereabouts … encourages a dangerous forgetting." For Marxists, fascism is inherently linked to capitalism, as asserted by both Renton (1999, 16)—"fascism is a recurrent feature of modern capitalism"—and Neocleous (1997, xi)—"fascism is first and foremost an ideology generated by modern industrial capitalism." As a result, one could logically conclude that as long as there is capitalism, fascism is possible.

Another argument for the coexistence of fascism and capitalism was presented by John Cammett in the 1960s. He argued that while fascism was the "fullest expression" of capitalism, it was "not identical at every stage … with monopoly capitalism … . As a Marxist, in order to eliminate the conditions for a revival of fascism, one would need to abolish capitalism" (Cammett 1967,

162). As Renton (1999, 16) concluded in true Marxist fashion: "The only decisive way to stop fascism is by fighting for a society where the potential of all humanity is fully realised and all forms of oppression are swept away."

Emile Durkheim's concepts of anomie and collective effervescence have often served as theoretical explanations for the rise of many groups and movements, but they cannot be applied universally, particularly in light of research identifying collective action as a logical act. Mancur Olson (1965) believed that all motivations were individualistic and that only a separate and "selective" incentive would ultimately inspire a rational individual to act as a group. While Durkheim believed that groups socialize individuals into their obligations to one another, Olson (1965) contended that members of groups did not act out of sentiment, loyalty, or a sense of belonging, rather they joined groups purely for the benefit they would derive as individuals. MF is a unique blend of benefit derivation: the goals of the group mirror those of the individual. What is beneficial to one is also beneficial to all: opportunity, preservation, power.

Nationalism, a key feature of the prospective MFGs, was once considered characteristic only of extremists and highly radicalized organizations. In 1960, British historian Elie Kedourie observed that nationalism was often associated with the radical right and therefore criticized as "an irrational doctrine with a fanatical vision and a propensity towards violence" (Halikiopoulou 2012, 7). Olson's research indicating the logic behind collective action does much to counter this erroneous concept which nonetheless lingers as a defining component of nationalism. Indeed, MF and the euroscepticism it embodies is very much a product of logic and rational thought, weighing costs against benefits.

MF is presented as the deliberate manifestation of groups campaigning against the status quo, in particularly the EU. Its emergence and relevance is extraordinary in style, trajectory, and platform. Though similarities to other ideologies exist, the unifying features of these groups are clearly an anomaly, unique not only in time and method, but manner.

Fascism as it existed in the twentieth century is no more. World leaders find themselves in positions of forced accountability. Any leader rising to infamy via acts of violence or genocide in the vein of traditional fascism would find himself or herself not only public enemy number one, but subjected to a very large bull's-eye and economic sanctions or boycotts. The modern-day immediacy and availability of information places everyone on a worldwide stage, under great scrutiny. As a result, the extreme nature of fascism in its purest, most primal form belongs to another time, another generation. Fascism in the twenty-first century is forced to take another form, a more societally palatable iteration. The groups of the right and left who continue to rapidly achieve not only success but also respect do not fit established molds.

In many cases they have achieved not only the unexpected, but also the seemingly impossible, and yet they remain an enigma.

It has been noted that fascism and euroscepticism have been, and continue to be, studied as separate ideologies. This disconnect was highlighted by Vasilopoulou (2011, 224) in this manner: "The issue of radical right EU attitudes remains under-researched in terms of content as well as underlying argumentation." I believe that merging the two fields would allow for more foundationally sound study and improved research in causal and explanatory factors, and I am not alone in my opinion. Renton asserted in 1999, that "any model of fascism must ask which factors within the societies in which fascism emerged enabled the fascist parties to grow … . The success of Le Pen … and Haider … suggests that fascism is again a threat" (Renton 1999, 4). Not only do I concur with this assessment, I contend that fascism has evolved into a modern idiom, enveloping and embodying the concept of euroscepticism.

To illustrate the need for this new version of fascism beyond the superficial, a review of voting trends and media mentions confirms the increase in popularity, and therefore significance, of far-right and Eurosceptic groups. Google Trends data visualization (Figure 4.1) reflected a steady increase in interest of far-right groups over time from 2005 through 2015 (Ramswell 2015). As a case example, Stockemer (2012) compared citizen group support for the Swiss People's Party (SVP) in the years 1995 and 2007 and found a significant increase in support. In fact, he found that support more than doubled in three of the four categories studied, with the fourth category results only slightly less than doubled.

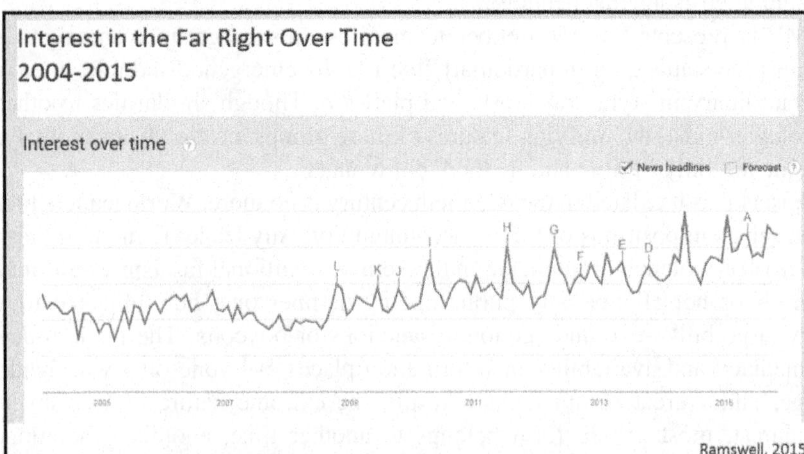

Figure 4.1 Interest in Far Right Over Time. The graph shows the increase in interest in Far Right groups over time. Ramswell 2015.

Greven's 2016 research compared right-wing populism in Europe and the United States. He found that "the spectrum of support of most right-wing populist parties, as well as the Tea Party and Donald Trump in the US, highlights a blurring of traditional left-right scales in the sense that presumed supporters of left-of-center parties, i.e., working class and unemployed voters, especially men, are embracing right-wing populist messages" (Greven 2016).

Such research makes it abundantly clear that not only is interest in these groups on the rise, so is support for them. As a result, it is important to recognize that they are distinctive and must be studied with that in mind. In 2013, Berntson noted that "the scope of fascist studies expands as new insights emerge, as more disciplines become involved, as new methods of inquiry are developed, and as new sources of data become available, such as archives in Russia and Eastern Europe after the fall of the Soviet Union." He also acknowledged that "many scholars are preoccupied by the possibility of fascism's return in today's extreme right in Europe" (Berntson 2013).

Such preoccupation neatly meshes with Griffin's frequently discussed "new consensus" of fascism, which he argued emerged in the 1990s and "conceptualizes fascism as a revolutionary form of ultra-nationalism that attempts to realize the myth of the regenerated nation" (Griffin 2012, 1; 1998; 2003). Scholars in the field, including Stanley Payne and Aristotle Kallis, concurred with Griffin's theory, and Pinto (2011) observed that the "'new consensus' of the 1990s … has only been extended and/or modified." By 2012, Griffin himself acknowledged the growth of the new consensus of fascism, stating he "would go even further and argue that by 2010 it has actually *emerged* and seems to have started spreading 'contagiously' to Marxist academic circles" (Griffin 2012, 13).

In 1991, a time of significant transition following the removal of the Berlin Wall, Griffin observed that ideological factors combined with historical conditions often make fascism seem a viable choice. He contended that these factors, coupled with ultra-nationalism and the political space for extra movements, further opened the door for fascism to emerge (Griffin 1991). The new millennium was host to these factors, making it quite hospitable to the formation of new parties. In particular, the aforementioned fall of the Berlin Wall and end of the Cold War served as major turning points. Of note, Griffin also acknowledged that a major theme of contemporary fascism was a "Europe of Nations." Whether consciously or ironically, the European Parliament political group comprised of Eurosceptics, co-chaired by Front National leader Marine Le Pen and Marcel de Graaff of the Netherland's Partij voor de Vrijheid, was christened the Europe of Nations and Freedom Group when it launched on June 15, 2015.

Why is there a need to recognize MF as a unique ideology? Quite simply, because—despite similarities to traditional fascism—they are different.

The means and methods inherent to this ideology are different, the goals are different, the perception and definition of success is different. Perhaps above all, their success and potential effect are so significant. Evidence of the need to examine MF became readily apparent in the aftermath of the 2014 European elections, if not before, and a deafening alarm was sounded in the wake of Brexit. Yet the 2014 election results lend themselves to an excellent starting point in discussing the significance of these groups.

As discussed in chapter 1, the 2014 European Parliamentary elections resulted in an influx of far-right and far-left Eurosceptic and Euroreject parties—a group which now forms an estimated 27% of the assembly. The UKIP was the clear victor, marking the first time since 1906 that a party other than the Labour Party or Conservative Party won the general election. Further, according to Reuters (Osborn and Faulconbridge 2014) it was also "the first time a party other than the Labour and Conservatives won the majority of seats in a national election since the December 1910 general election."

In France, the far-right Front National (Front National is often called National Front) Party won a historic victory with 25% of the French vote (compared to the 6% it garnered in 2009), besting more moderate pro-EU parties who had dominated the elections five years prior (CNN 2014). In Greece, the rise of the Golden Dawn (Χρυσή Αυγή) has drawn many comparisons to the rise of the Nazi regime in the 1930s (Fallon 2014). Observed Mansheim (2014): "Swept into popularity by the current lack of faith in the EU among Greeks, the aggressively neo-fascist party is now the third most popular political party in Greece, and is making inroads on its mainstream opponents." In May 2015, "the party received seven percent of the vote, and 6.9 percent in June, granting it 21 and 18 parliamentary seats out of 300 respectively; they retained their support in the 2014 European Parliament Elections receiving 9.38 per cent of the vote and hold the third greatest number of seats (17) in Greek Parliament" (Vasilopoulou and Halikiopoulou 2015).

Further, there are concerns about increased connections to Russia. Observed Kreko (2014):

> Russia supports increasingly popular anti-EU parties on the far left and far right, hoping to have pro-Russian caucuses in the next Parliament to help articulate Russian views, and to have an impact on decision-making processes. … Fifteen out of 25 major European far-right parties are vocal and open supporters of Russia and Russian interests, while seven can be classified as "open" and only three as hostile towards Russia. (Kreko 2014)

Perhaps more alarmingly "the Hungarian Jobbik party has supported Russia since it was elected to the European Parliament in 2009. The party's 2010 election program described the establishment and maintenance of good relations with 'an increasingly influential Russia' as vitally important" (Kreko 2014).

Halikiopoulou, et al. (2012) rightfully observed that research has led scholars to stress the compatibility of many aspects of nationalism with right-wing radicalism (Breuilly 1993; Freeden 1998; Hechter 2000; and Kedourie 1960). Walsh (2014) contended that "the vote for anti-EU populists and socialists, even for right-wing extremists and assorted oddballs, is a rejection of high-handed governance that pays little attention to people's needs and desires." In 2014, Gifford added, "populist eurosceptic mobilizations have become an established response to the underlying crises of legitimacy faced by both British mainstream parties. These have occurred when the weaknesses in the British governing position on Europe has been particularly exposed, such as the struggle for membership on acceptable terms and the failure of Conservative governments to halt or influence the drive for Economic and Monetary Union."

Jim Wolfreys, Senior Lecturer for contemporary French politics at King's College London, used the example of the Front National to explain how far-right parties manage to be accepted by the electorate: "The founders of [the Front National] consciously attempted to mask direct affiliation of fascism behind a language and an appearance that courted respectability" (Schwab and Joyner 2015). The authors contended that "these movements benefited from the dissatisfaction with mainstream parties, but they were also helped by the fact that the right-wing parties of today are very different to those of previous decades" (Schwab and Joyner 2015).

Categorizing fascism and its various forms Renton (1999, 43) observed: "fascism remains a force in European society, and a theory of it is needed which grasps the processes and dynamism of fascism as it continues to exist." The impact of MF is obvious. Euroscepticism has made an ineradicable mark on society and on the European political landscape. With agendas and ideologies echoing the sentiments of fascism, and paths that mimic the rise of the most notorious fascist groups in history, it is incumbent on us to identify these groups as unique and thoroughly explore their rise and impact. There is much evidence to support that these groups are unique, a new generation of political ideology and methodology. The argument for MF as a relative of fascism is based on the contention that the groups rising and gaining power today are at once distinctive and reborn from strains of traditional fascism. MF and traditional fascism may share many primary features, but they also diverge on many levels. MF is the result of the unique new millennium convergence of political opportunity, populism, nationalism, and euroscepticism.

How can Millennial Fascism best be described? In order to establish a definition of MF, it is important to review and discuss the elements and descriptors of traditional fascism and its derivatives. The reasons for this are twofold: it is necessary to note similarities and potential differences between MF and its predecessors, and it will serve as a foundation for and springboard into the rationale for creating this new category of fascism.

TRADITIONAL FASCISM

The term "fascism" is from the Latin *fascis* and Italian *fascio,* meaning *bundle* or *political group*. In the chapter on the evolution of fascism, the difficulty scholars have in isolating a single definition of fascism as a result of these connotations and associated historical influence was discussed. The word has become exceptionally difficult to define as a result of the meanings ascribed to it and their evolution. In 1996, Roger Eatwell logically argued that fascism "must be seen primarily as a series of ideas" (Renton 1999, 19). There was, he argued, "no other way to interpret fascism." Eatwell believed that "fascism could not be viewed as a form of regime; moreover, fascism cannot be defined as a species of political movement, because such movements 'exhibit time and context specific features' which draw attention away from the decisive core of fascist ideas" (Renton 1999, 19). Using the argument that fascism was primarily an ideology, Eatwell (1996, 303–319) contended that fascism was best defined in these terms: "Generic fascism, transcending place and time, is identified as 'an ideology that strives to forge social rebirth based on a holistic national radical Third Way, though in practice fascism has tended to stress style, especially action and the charismatic leader, more than detailed programme, and to engage in a Manichaean demonisation of its enemies.'" Eatwell's description of an ideology that strived to forge "rebirth" is particularly apropos with respect to euroscepticism, especially when juxtaposed with Griffin's (1991) concept of "palingenetic ultranationalism" (also a rebirth but on a national level) and his observation that "fascism emerged when a nation perceived itself to be in crisis." Indeed, Vasilopolou and Halikiopoulou (2015) discussed this concept as it related to the far-right Greek group "Golden Dawn":

> The success of Golden Dawn must be understood precisely within this context: as dependent on the extent to which it was able to propose plausible solutions to the three sets of crises—economic, political and ideological—that befell Greece and culminated in an overall crisis of democracy to which Golden Dawn offered a nationalist solution. This can be shown by drawing upon the theories of fascism developed by authors such as Michael Mann and Roger Griffin. We argue that the nature of the Greek crisis and the fact that its economic, political and ideological dimensions challenged the Greek nation-state at its core, opened up a political opportunity for Golden Dawn to present itself as the saviour of the nation and defender of the national mission. Like fascist movements of the past, Golden Dawn puts forward "a 'palingenetic myth' of populist ultra-nationalism, seeking a nation rising Phoenix-like from the ashes of an old decadent social order." (Vasilopoulou and Halikiopoulou 2015)

Eatwell and Griffin's explanations of fascism highlight its stark parallels to euroscepticism and the proposed concept of MF. Further, the formation of movements with strategies and goals (Kitsikis 1988; Payne 1980), and the idea of a new generation of intellectuals rising against liberal society (Sternhell 1995), provide further evidence in a case for MF. Noted Leonard, et al. (2013):

> The old explanation for euroscepticism was the alleged existence of a democratic deficit within the EU. Decisions, critics said, were taken by unaccountable institutions rather than elected national governments. But the current crisis is born not of a clash between Brussels and the member states but a clash between the democratic wills of citizens in northern and southern Europe—the so-called centre and periphery. And both sides are now using EU institutions to advance their interests. (Leonard, et al. 2013, 1)

The similarities between fascism and euroscepticism cannot be ignored: nations in social and political turmoil, a rebirth of nationalism, group formation and rise, and a new generation in a state of revolt.

With such sweeping concepts and identifiers, it is easy to see how selecting one overarching yet concise definition of fascism has proven problematic. Efforts to develop a more succinct definition, therefore, have tended to focus on commonalities. Therefore, for classification purposes, we shall consider fascism and, more specifically, fascist groups as any group exhibiting nationalism and unity by way of a desire to transform, cleanse, and expand its personal community, under an authoritarian leadership willing to use force and viewing itself as superior to others, and which existed before World War II.

NEO-FASCISM

During the twentieth century, fascism developed subcategories that contained its central tenets, yet established identities of their own. The subgroups "neo-fascist" and "neo-Nazi" are the two most widely accepted offshoots of their ideological progenitor. Unfortunately, the difficulty in isolating a universally accepted definition of fascism has not been limited to the term "fascism." Selection of a unifying definition for neo-fascism is only slightly less problematic, thanks in part to the parameters created by selecting a date or timeframe as a dividing line.

The term neo-fascism has become quite generic, embracing many groups with many different mantras. In its simplest, and perhaps most widely accepted, form neo-fascism is defined as a fascist group existing post World War II. *The Oxford Handbook of Fascism* (2009) ascribed the term *neo-fascism* to "those political and ideological groups and parties that operated after 1945, especially in Europe, and which were directly inspired by the experience of the inter-war fascist and Nazi regimes in Germany, Italy, and other European countries."

The Encyclopedia Britannica (2009) described neo-fascism as "a political philosophy and movement that arose in Europe in the decades following World War II, advocating extreme nationalism, opposing liberal individualism, attacking Marxist and other left-wing ideologies, indulging in racist and xenophobic scapegoating, and promoting populist right-wing economic programs." It was noted that the National Front in France and the Liberal Democratic Party in Russia were often cited as examples of neo-fascist groups (*Encyclopedia Britannica* 2009).

The difficulty in defining neo-fascism lies in the inclusion or exclusion of the hereto defined fascist groups, now who must be further delineated based on ideology. This characteristic already serves as a point of division among scholars of fascism, some of whom contend fascism is not an ideology but a form of governance or a way of life. In fact, noted Italian fascist theorist Giovanni Gentile believed that fascism was best viewed as "authoritarian democracy." In adhering to a "keep it simple" strategy and avoiding overcomplicating the issue, date will serve as the primary divider between fascism and neo-fascism, while ideology will serve as the separator between neo-fascism and neo-Nazism (which will be discussed next). Thus, neo-fascism shall be described as fascism (as defined above) occurring post World War II.

NEO-NAZISM

Griffin (1998) argued that fascism and Nazism were different from one another though at the same time linked through a "common mythic core." He asserted that since 1945, many racially motivated fascist organizations have been inspired by Nazism and, further, that these new Nazi movements were referred to as neo-Nazis because they used Adolf Hitler's Nazi movement as inspiration but modified the original Nazi ideological doctrine (Griffin 1991). Indeed, neo-Nazism could be considered a sub-group of neo-fascism. Accordingly, ideology will serve as the primary qualifier distinguishing between neo-fascism and neo-Nazism—a distinction many scholars do not make.

Nazism, in its purest form as characterized by Hitler, is considered part of traditional fascism. However, as a post–World War II incarnation, there is a distinction between fascism and Nazism. A group determined to meet the characteristics of neo-Nazism shall be included in that category rather than neo-fascism. It is in this vein that a distinction between neo-fascism and MF will also be constructed.

To be considered neo-Nazi, a group will boast a Nazi ideology/refrain with a stated tenet of "scientific racism" and/or anti-Semitism. Further, any group formed post World War II promoting scientific racism will automatically be categorized as a neo-Nazi group. For clarification, Garrod (2006, 54) defined scientific racism as "a scientific tradition in which biology is used not only to prove the existence of race, but also, to maintain existing social hierarchies." He explained:

> While science has the reputation of objectively testing theories using the scientific method, scientific racism is the exact opposite. It seeks to create definitions of race and culture based on opinion and extremely questionable evidence: "Supposed scientific evidence was marshalled, to establish both the existence of different racial types, and their depiction within a hierarchy of superior and inferior, where the Black was regarded as inferior." (Garrod 2006, 55, citing Anthias and Yuval-Davis 1992)

As such, the parameters for neo-Nazism are fairly straightforward. Those groups adhering to the Nazi ideology, a belief in scientific racism or anti-Semitism, and who exist post World War II will be considered neo-Nazi.

MILLENNIAL FASCISM

The need to view this turn-of-the-century rise in Eurosceptic nationalism through a different lens has three vocal proponents: experts who have clearly acknowledged a need for combined study; the political parties who have risen and altered the political atmosphere in Europe; and the undeniable similarities between euroscepticism and fascism. MF serves as the response to this need.

Millennial Fascism is NOT traditional fascism. As noted, it incorporates some of the central principles of traditional fascism, but is quite distinct and evolved from it. The issues associated with creating a universally accepted definition can often be found in the elements being used as descriptors, as the elements themselves are often challenged by thinkers embracing different perspectives.

With any group, consideration of cultural, environmental, and historical conditions is important, but so are goals, methods, and long-term strategic plans. Cunningham (2012) acknowledged that the conceptualized categories and definitions of fascism prove problematic. He asserted that "dismissing the need for a shared conceptual definition of fascism risks the overextension of the term to any national movement bearing vague similarities" (Cunningham 2012, 379).

Also of import is recognizing that MF is a modern view of fascism, fascism in the new millennium, a new perspective on a centuries-old concept. One of the hurdles in retaining the term "fascism" is overcoming its negative connotation. BBC (10/20/09) reported that though it has been "more than six decades since the end of World War II and the fall of Nazi Germany, those events remain the prism through which the word 'fascism' is still viewed." When describing the difficulty faced in overcoming its historical association, Griffin (2012) eloquently acknowledged that

> many representatives of an older generation of scholars would doubtless persist in seeing fascism as essentially nihilistic, barbaric, anti-modern, and lacking an ideology apart from the cult of action, violence and destruction, or, if they were Marxists, as basically (petty) bourgeois or capitalist reaction. But I argued that within the emerging consensus it was increasingly accepted that "like conservatism, anarchism, liberalism, or ecologism, fascism is definable as an ideology with a specific 'positive', utopian vision of the ideal state of society, a vision which can assume a number of distinctive forms determined by local circumstances while retaining a core matrix of axioms." (Griffin 2012, 6)

Perhaps it is best to not attempt to overcome the word's reputation. Rather, focus on the evolution of fascism. Indeed, the concept of MF is that it is at once the same as and different from classic fascism; it retains symbolic strands of its predecessor while exhibiting a pivotal distinction: widespread acclaim. In fact, *Oxford English Dictionary* now offers several definitions of fascism including "[loosely] a person of right-wing authoritarian views" and "a person who advocates a particular viewpoint or practice in a manner perceived as intolerant or authoritarian" (BBC 10/20/09).

In 1997, Historian Walter Lacqueur asserted that if fascist regimes were to come into power in the future, they would not take their earlier form. Indeed, many scholars left room for future delineation of fascism with expansive typologies and consensus definitions. MF has been constructed as a modern-day form of fascism, a derivative and variation of classic fascism. Its distinction from other types of fascism lies within the unique elements that have allowed for its rise, acceptance, and relative success among the plethora of social movements throughout Europe. Acceptance of this concept serves to eliminate MF from established categories, but, in what ways? What aspects of these groups have allowed them to stand on their own?

Euroscepticism is held to be the primary characteristic of MF and, for purposes of this research, euroscepticism will be defined as Taggart (1998, 366) described it: "The idea of contingent or qualified opposition, as well as incorporating outright and unqualified opposition to the process of European integration."

Several other traits are intrinsic to MF, such as nationalism, populism, reformism, mainstream appeal, popular agendas, and right-wing inclination. This brings us to a decision point. In Europe and European Parliament, there are a number of left-wing Eurosceptic parties who have gained notoriety, including Greece's SYRIZA. In fact, EP contains Eurosceptic groups from across the political spectrum, including the "European Conservatives and Reformists group, typified by center-right parties such as the British Conservative Party (considered to be a soft Eurosceptic group), and the European United Left–Nordic Green Left which is an alliance of left-wing parties" (Szczerbiak 2008, 418). This gives pause, as the original conception of MF was as right-wing Eurosceptic groups.

In an effort to remain true to the original and successive forms of fascism, I initially believed it important to continue the tradition of fascism as a purely right-wing phenomenon. However, MF is a new, modern interpretation of a century-old concept. Deliberation led to a review of Mussolini's intentions and objectives as founder of the fascist party. In 1919, Mussolini famously described fascism as "a movement that would strike against the backwardness of the right and the destructiveness of the left," yet it is these words spoken in 1922 which served as the tipping point in the debate:

> Fascism, sitting on the right, could also have sat on the mountain of the center. … These words in any case do not have a fixed and unchanged meaning: they do have a variable subject to location, time and spirit. We don't give a damn about these empty terminologies and we despise those who are terrorized by these words. (Mussolini 1922)

Therefore, the decision was made to not automatically disqualify left-wing groups from an MF classification.

In an effort to better quantify MF, it is necessary to include disqualifiers —traits which, if present, will serve to eliminate a group from inclusion. Disqualifiers that serve to remove a group from the category of MF are: stated platform of anti-Semitism or scientific racism (as explained above), and violent acts/terrorism with the intention of forcing compliance or surrender.

Utilizing the characteristics and disqualifiers described above, we can now define MF based on certain necessary criteria. As Griffin wrote in 2003: "I believe any new theory of fascism should meet the challenge of being summarized in a sentence if it is not to be a work of obfuscation rather than clarification … the most recent offerings from Laqueur, Renton, and Gregor all failed this test" (8). In crafting a definition of MF, I believed it important to adhere to Griffin's conception of a concise yet accurate description. Therefore, the following description was developed: Millennial Fascism is a post–Cold War political philosophy founded on a non-violent, non-anti-Semitic/

racist/homophobic ideology that embodies euroscepticism and the promotion of nationalism and reform.

The similarities between traditional fascism and Millennial Fascism cannot be ignored, yet there are unquestionable differences. These differences provide a natural progression, an evolution, of fascism embodying the political elements and atmosphere of the present day. Millennial Fascism is at once unique and familiar. It's not your mom and pop's fascism, nor their wayward child. Millennial Fascism is a distinctive manifestation of old and new.

It is important to note that creation of a category which is representative of these groups does not imply a recoding of radical right populism or neo-populism, nor does it imply that other such classifications are obsolete, inaccurate, or do not apply. MF can be extremist, right-wing, populist, and neo-populist but it can also be nationalist, left-wing, reformist, and a host of other descriptors.

To identify it solely as neo-populism or radical right-wing populism would be erroneous. MF is a new classification for a segment of the population that could, possibly, include radical right-wing populists and neo-populists. The distinction is important. A point to consider: Eurosceptics and Millennial Fascists may also be populists, but not all populists are Eurosceptics or Millennial Fascists. No vital taxonomic distinctions have been blurred and remain solidly intact. Rather, such distinctions have been utilized to identify characteristics that better serve as unique identifiers for a new category.

Now that a distinction has been made between categories, we turn to the task of determining which groups should be considered Millennial Fascist Groups and the shared features that have led to their rise.

Chapter 5

Examination of the Threat

Qualification and Determination of Millennial Fascist Groups (MFGs)

In the previous chapter, we developed descriptions of fascism, neo-fascism, neo-Nazism, and Millennial Fascism (MF) for classification purposes. Now begins the process of determining which groups should be considered Millennial Fascist Groups (MFGs). A case study approach will be utilized to analyze 27 parties, in a systematic process that will determine whether a party meets the necessary criteria and qualifies as a MFG. Parties meeting the criteria of a MFG will then serve as the subject cases as we examine the factors leading to the rise of MF. The following groups were chosen from active fringe groups/ parties in Europe in 2016, and will be researched and analyzed utilizing a set of variable requirements:

- Alternative for Germany-AfD (Germany)
- ATAKA (Bulgaria)
- Congress of the New Right (Poland)
- Danish People's Party-DF (Denmark)
- Dutch Freedom Party-PVV (Netherlands)
- English Defence League-EDL (England)
- Fascism and Freedom Movement-National Socialist Party (Italy)
- Finns Party aka Perussuomalaiset (formerly True Finns)-PS (Finland)
- Freedom Party of Austria-FPÖ
- Front National (France)
- Golden Dawn (Greece)
- Jobbik (Hungary)
- LAOS (Greece)
- Lega Nord (Italy)
- National Democratic Party of Germany (NPD)

- Party of the Swedes (Sweden)
- Pegida (Germany)
- Podemos (Spain)
- Republican People's Party-Cumhuriyet Halk Partisi-CHP (Turkey)
- Right Sector (Ukraine)
- Slovak National Party-SNS (Slovakia)
- Svoboda (Ukraine)
- Swedish Democrats (Sweden)
- Swiss People's Party (Switzerland)
- SYRIZA (Greece)
- UKIP (England)
- Vlaams Belang aka Flemish Interest (Belgium)

We have distinguished MF as a post–Cold War political philosophy founded on a non-violent, non-anti-Semitic/racist/homophobic ideology that embodies euroscepticism and the promotion of nationalism and reform. Utilizing this description, five variables were selected as either qualifying or disqualifying criteria. Each group/party will be analyzed to determine which, if any, of the five variables are applicable to that group. Groups that are identified as meeting all five conditions shall be determined to have met the requirements necessary for classification as an MFG. By default, groups not meeting the criteria of MF would be categorized as neo-Nazi or neo-fascist. The characteristics serving as variables, as well as their descriptions, are detailed below. The method to be utilized in determining whether a group meets a particular criterion will follow each description.

VARIABLES

A. *Occurring post-Cold War.* Identified as: formation or restructured ideology occurring in 1990 or later; Determined through: review of group's history, vision/ideology, official website(s)/publications.

B. *Non-Violent.* Identified as: strategy and ideology that does not promote violence or terroristic acts;

   Determined through: review of group's mission, vision, official website(s)/publications, media reports; neither promotion of nor participation in violence by leadership or its members.

C. *Non anti-Semitic/racist/homophobic.* Identified as: mission and vision do not specifically contain anti-Semitic, racist or, homophobic ideology;

Determined through: review of group's mission, vision, official website(s)/publications, media/news reports.

D. *Eurosceptic.* Identified as: contingent or outright oppositions to the process of European integration, austerity measures, or the EU and European project;

Determined through: Review of group's mission, vision, official website(s)/publications, media/news reports.

E. *Nationalist/Reformist.* Identified as: belief that the interests of the nation-state are of primary importance; a desire to reform the policies of the EU;

Determined through: review of group's mission, vision, official website(s)/publications, media/news reports.

At this juncture, I believe it important to provide a few points of clarification. People have a tendency to misuse the word racist, particularly when discussing Islamophobia, defined by *Oxford English Dictionary* as "the dislike of or prejudice against Islam or Muslims, especially as a political force." The media perpetuates this misuse which has, in many cases, led to a party's erroneous labeling as "racist." The *Oxford English Dictionary* defines race as "each of the major divisions of humankind, having distinct physical characteristics," and racism as "prejudice, discrimination, or antagonism directed against someone of a different race based on the belief that one's own race is superior."

Some of the groups researched were found to promote anti-Islam/anti-Muslim platforms. These groups were almost always referred to as "racist." As delineated above and underscored by the Religion of Peace (2015), "Race is the arbitrary classification of individuals according to physical traits that presumably have a genetic pattern. Muslims are not a race, as is often implied but if they were then it would make Islam the world's most dangerous race-based supremacist ideology."

Similarly, some groups studied are accused of xenophobia, which is also used interchangeably with the term racism. According to *Oxford English Dictionary*, xenophobia is the "intense or irrational dislike or fear of people from other countries." Again, xenophobia is different from racism. A person whom is xenophobic could very well dislike someone of their own race simply because they are from a different country. Xenophobia is a location-based fear, not a race-based fear.

Therefore, there will be a distinction made between racism, xenophobia, and religious prejudice. For variable C, religious prejudice and xenophobia (absent racism), will not disqualify a group from meeting the required conditions.

ANALYSIS AND QUALIFICATION

Alternative for Germany (Alternative für Deutschland—AfD), Germany

According to the BBC (Hill, 2015), "AfD was founded in 2013 by Bernd Lucke, Alexander Gauland and Konrad Adam to oppose German-backed bailouts for poorer Southern European countries. … The party became the first anti-euro party to win seats in a German regional parliament, receiving almost 10% of the vote in the eastern German state of Saxony in 2014, and has gone on to win seats in other states" (Hill, 2015). "The party had seven MEPs elected in the 2014 European elections and is currently part of the European Conservatives and Reformists Group" (Hill, 2015).

Frauke Petry replaced Lucke as party leader following his departure in early July 2015, arguing that AfD had become increasingly xenophobic (Hill, 2015). The party has been called the "Party of Professors" (due to the high percentage of members holding doctorates—including founder Lucke) and the German Tea Party by various media including the BBC, Deutsche Welle, the *Frankfurter Allgemeine Sonntagszeitung*, and UK's *Guardian*.

A. *Occurring post-Cold War.* AfD was founded in 2013. Condition: met.
B. *Non-Violent.* AfD carefully screens its membership for evidence of right-wing extremism or radicalism. The group is not considered violent nor a perpetrator of violence. Rather, the party has been the target of several acts of violence by others. Reported *Spiegel* (Heine, 2013): "AfD campaigners have received threatening phone calls, been subjected to verbal abuse and—in some cases—physical attacks. … Though the AfD has complained of such incidents in a number of cities including Berlin, Lübeck, and Nuremberg, the party points to a particularly brutal confrontation at a campaign stand in the eastern town of Göttingen [in 2013]." Party leader Lucke has warned against the opposition's tendency toward attribution error: "A violent crime committed by two extremists should not be attributed to an entire religious community, the majority of which consists of peaceful, respectable people" (Sagener et al, 2015). Condition: met.
C. *Non anti-Semitic/racist/homophobic.* The Economist (2/23/2015) noted that AfD is a group that "calls for dissolving the euro and which often uses anti-immigrant and homophobic innuendo in its campaigns." However, once again, anti-immigrant is a term many use in response to a nationalist platform. Innuendo is subjective and not factual. In fact, the *Guardian* (Oltermann, 2014) reported that AfD "MEP Beatrix von Storch, who is considered one of the leading voices of party's conservative faction, frequently asserts that she sees the AfD as founded on a 'Christian view

of humanity'." Von Storch has described support networks for young gay people at German schools as "forced sexualisation." However, Von Storch (2011) clarified her comments, stating that "I condemn not, there are people who live differently than oneself or as you would expect. That's not what it is about. It's about the government mission statement."[1]

AfD has been the target of accusations of anti-Semitism. However, in 2014, AfD-state board unanimously launched party exclusion proceedings against the Uckermark district chairman and designated MEP Jan-Ulrich Weiss after he posted an anti-Semitic cartoon on his Facebook page. The caricature was considered reminiscent of the Nazi paper *Der Stuermer* (Dvorin, 2014). Ultimately, speculation abounds but AfD does not promote an anti-Semitic/racist/homophobic agenda. Condition: met.

D. *Eurosceptic.* Party spokesman Alexander Gauland acknowledged that "there are differences between being euro-critical, EU-critical, and Europe-critical. We are critical of the euro and the EU, but we are pro-European" (Knight and Goebel, 2014). EurActiv (Sagener et al, 2015) classified the group as "the Eurosceptic Alternative for Germany (AfD)." Condition: met.

E. *Nationalist/Reformist.* AfD is classified as a nationalist conservative party (Bundeswahlleiter, 2015). Observed Lochocki (2015): "The AfD's party platform largely follows the formula of classic European right-wing populists, positioning itself as for the nation and against the existing political establishment." Condition: met.

AfD: ALL CONDITIONS MET

ATAKA (Атака), Bulgaria

ATAKA, or "attack," is a Bulgarian party which has gained increasing notoriety since its formation in 2005. The party touted a concise platform of 20 Principles which, "in June 2005, catapulted them into the 40th parliament (2005–2009) with 8.94% of the popular vote and 21 seats" (ATAKA, 2015). The group's mantra "Let's regain Bulgaria for the Bulgarians!" is one that resounds with many Bulgarians. Its founder and leader, Volen Siderov, is a former journalist whose television program was also called "Ataka."

Siderov was one of the first who started anti-EU campaigning because of the closure of four blocs of "Koslodui" nuclear power plant. He also "was the first who openly gave an ethnic adjective to the criminal [in Bulgaria]. … In [*sic*] the same time he accused the Government, the EU and the Roma organisations for money laundering [*sic*] and redirecting of that money to private pockets, on [*sic*] expense of Bulgarians" (Novaković 2008, 53).

A. *Occurring post-Cold War.* The ATAKA party was established by Siderov in 2005 as "a patriotic formation to stand up against globalization" (Feffer 2013). Condition: met.

B. *Non-Violent.* In 2011, a violent protest by supporters of the far-right party ATAKA led party leader Siderov to state that he had "never incited ethnic or religious hatred … and that the people who clashed with Muslims at the mosque are not members of his party" (Dzhambazova 2011). In a 2011 Human Rights Report, it was noted that "despite the widespread condemnation of Ataka for the incident and the prosecuting authorities opening of pre-trial proceedings against several assailants arrested on the scene, it merits mention that the proceedings define the ultra-nationalists' actions as 'hooliganism' rather than discriminatory violence on the grounds of religion." "Hooliganism, as defined by the Criminal Code of Bulgaria (Article 325), constitutes acts against 'public order'" (Bulgarian Helsinki Committee 2011). Condition: met.

C. *Non anti-Semitic/racist/homophobic.* In 2013, leaders of the party distributed pamphlets detailing the group's manifesto: "ATAKA is neither a racist nor xenophobic party and this can be seen by every objective observer who reads our pragramme [*sic*] and gets familiar with our activities," noted ATAKA MP Magdalena Tasheva (www.ataka.bg).

This position seemingly contradicts actions of the group in its early years: "ATAKA, which employed racist and discriminatory rhetoric during the 2005 and 2006 electoral campaigns, published anti-Semitic and anti-Muslim material in its newspaper, on its Web site, and on its cable television mouthpiece *Skat*" (US Department of State, 2008). In a 2013 interview, Volen Siderov, leader of ATAKA, stated, "We do not have the difference between blacks and whites here. Racism was never an issue in Bulgaria. However, when crime rates rise, and all this crime originates in these ethnic groups, people start having negative sentiments. So there is not a single village in Bulgaria that has not been robbed by the Gypsy groups" (Feffer 2013).

Further, in 2014, Siderov proposed "amendments to Bulgaria's Penal Code … that would have imposed jail and huge fines for 'public manifestations of homosexuality' such as taking part in gay parades" (Leviev-Sawyer 2014). Thus, unless ATAKA is splitting hairs and viewing a racist ideology as different from an anti-Semitic/anti-Roma ideology, the group is clearly misrepresenting their beliefs. In this instance, an official stance is overruled by action and circuitous statements. Condition: unmet.

D. *Eurosceptic.* Interestingly, according to Euractiv "Bulgarians are broadly pro-European, largely because they trust EU institutions more than those of their own country. The latest Eurobarometer poll shows that Bulgaria is among the countries that is the most positive about the future of the EU, at 61%, with 27% pessimistic. … The EU average is 53% optimist, versus 40% pessimist" (Euractiv.com 2014). Nonetheless, ATAKA is considered "the key progenitor of the Eurosceptic undercurrent" (Dandalov 2014).

Accordingly, Number 16 of Ataka's "20 Principles" states: "Reconsideration of the closed chapters in the accession negotiations with the EU; renegotiation of all unfavourable clauses, damaging Bulgaria's interest. Cancellation of any agreements, accords or memoranda implying or demanding the decommissioning of the Kozlodui NPP" (ATAKA 2015). The party affirmed their stance in 2013, stating: "Yes, we are a Eurosceptic and anti-globalist party" (ATAKA 2015). Condition: met.

E. *Nationalist/Reformist.* The group is often characterized in the media as ultra-nationalist (Yahoo, BBC, *The Guardian*). Party leader Siderov has stated, "The struggle of our party is to make the Bulgarian nationality a category of prestige, so that the inhabitant of a ghetto would be proud to call himself Bulgarian" (Feffer 2013). The party's official website proclaims as one of its twenty principles: "Every Bulgarian investor, entrepreneur, and/or manufacturer shall have precedence over any foreign one, up until Bulgaria's living standards reach the average European level. Bulgaria's production, commerce, banks and all other means of production should be in Bulgarian hands" (ATAKA 2015). In fact, the group's first stated principle is: "Bulgaria is a unitary, monolith state, not liable to secession on neither religious, ethnic, cultural, or any other basis. Differences by origin or faith shall have no priority over nationality. Whoever violates this principle, detaches oneself off from the Bulgarian nation and the Bulgarian state and shall not be eligible to lay any claims to both of them" (ATAKA 2015). Condition: met.

ATAKA: ALL CONDITIONS NOT MET

Congress of the New Right (Kongres Nowej Prawicy, Nowa Prawica-KNP), Poland

KNP was founded on March 25, 2011 by Janusz Korwin-Mikke, who finished in the 4th place in Poland's 2010 presidential election. KNP was "a result of a merger of the Freedom and Lawfulness (WiP) with several members of the Real Politics Union (UPR)" (Dutch News, 6/19/14). It was considered a radical libertarian party and sought decriminalization of the use and production of all drugs (Dutch News, 6/19/14). The Democratic Society (5/13/2014) noted that Korwin-Mikke has conservative views on women and homosexuality and has previously suggested that women should not have the vote. In the 2014 KNP election program, Korwin-Mikke claimed that "KNP is the only anti-EU party in Poland, consistently and without compromise. Our goal is to dissolve the EU by reducing this artificial, statist, fiscal, and ideological construct to a free trade zone—the original European Economic Community, which was the source of the economic success and prosperity of the West after World War II." The 2014 election resulted in KNP garnering 7.06% of the vote, finishing 4th in the national poll and earning four MEPs (Lesniak 2014). KNP joined the Europe of Freedom and Direct Democracy group in 2014. In January 2015, Korwin-Mikke was ousted from KNP and created a splinter party called Korwin. Since that time, Korwin holds two seats and KNP the other two (KNP 2015).

A. *Occurring post-Cold War.* KNP was founded in March 2011 by Janusz Korwin-Mikke. Condition: met.
B. *Non-Violent.* "If someone gives money to an unemployed person he should have his hand cut off because he is destroying the morale of the people," Korwin-Mikke said, adding, "Europeans were very aggressive and now the boys are taught not to be aggressive. … Give them the pistol, give them a sword" (Graham-Harrison 2014). In 2014, it was widely reported that Korwin-Mikke "slapped a leftwing Polish politician in the face" (Graham-Harrison 2014). As noted in Bachrynowski (2015), Korwin-Mikke is even unwilling to condemn China for cruel acts of violence toward citizens, if those actions work to the economic benefit of the country. Condition: unmet.
C. *Non anti-Semitic/racist/homophobic.* In his 2014 electoral interview to the EU parliament, Korwin-Mikke expressed his belief that there is no proof that Hitler did know anything about Jews' extermination which is a reference to the assertion of British historian David Irving (Open Europe 2014).

   According to the *Jewish Chronicle* (Tzur 10/21/2014), "While Korwin-Mikke claimed he was 'against any restrictions on minorities', he explained this by saying: 'For us there are no minorities, there are only Polish citizens. We are against special rights for minorities. The same with Jews.'" Further, Tzur (2014) stated: "Korwin-Mikke said that Jews' efforts to win back property stolen during World War II often amounted to a 'Holocaust industry' and that the only Jews left in Poland were 'Jewish communists,'" adding, "Jews are very talented people, and therefore are our worst enemies, because they are talented communists. This is why the Poles have a specific image of Jews. They don't know the real Jews, only the Communists ones who stayed here." KNP also opposes gay marriage and advocates for the disfranchisement of women because they are "not as clever as men" (Bachrynowski 2015). Condition: unmet.
D. *Eurosceptic.* As noted above, Korwin-Mikke boasted that "KNP is the only anti-EU party in Poland" (KNP 2014). According to Open Europe (2014), Korwin-Mikke commented in 2014, "We are going to the European Parliament to show what a nonsensical institution it is. It's not possible to achieve anything sensible there." Further, Open Europe (2014) reported that Korwin-Mikke declared that "the party would go into the parliament in order to detonate a bomb inside it, while one of his MEP candidates claimed that the European Parliament is a brothel, a role for which it is ideally suited" (Open Europe 2014).

Lesniak (2014) noted that KNP is "against adopting euro as polish official currency and strongly discourage from further integration within the European Union."

Condition: met.

E. *Nationalist/Reformist.* Party founder Korwin-Mikke is a well-known Polish nationalist with a long history of activism on behalf of Poland. Korwin-Mikke "advocates national self-interest and the instrumentalisation of political" (BBC April 28, 2014). Lesniak (2014) noted that KNP "embraces the standpoint of disbanding minimal wage and privileges of labour unions. The party also demands constitutional amendment imposing on future governments to balance national budget (preventing incurring debts)."

Condition: met.

KNP: ALL CONDITIONS NOT MET

Danish People's Party (Dansk Folkeparti-DF), Denmark

According to the party's website, the Danish People's Party (DF, though alternatively abbreviated DPP in English) was founded at Christiansborg on October 6, 1995, with co-founder Pia Kjærsgaard unanimously elected as party chairman (DF 2015). The party is viewed as populist, nationalist, and Eurosceptic, and has been led by Kristian Thulesen Dahl since 2012. In 2001, the party won 12% of the vote and 22 seats; by 2007, it had claimed 13.9% of the vote and 25 seats. In 2015, DF "jumped to 21.1% from 12.3% in 2011" (*Economist* 6/19/15). DF is a member of the Europe of Freedom and Democracy group in the European Parliament.

A. *Occurring post-Cold War.* The party was formed in 1995 when its founders separated from the Progress Party (DF 2015). Condition: met.

B. *Non-Violent.* The DF opposes violence and favors stricter laws on crime. The party's website notes, "Preservation of law and order is of great importance in a society founded on the rule of law, and therefore there must be coherence between crime and punishment" (DF 2015). Counterpoint (2014) rated the group as a low danger for violence. Condition: met.

C. *Non anti-Semitic/racist/homophobic.* In 2003, Pia Kjærsgaard "lost a 2003 libel action against a political opponent who accused the party of having 'racist policies'" (Europhobia 2009). The courtroom loss resulted in many opponents labeling the group as an officially racist organization (Europhobia 2009). Pfisterer (2011) noted that "the DF rejects multiculturalism and … demands increasingly stronger rules for immigrants: last year DF party leader Pia Kjærsgaard even proposed banning satellite dishes in order to prevent people living in Denmark from watching 'anti-western' TV channels such as Al-Jazeera and Al-Arabia."

Despite accusations and speculation, research indicates DF does not propagate a platform of racism, anti-Semitism, or homophobia. Condition: met.

D. *Eurosceptic. The Economist* (6/19/15) described the party as an "anti-European Union, anti-immigration party." Further, DF "calls for the re-establishment of border controls, and opposes scrapping Denmark's current opt-out from EU judicial co-operation" (*Economist* 6/19/15). "The Danish People's Party wishes friendly and dynamic cooperation with all the democratic and freedom-loving peoples of the world, but we will not allow Denmark to surrender its sovereignty. As a consequence, the Danish People's Party opposes the European Union" (DF 2015). Condition: met.

E. *Nationalist/Reformist.* On the party's official website, Dahl proclaims, "The aim of the Danish People's Party is to assert Denmark's independence, to guarantee the freedom of the Danish people in their own country, and to preserve and promote representative government and the monarchy" (DF 2015). Further, "the essence of the party program is a warm and strong love of our country … . Denmark belongs to the Danes and its citizens must be able to live in a secure community founded on the rule of law, which develops along the lines of Danish culture." Following the 2014 EP elections, DF joined the European Conservatives and Reformists Group (European Parliament 2015). Condition: met.

DF: ALL CONDITIONS MET

Dutch Freedom Party—(Partij voor de Vrijheid-PVV), Netherlands

In 2004, Geert Wilders left the right-wing party "Volkspartij voor Vrijheid en Democratie (VVD), angered in part by the party's support for Turkish membership in the European Union" (de Jong 2015). Two years later, Wilders formed the Partij voor de Vrijheid (PVV). Wilders and, by extension, the PVV, believe "Muslims should be subjected to other, more oppressive laws and regulations than people in the 'in-group'; their holy book should be banned, there should be a special tax for wearing head-scarves, unlike other religious groups they should not be allowed to organize their own schools, and recently the party called for closing all mosques in the Netherlands. … The PVV doesn't have members, branches or other publications than a website" (de Jong 2015). Terry (2014) noted: "Under Dutch law, a political party must have at least two members. Hence, "the PVV has exactly two members: Geert Wilders, and the Geert Wilders Foundation. … PVV policy is set by Wilders. All the party's candidates for office are only accepted onto its lists after heavy vetting by Wilders personally" (Terry 2014).

The BBC (2009) observed that the PVV went "from winning nine seats in the 2006 election to 24 in 2010, taking a bigger share of the vote than the Christian Democrats—the main party in the outgoing government." According to the Netherlands House of Representatives, in the 2012 election, the party only won 15 seats. The number of seats they held in European Parliament remained at four following the 2014 elections.

A. *Occurring post-Cold War.* As noted above, Wilders formed PVV in 2006. Condition: met.
B. *Non-Violent.* In an interview with BBC (October 2009), Wilders proclaimed, "It's not my intention to have anything at all to do with violence. ... On the contrary, I despise violence—I just want a debate." Counterpoint (2014) ranks the group as a low danger for violence. Condition: met.
C. *Non anti-Semitic/racist/homophobic.* In the October 2009 BBC interview, Wilders, whose wife is Hungarian, was adamant that he is not a racist. He told the BBC his intention had only ever been "to have a debate about freedom of speech and the threat of Islamisation of our Western societies" (BBC 2009).

   "Our culture is based on Christianity, Judaism and humanism and (the Israelis) are fighting our fight," Wilders told *Reuters*, adding that "if Jerusalem falls, Amsterdam and New York will be next" (Heneghan 2010). Noted the BBC (2009), "Unlike other figures on the fringes of European politics, he has never been accused of anti-Semitism." Further, Wilders "styles himself as a promoter of gay rights, which he sees as in line with traditional Dutch values" (Polyakova 2014).

   Bahceli (9/16/15) reported that "In a September 2015 debate, Wilders called the wave of refugees passing through Hungary and other countries 'an Islamic invasion of Europe, of the Netherlands … . Masses of young men in their twenties with beards singing Allahu Akbar across Europe. It's an invasion that threatens our prosperity, our security, our culture and identity.'" Such rhetoric has been called racist, though, as noted above for FPÖ, Islam is a religion not a race. Wilders' words are certainly inflammatory, particularly his reference to appearance, but are not directed at a particular race.

   Similarly, in June 2014, Wilders asked his supporters: "Do you want more or fewer Moroccans in this city and in the Netherlands?" The response came loud and clear: "Fewer! Fewer! Fewer!" "We'll take care of that," their leader replied (McDonald-Gibson 2014). Once, again, is this rhetoric directed at a race? Though his words were certainly disparaging to Moroccans, Wilders' obvious point was immigration. Condition: met.

D. *Eurosceptic.* Wilders has suggested that "the Netherlands take back its national border and immigration control from the Shengen system of 26 European countries that has enabled free transit for European recruits to join the Islamic State. … He has also suggested that any returning Dutch veterans of the ISIS be barred from entry and deprived of Dutch citizenship" (New English Review 2015). Terry (2014) noted that "since 2011 Wilders has also increasingly positioned himself as an opponent of EU austerity, but even his opposition to austerity is coached in nationalist terms. Since 2012 he has become an uncompromising advocate of total withdrawal from the EU." *The Huffington Post* (Robins-Early 2015) reported "Wilder's PVV party is anti-European Union, anti-euro, anti-Islam and anti-multiculturalist. The party wants the Netherlands to leave the European Union so The Hague can independently decide on its immigration and fiscal policies." Condition: met.

E. *Nationalist/Reformist.* "The party has a populist economic program, but is socially conservative—advocating the protection of Dutch tradition" (Robins-Early 2015). Oudenampsen (2013) referred to the group as nationalist and populist.

Condition: met.

PVV: ALL CONDITIONS MET

English Defence League (EDL), England

According to the EDL official website, the English Defence League is a "human rights organisation that was founded in the wake of the shocking actions of a small group of Muslim extremists who, at a homecoming parade in Luton, openly mocked the sacrifices of our service personnel without any fear of censure" (EDL 2015). Thus, as Goodwin (2013) identified, the group is "a prime example of what Eatwell (2006) described as 'cumulative extremism,' whereby the activities of one extremist group trigger the formation of another manifestation, and possibly thereafter a spiral of counter-mobilization or even conflict."

The group was formed in Luton in 2009 by cousins Kevin Carroll and Tommy Robinson. Tommy Robinson is also known as Stephen Yaxley-Lennon and is a former BNP member. The EDL is vigorously anti-Islam and part of what Goodwin (2013) terms the "counter-Jihad" wave of movements. The EDL believes that "British Muslims should be able to safely demand reform of their religion, in order to make it more relevant to the needs of the modern world" (EDL 2015).

Though the group was originally dismissed as a band of violent hooligans and street thugs, Goodwin (2013) observed that "between 2009 and 2012 the EDL organized over 50 street-based demonstrations that often mobilized between 1,000 and 3,000 activists … in only a short period, the EDL established a national media profile and more than 80 local divisions, and attracted over 80,000 Facebook followers."

A. *Occurring post-Cold War*. The EDL was created in 2009 in Luton, England. Condition: met.
B. *Non-Violent*. On the official EDL website, the group proclaims, "We are an inclusive movement dedicated to *peacefully* [emphasis my own] protesting against Islamic extremism." However, media such as the *Independent* has reported multiple violent incidents involving EDL leadership and members, including then leader Tommy Robinson head-butting a fellow member at an EDL march in Blackburn and 172 EDL members arrested at one march on Whitehall in London (Rawlinson 2011).

   The BBC reported in 2015 that 50 convictions had resulted from a 2013 gathering of 2,000 EDL supporters in Centenary Square where missiles and bottles had been thrown at police, and the *Guardian* has highlighted the EDL's regular staging of violent protests (Taylor 2010).

   Channel 4 News (2013) reported that "EDL supporters are more likely to believe that violence is justifiable and inevitable: 72 per cent say that violence between different groups is 'largely inevitable', compared with an average of 46 per cent." Observed Goodwin (2013): "While most supporters say they would never personally engage in violence (only five per cent would), the picture changes when violence is framed as a response to other forms of extremism: 38 percent agree that 'violence against extremists is justified', a figure significantly higher than the wider average of 21 per cent." Further, "the vision that they offer to supporters is one in which different ethnic, racial and religious groups are embroiled in communal violence, and where violence may be called for (and justified) in order to protect the native group" (Goodwin 2013). Condition: unmet.
C. *Non anti-Semitic/racist/homophobic*. The court of public opinion holds the EDL as racist and fascist. However, according to Goodwin (2013), the EDL has "specifically sought to rally support among Jewish, Sikh and Pakistani Christian communities, as well as lesbian, gay, bisexual and transsexual ones." The EDL acknowledged it is "keen to draw its support from people of all races, all faiths, all political persuasions, and all lifestyle choices. Under its umbrella, all people in England, whatever their background, or origin, can stand united in a desire to stop the imposition of the rules of Islam on non-believers" (EDL 2015). They note, ironically, "The time for tolerating intolerance has come to an end: it is time for the whole world to unite against a truly Global Jihad" and "the EDL will continue to work to protect the inalienable rights of all people to protest against radical Islam's encroachment into the lives of non-Muslims" (EDL 2015).

The EDL notes that "there is a little understanding of what it is to be an 'Islamic extremist', and critics are all-too-often unfairly labelled as 'racists' or 'Islamophobes', again without any real understanding of what the terms mean" (EDL 2015). Reported Goodwin (2013): "Only a minority of those who agree with the platform of the EDL endorse classical or 'biological' racism. Few endorse open expressions of racial supremacism: 58 per cent agreed that non-white citizens who were born in the country are just as 'British' as white citizens, while 56 per cent said there is no difference in intelligence between black and white citizens."

Then party leader Robinson told *Channel 4 News* (May 28, 2013) that the EDL "is not a fascist organisation." "We oppose a fascist ideology. I hate Nazis as much as I hate Islamists, but Nazism isn't a problem in this country." He also insisted that the EDL is not racist: "The truth cannot be racist," adding "You can be any colour, but you can be a terrorist Muslim" (*Channel 4 News* 2013).

Thus, once again, we have a group with an anti-Islam/Muslim agenda, (specifically, an anti-Islamic extremist agenda) and we face the question of racism versus religious prejudice. As in the prior cases, it is determined that the two are not synonymous. Condition: met.

D. *Eurosceptic.* The EDL is considered to be Eurosceptic because of their anti-immigration stance. In 2013, EDL leader Robinson endorsed UKIP, stating "They are saying exactly what we say, just in a different way" (Stanley 2013). UKIP, as examined above, has "one key policy—to leave the European Union" (BBC Nov 21, 2014). However, as EDL has no seats in EP and has no official EU position, they cannot be determined to meet the required conditions to be considered Eurosceptic. Condition: unmet.

E. *Nationalist/Reformist.* Goodwin (2013) noted that the EDL has garnered support by "framing the religion as a fundamental threat to the national way of life and to Europe generally." *Channel 4 News* (May 28, 2013) noted that the EDL "sees itself as a defender of British values, which includes the army." EDL is widely recognized as a nationalist and even ultra-nationalist group. Condition: met.

EDL: ALL CONDITIONS NOT MET

Fascism and Freedom Movement-National Socialist Party (Movimento Fascismo e Libertà–Partito Socialista Nazionale, MFL-PSN), Italy

The Fascism and Freedom Movement-National Socialist Party was formed on July 25, 1991 by Senator Giorgio Pisanò with the motto "L'unico movimento del e per il popolo italiano!" or "the only movement of and for the people of Italy" (Freebase 2015). The group's leader has been Carlo Gariglio since December 2001. The group embraces fascism and Benito Mussolini's political thought, and is the only group in Italy to incorporate the fascist symbol in its logo (Milesi et al. 2006). The party is most often referred to as, simply, the Fascism and Freedom Movement. Note: Information on this group was exceptionally difficult to find. As a result, most references are from the party's official website (in Italian and translated to English for this research).

A. *Occurring post-Cold War.* The party was formed in 1989 as a political movement within the Italian Social Movement, becoming its own party in 1991 (Freebase 2015). In 2009, it added the "National Socialist Party" (NSP) to its name (Cyclopaedia 2015). Condition: met.
B. *Non-Violent.* No explicit references to the group either condemning or condoning violence could be located. There are various reports of members in attendance during protests or public addresses which turned violent, but no definitive links. As such, it is concluded that the group will meet the condition. Condition: met.
C. *Non anti-Semitic/racist/homophobic.* The party adheres to an ideology of anti-Americanism and anti-Zionism, and it outspokenly, unapologetically fascist. It is widely in the media as neo-Nazi and neo-fascist (Cyclopaedia 2015). Acknowledges the party, "The MFL-PSN favors adherence to the ideals of fascism over skin color, nationality and religious belief: for us a Fascist of color and who is Islamic is worth a thousand times more than a non-fascist who is white and Catholic."[2]

   Interestingly, the party states on its website that "Il MFL-PSN, infatti, chiarisce subito di non essere razzista," which translates to "the MFL-PSN, in fact, makes it clear that it is not racist" (Fascismo e Liberta 2015).

   The party does not specifically reference homosexuality though, by its strict adherence to fascist principles, it follows that MFL-PSN would echo classic Italian fascist beliefs. Wrote Quine (1995): "Fascist Italy considered homosexuality a social disease ... it condemned pornography, most forms of birth control and contraceptive devices (with the exception of the condom), homosexuality, and prostitution as deviant sexual behaviour."

   Further, because of its status as a fascist party, it would be disqualified from consideration as a MEPG, and categorized as a neo-fascist party. Condition: unmet.
D. *Eurosceptic.* The party's official website asserts that the MFL-PSN knows that the enemy is not the refugee, stowaway or immigrant (call it what you will) but the SYSTEM that allows a foreigner to enter Italy undisturbed. In fact, the system that favors unrestricted immigration (as well as the introduction of gay marriage, the gender theory and the Jobs Act) is a capitalist system (translated by the author from Italian).[3] Condition: met.

E. *Nationalist/Reformist.* The party "makes explicit reference to the ideals of the Italian Social Republic as corporatism, the socialization of the economy, taxation and monetary nationalism (Freebase 2015). Their website notes, "We believe that fascism is, in its essential and fundamental purpose (defense identity, exaltation of the concept of national sovereignty, nationalization of enterprises, defense of the community with a great attention to social issues and weaker sectors of the population) the solution to problems facing an Italy which, thanks to this class of politicians has become only poorer, more insecure, weaker economically, socially and in relations with other states"[4] (Fascismo e Liberta 2015). Condition: met.

MFL-PSN: ALL CONDITIONS NOT MET

Finns Party formerly True Finns (Perussuomalaiset-PS), Finland

The Finns Party claims that it is "both the youngest—established in 1995—and one of the oldest—with roots going back to the 19th century" party in Finland (PS 2015). The party has experienced multiple iterations and name changes. Observed the BBC (Sundberg, 2015), "The party's origins lie in a split in the Centre Party (then known as the Agrarian League) in 1959, when charismatic former cabinet minister Veikko Vennamo resigned in protest at what he saw as Finland's too-friendly relations with the Soviet Union."

After a period of instability and several name changes, he established the Rural Party in 1966, which also splintered years later. The party dwindled away and "by 1995, the party was in ruins, and the True Finns Party was established from its ashes" with Timo Soini taking over as chairman in 1997 (Sundberg 2015).

As noted on the party website, the Finns Party "according to a Finnish Broadcasting poll in September, 2013, is the second most popular party in Finland. It is, from the general election of 2011, the third largest party in the national parliament (Eduskunta)—and the largest party in opposition. ... The party has one MEP in the European Parliament as well as representatives in significant international organisations such as the Council of Europe, OSCE, Arctic Council, Inter-Parliamentary Union, and Nordic Council" (PS 2015).

A. *Occurring post-Cold War.* Though it has origins as far back as 1959, the party in its current form and revised agenda was established in 1995 (PS 2015). Condition: met.
B. *Non-Violent.* In an August 2015 speech, party chairman Soini emphasized: "No violence or hate speech against anyone, not even against the Finns Party," he stated, demanding that the actions of both the far right and far left be condemned (*Helsinki Times* August 10, 2015). Soini further declared that "such ideas and actions have no place in the Finns Party"

(*Helsinki Times* August 10, 2015). The party's 2015 manifesto asserts that "enforcement and punishment related to laws should be applied equally to all—with no consideration given to different economic and political standing of those violating laws" (PS 2015). Counterpoint (2015) ranks the group as a low danger for violence. Condition: met.

C. *Non anti-Semitic/racist/homophobic.* As discussed previously, most oppositionist groups are quick to be labeled racist, homophobic, and xenophobic, particular when they embrace restrictions on immigration. Such labels proliferate when comments are taken out of context, are lost in translation, or are the comments of one member or associate and are wrongly attributed to the organization as a whole. As the Finnish Department of Ministry (Finland.fi 2015) acknowledges, "To be sure, individual extremist voices are often heard from the party's rank-and-file."

As an example, on July 25, 2015, "a True Finn's Member of Parliament, Olli Immonen, released a Facebook update where he openly declared to be against a multicultural Finland. The text was posted in English and it is included below in its original form: *I'm dreaming of a strong, brave nation that will defeat this nightmare called multiculturalism*" (Joukahainen 2015). As expected, adversaries pointed to the comment as evidence of the party's racism.

However, the party's manifesto clearly stipulates: "'Justice for all' is a concern that permeates the Party's whole platform and policy … the basic foundation of the Party is a recognition of the Progressive traditions of equality of opportunity for all," and their 2011 manifesto declared that "hate crime is not to be tolerated and legislation is needed" (PS 2015). Condition: met.

D. *Eurosceptic.* The BBC characterizes the Finns Party as a populist and Eurosceptic party (Sundberg 2015). Indeed, the Finns Party makes no secret of their disdain for the EU: "The Finns Party is a leading EU-skeptic party in Finland. The Party argues that the European Union is working far below its capability and much could be done for improvement. Its opinion is that the EU meddles too much into citizens' every day affairs and is creating excessive central governance in Brussels" (PS 2015).

Further, the party presented a list of five main concerns ahead of the Finnish parliamentary elections in 2015. Among these concerns was a desire to stop bullying, particularly as it related to "Termination of detrimental EU-bureaucracy" (PS 2015). Condition: met.

E. *Nationalist/Reformist.* The party presented an elaborate manifesto of reforms ahead of the 2015 elections. As part of their economic platform (PS 2015), the Finns Party "believes the most important function of government is assuring the security and welfare of the ordinary Finnish citizen—thus budget cuts must come from decreasing migration—support and foreign development aid as well as other 'make a better world' -type spending." This priority is revisited during the presentation of their platform "Five Main Concerns."

Further, the party website proclaims that "the Finns Party does not accept outsiders setting up standards for how people judge themselves" (PS 2015). Sundberg (2015) observed that "beneath the strong Euroscepticism lies a brand of Finnish nationalism that targets refugees, immigrants and the Swedish population in Finland."

The party has also established a language policy: "The Finns Party believes that the Finnish language supports, nurtures and unifies Finnish citizens and their society. Promotion of proficiency in the Finnish language and its protection and development should be incorporated into national legislation. Such policy includes requirements such as 'Satisfaction competency in Finnish must be shown for extension of residency permission'" (PS 2015). Condition: met.

FINNS PARTY: ALL CONDITIONS MET

Freedom Party of Austria (Freiheitliche Partei Österreich-FPÖ), Austria

The US Library of Congress reported that "the Freedom Party of Austria (Freiheitliche Partei Österreichs-FPÖ) was founded in 1956 by Anton Reinthaller, who had served in the Seyss-Inquart national socialist government formed in collaboration with Hitler after the Anschluss in 1938" (Solsten 1994). During an FPÖ convention in spring of 1986, Jörg Haider, leader of the Carinthian branch of the party, launched a successful coup against leader Norbert Steger and became the new chairman (Solsten 1994). The *Encyclopedia Britannica* (2015) stated that

> in 1999–2000 a series of electoral successes … created a storm of controversy and produced widespread protests in Austria and abroad, largely because of perceptions that the leadership of the party, including Haider himself, was sympathetic to Nazism. Haider, whose father had been a leading member of the Austrian Nazi Party before and during World War II, became notorious for his praise of Hitler's employment policies and his remark, made to a group of Austrian veterans of World War II, that the Waffen-SS deserved "honour and respect." Arguing for stricter controls on immigration, he warned against the "over-foreignization" of Austrian society, pointedly borrowing a term—*Überfremdung*—used by Joseph Goebbels, Hitler's minister of propaganda.

Today, the Freedom Party is a self-proclaimed Eurosceptic group which has campaigned under an anti-immigrant platform and has raised slogans such as "Too much EU is dumb" (Bell 2014). The party is part of EP's newly formed Europe of Nations and Freedom party, a bloc of right-wing, Eurosceptic nationalist parties.

A. *Occurring post-Cold War.* The Freedom Party was originally founded in 1958. Because this pre-dates the end of the Cold War, the FPÖ is disqualified from consideration as a MEPG unless the party underwent an ideology change when Haider's assumed leadership. Morris, et al. (2014) noted that Haider succeeded in "transforming the FPÖ into a radical right-wing protest party that positioned itself against the mainstream." Indeed, 1993 served as a transformational year for the FPÖ.

   According to Meret (2010), "In 1993, the FPÖ launched a popular initiative on the topic of immigration called 'Austria First!'. The aim was to collect signatures in favour of a popular referendum on … restrictions and control in relation to immigration. The initiative was considered very controversial and provoked the exit of five party MPs, among them Heide Schmidt, who later launched the new party Liberal Forum (LiF). In the same year, relations between FPÖ and the Liberal International group—of which the party was a member since 1979—became more difficult. In 1993, the Liberal International executive recommended the expulsion of the FPÖ from its ranks, but the measure was preceded by the decision of the FPÖ to withdraw its membership."

   Thus, as a result of the pivotal changes in platform, rhetoric, and ideology during the early 1990s, FPÖ will be determined to meet the condition of restructured ideology. Condition: met.
B. *Non-Violent.* An article in *Reuters* acknowledged that the FPÖ "continues to attract a neo-Nazi fringe which has no other party to join and warns continually of an 'Islamicisation' of Catholic Austria. … There is, however, no evidence of any association with anti-foreigner violence, which remains rare in Austria" (Prodhan 2013). Similarly, reports of violence by members are spotty and circumstantial. Condition: met.
C. *Non anti-Semitic/racist/homophobic.* Freedom House (2013) reported that "the far-right FPÖ has been accused of anti-Semitic rhetoric in recent years. … Additionally, the FPÖ has been criticized for fueling anti-Muslim feelings in Austria through controversial ad campaigns." FPÖ believes "that the influence of the outsiders must be reduced or eliminated" (Morris, et al. 2014). The Anti-Defamation League reported in 2004 that "Haider has fended off accusations of anti-Semitism since the 1980's, but his insensitivity to Nazi brutality and a refusal to appreciate the suffering endured by those who lived under Nazi rule is well documented."

   Current party leader Heinz Christian Strache has taken strides to dispel party links with anti-Semitism. During a visit to Israel with Rene

Stadtkewitz (leader of the German Freedom Party), Kent Ekeroth (Sweden Democrat MP), and Filip Dewinter (head of Belgium's Vlaams Belang) he "denied they were stoking Islamophobia with their statement of support for Jerusalem," noting that Israel faced "an Islamic terror threat that aims right for the heart of our society" (Heneghan 2010).

However, in a 2008 interview with Britain's *Telegraph*, Strache stated "It is not about keeping Austria white, just about protecting its traditional community. ... We see Europe as Christian, and we believe it's at risk of Islamization" (McHugh 2015). Obviously, Islam is a religion and not a race/ethnicity.

Many analysts point to the FPÖ's definition of family as a sign of the party's homophobic leanings since the party defines family as "a partnership between a man and woman with common children." They offer as further evidence the party's opposition to crosswalk signals depicting same-sex couples. However, in "November 1996, when the reform of three anti-homosexual provisions in the Austrian penal code was on the agenda of the Parliament, the FPÖ voted in favour of repealing the ban on gay and lesbian organisations (Article 221) ... and also proposed to lower the age of consent for gay men to 16" (Hosi Wien 2015).

As with Front National, the FPÖ asserts that any accusations of racism and anti-Semitism stem from a misinterpretation of their tough immigration stance or isolated statements made by party members rather than official rhetoric. Coupled with the philosophically different leadership of Strache, a leader without close ties to the Nazi party, and the waters are muddied even further.

However, in the absence of a stated platform of homophobia, racism, or anti-Semitism, and derogatory attributions based on oppositional inference, it is determined that FPÖ will be deemed to have met this condition. Condition: met.

D. *Eurosceptic.* FPÖ's platform holds that international institutions like the EU have no right to intrude excessively in Austria's affairs (Morris, et al. 2014). The FPÖ has adopted a critical position of the European Union and the enlargement in particular. In campaign materials, the party utilized the slogan "EU critics vote blue. The FPÖ stands for an Austria without ifs and buts" (Meret 2010). Condition: met.

E. *Nationalist/Reformist.* FPÖ embraces several key core institutions held to be extremely valuable: the family, the nation (or "fatherland"), and the welfare state (Morris et al. 2014). Further, FPÖ is "committed to protecting our homeland of Austria, our national identity and autonomy as well as our natural livelihood" (Morris, et al. 2014). Freedom House (2015) categorizes the party as "the country's far-right, nationalist, and anti-immigration" party. Condition: met.

FPÖ: ALL CONDITIONS MET

Front National FN, France

Front National (FN) has been one of the "success" stories of euroscepticism. Originally founded in 1972 by Jean-Marie Le Pen, FN is considered to be Europe's oldest political far-right party (Ivaldi 2012). Le Pen earned the nickname "Devil of the Republic" as a result of his extreme right-wing views; his daughter, Marine Le Pen, has subsequently been referred to as "the devil's daughter." Craw (2015) wrote that under Jean-Marie Le Pen, FN "vehemently opposed to immigration, the European Union and same-sex marriage and in favour of the death penalty and promoting anti-globalisation in traditional values—views which saw him targeted by a car bomb outside their home when Marine was eight years old." Marine Le Pen assumed leadership of the party in 2011, having already made significant strides in reframing and redefining the party's tenets and vision. Her efforts to "normalize" the party are the result of a softer line that has increased political acceptance (Ivaldi 2012).

In his 2013 study on the ideological changes within Front National, Almeida observed that "academic analyses of the French radical right tend to converge in their assessment that, since Marine Le Pen took over the campaign management of the 2007 presidential election and succeeded her father as party president, the Front National has undergone a path of image change and ideological deradicalization or, at least, that most radical and polemic stances have been toned down." Ivaldi (2012) concurred, writing that "criticism of Islam has been tactically reframed into a pseudo-liberal agenda of tolerance or gender equality, borrowed in part from France's tradition of *laïcité* (secularity)" though the "concept of 'national priority' remains cornerstone to the party's ideology." Indeed, many of the ideas of FN resonate throughout Europe. In January 2015, Le Pen formed the new anti-EU bloc ENF after recruiting enough MEPs to meet a requirement that political groups have members from at least seven different EU countries (de la Baume 2015).

A. *Occurring post-Cold War.* FN was founded in 1972 which would disqualify it from meeting the conditions of this variable. However, FN has had a significant change in ideology and political stance, underscored by a change in leadership in 2011. This philosophical overhaul and subsequent softer, more appealing approach is widely documented and recognized by mainstream media worldwide such as the BBC, the *Economist*, and the *Guardian*. Marine Le Pen's incarnation of FN serves as a reinvention of the party, thus allowing for the post–Cold War condition to be met. Condition: met.
B. *Non-Violent.* Since Marine Le Pen assumed leadership of FN, none of the group's official press/website has promoted or encouraged violence. In

a 2011 statement, Le Pen noted her party's determination to fight mercilessly against all forms of violence and barbarity (Front National 2015). Counterpoint (2014) rates FN in the category of lowest risk of violence.

Although there is a fine line between not discouraging and encouraging, because the group does not condone acts of violence this condition is determined to have been met. Condition: met.

C. *Non-anti-Semitic/racist/homophobic.* Under Jean-Marie Le Pen, anti-Semitism was rife. Jean-Marie has been described as "a political provocateur convicted multiple times for hate speech and Holocaust denial" (Liphshiz 2014). However, the new FN under Marine Le Pen repeatedly has "condemned anti-Semitism and punished a party official who made anti-Semitic statements. In 2011, Le Pen dispatched her life partner and National Front Vice President Louis Alliot on a bridge-building mission to Israel" (Liphshiz 2014).

Though some people contend that the non-racist rhetoric is part of a rebranding strategy, Marine Le Pen has continually stated that FN is not racist (BBC News 2014). Since Marine Le Pen assumed leadership of FN, none of the group's official press/website has promoted racism or anti-Semitism, focusing instead on immigration. Counterpoint (2014) rates FN as lowest possibility for anti-Semitism, and moderate risk for homophobia and racism. Condition: met.

D. *Eurosceptic.* FN is unapologetically Eurosceptic. In a 2014 interview, Le Pen stated: "I want to destroy the EU, not Europe! I believe in a Europe of nation-states. I believe in Airbus and Ariane, in a Europe based on cooperation. But I don't want this European Soviet Union. ... The EU is deeply harmful, it is an anti-democratic monster. I want to prevent it from becoming fatter, from continuing to breathe, from grabbing everything with its paws and from extending its tentacles into all areas of our legislation" (Spiegel 2014).

Further, Le Pen has readily acknowledged her party's anti-immigration stance, adding that it is not because of a hatred of foreigners, rather it is because of an inability of the government to assist those already in France. "We have millions of unemployed and cannot afford any more immigration ... we support putting a stop to immigration" (Speigel 2014).

Lesniak (2014) noted of FN that "since the 1990s, its stance on the European Union has grown increasingly Eurosceptic. The party's opposition to immigration is focused on non-European immigration, and includes support for deporting illegal, criminal, and unemployed immigrants." Condition: met.

E. *Nationalist/Reformist.* Marine Le Pen asserted in 2014: "We want to represent all the French people with ideas that are neither left nor right: patriotism, defense of the identity and sovereignty of the people. If a person like me is described as being extreme left and extreme right at the same time, then that isn't far off the mark" (Spiegel 2014). Lesniak (2014) observed that "the party's ideology has been broadly described by scholars such as Shields as authoritarian, nationalist, and populist." Condition: met.

FRONT NATIONAL: ALL CONDITIONS MET

Golden Dawn (Χρυσή Αυγή), Greece

In 2015, the London School of Economics reported that "Golden Dawn is an extreme, ultra-nationalist and racist party. Among current far-right parties in Europe, it is the one that most resembles fascism, and in particular Nazism, in its outright espousal of National Socialism: the endorsement of what it terms the 'third biggest ideology in history', i.e. nationalism, combined with support for an all-powerful state premised on 'popular sovereignty'" (Vasilopoulou and Halikiopoulou 2015).

The UK's *Telegraph* has noted that the group's founder and leader, mathematician Nikos Michaloliakos, is "a former nationalist youth leader, who was close to the army dictators who ruled the country from 1967 to 1974… . In 2010, he caused controversy by giving fascist salutes in the city council in a taunt to a Left-wing councilor who had called him a fascist."

Further, it was noted that, in 2012, "the party exploited widespread anger over immigration and austerity reforms imposed by the EU and IMF and won 18 seats in parliament" (Squires 2015). In 2015, scores of Golden Dawn supporters went to trial on charges ranging from murder to participation in a criminal organization (Squires 2015).

A. *Occurring post-Cold War.* Golden Dawn was borne from ideas generated from Nikolaos Michaloliakos in the 1980s, though it wouldn't be until 1993 that the group would formalize and register as a political party. Condition: met.
B. *Non-Violent.* In 2013, the BBC profile on Golden Dawn reported that in 2012, "most of the 154 recorded racist attacks in Greece were attributed to Golden Dawn members, as were most of the 104" attacks reported through mid-2013. The BBC (2013) reported that in 2012 "party spokesman Ilias Kasidiaris, caused outrage last year when he attacked two female left-wing politicians during a live TV debate, slapping one and throwing water over another."

   Unfortunately, such incidents pale in comparison to charges against members that include murder. In 2015, 69 alleged members of Golden Dawn are on trial for charges that include a variety of serious charges, including murder. "Golden Dawn has already taken the line that even if some of its members are indeed guilty of the crimes of which they are accused, this has nothing to do with the party itself. The wrongdoers, the claim goes, are bad eggs, members gone rogue, or caught up in the wrong moment. If this claim is successful then the party itself is politically exonerated and ducks a blow that might irreversibly undermine its continued existence" (Melissaris 2015).

In the face of such diametric positions, the argument becomes one of whether those involved in these heinous acts are merely supporters and "wanna-bes" or active members, further, if they are found to be members are they acting on their volition or at the behest and encouragement of the Golden Dawn leadership. The BBC (2015) reported: "Police say they found evidence linking the killer of Pavlos Fyssas to the Golden Dawn leadership. In the homes of MPs arrested, they said they uncovered photos of Adolf Hitler and swastika flags. Witness testimony told of a 'Fuehrer-like' party structure, commanding hit squads that drove through Athens attacking migrants" (Lowen 2013).

Ultimately, there is too much evidence pointing to, at the least, an attitude of turning the other cheek if not outright acceptance of violence as a permissible method to achieve the group's goals. Condition: unmet.

C. *Non anti-Semitic/racist/homophobic.* Golden Dawn does not openly tout a racist platform. However, they are widely regarded as racist, homophobic, and anti-Semite. Lesniak (2014) noted that "according to academic sources, the group is racist and xenophobic." Reported the BBC in October 2013, "Golden Dawn may officially deny being a neo-Nazi movement but its badge resembles a swastika and some of its senior members have praised Adolf Hitler. ... Mr. Michaloliakos himself has denied the existence of gas chambers and crematoria at the site of the Auschwitz death camp."

Further, in 2014, Golden Dawn MP Ilias Panagiotaros extolled "the virtues of a one-race nation, and lashed out at the minorities the party considers deviant in the *60 Minutes* interview, describing Muslim immigrants as jihadists and gays as 'faggots'" (Smith 2014). He further stated that "until 1997, [the] international association of doctors, and I don't know what, considered homosexuality a sickness, illness, which it is" (Smith 2014). Condition: unmet.

D. *Eurosceptic.* The party was, and remains, adamantly opposed to the EU. At the exit polls in 2014, party spokesman Ilias Kasidiaris delivered a message from Michaloliakos stating: "I congratulate you for managing to resist the government's terrorism and for not believing their lies ... . We are the only political power that actually stands up against our state being run by foreign powers" (Govan 2014). Condition: met.

E. *Nationalist/Reformist.* The Golden Dawn website (Golden Dawn 2015) states "GOLDEN DAWN is a Popular and Nationalist Movement, with structures, principles and positions … nationalism is the only absolute and true revolution because it seeks the birth of new ethical, spiritual, social and mental values. The right and left solutions supposedly fighting each other, are just a fake theater of two partners who perpetuate the dominance of cosmopolitan internationalists, anti-national and anti-social forces." Lesniak (2014) affirmed that "the party's leader has openly identified it as nationalist and racist."

The group's nationalist platform is one aspect of the party on which nearly everyone can agree. Condition: met.

GOLDEN DAWN: ALL CONDITIONS NOT MET

Jobbik, Hungary

According to its website, the Jobbik Movement for a Better Hungary formed as a party in October 2003, from a movement of the same name (Jobbik 2015). Its founders were primarily Christian university students. Jobbik is a "principled, conservative and radically patriotic Christian party. Its fundamental purpose is protecting Hungarian values and interests" (jobbik.com).

The group has seen its popularity continue to rise. Notes its website: "At the 2009 European parliamentary elections, Jobbik won 3 seats with 15% of the votes and in doing so came close to beating the ruling Hungarian Socialists into third place. Hungary's 2010 parliamentary elections saw Jobbik cement its position as the nation's 3rd largest party, doubling the vote it had received in the previous year and getting just three seats short of the previous ruling party. Jobbik reached nearly 18% of the votes and delegated 47 deputies into the Hungarian Parliament" (Jobbik 2015).

A. *Occurring post-Cold War.* The group was formed in October 2003 (Jobbik 2015). Condition: met.
B. *Non-Violent.* In a letter sent by Jobbik leadership to *Reuters* in 2014, the group proclaimed "Jobbik condemns violence, and its members cannot be linked to such acts either," (Business Insider 2014). Counterpoint (2014) rated Jobbik as a medium danger for violence, contending "that the party is connected with violent groups and/or party leaders have made comments encouraging violence, although there is little evidence that members of the party leadership are themselves violent." They noted that Jobbik was "connected to the banned paramilitary group Magyar Garda, but party leaders have denounced violence." Condition: met.
C. *Non anti-Semitic/racist/homophobic.* Jobbik (2015) states: "What everyone knows but is silenced by: 'political correctness'—that 'phenomenon of "gypsy crime" is real'. It is a unique form of delinquency, different from the crimes of the majority in nature and force." In an official statement

on its website, the party states "Jobbik has never denied the holocaust, and persistently refutes as absurd the idea that it is anti-Semitic … [we] maintain that the charge is a completely invalid one, because the religious adherence or not of any of the parties involved, has absolutely no bearing or relevance whatsoever to these matters, only the facts, and people's actions do."

However, perhaps Germany's *Spiegel* stated it best, noting that deputy parliamentary floor leader Márton Gyöngyösi regularly devolves "into tiring marathons of relativization. … He's not an anti-Semite, he insists, but the Jews … he's not against the Roma, but the Gypsies" (2012).

Counterpoint (2014) rated Jobbik as a high danger of homophobia, anti-Semitism and racism. They noted that "there is clear evidence—either from the party manifesto or comments by the party leadership—that the party discriminates against people on the basis of race or ethnic group, stokes fears of Jews, and discriminates against gay people." Condition: unmet.

D. *Eurosceptic*. Jobbik (2015) states that "Jobbik rejects the Lisbon treaty accepted by each party in the Hungarian Parliament and renounces the cynical tactics of the political elite to force the EU Constitution upon the peoples of Europe, despite it failing to ratify in France and the Netherlands … we endorse the Europe of Nations concept instead of the United States of Europe agenda." Jobbik is openly Eurosceptic and regarded as such by media outlets worldwide (BBC, *Washington Post, The Guardian*, etc). Condition: met.
E. *Nationalist/Reformist*. Jobbik's fundamental purpose, as asserted on its website, is "protecting Hungarian values and interests … the party considers the protection, replenishment and expansion of the national resources crucial. These include the physical and mental condition of the nation, patriotic togetherness and solidarity" (Jobbik 2015). Freedom House (2015c) referred to the group as "the radical-nationalist and Euroskeptic" Movement for a Better Hungary (Jobbik). Condition: met.

JOBBIK: ALL CONDITIONS NOT MET

LAOS Popular Orthodox Rally (Λαϊκός Ορθόδοξος Συναγερμός-LAOS), Greece

"LAOS is the Greek name for the Popular Orthodox Rally (also translated as the Popular Orthodox Alarm), an extreme right-wing party in Greece" (JTA 2014). Founded on September 14, 2000 by Georgios Karatzaferis, the party began as a split from New Democracy" (Project Gutenberg 2015). In 2007, "LAOS won 10 of the 300 seats in Greek Parliament, making it the first extreme-right party in Greek Parliament since 1974" (JTA 2014). Since

2009, the party has been a member of the EP group "Europe of Freedom and Democracy."

A. *Occurring post-Cold War.* LAOS was founded in September 2000 (Project Gutenberg 2015). Condition: met.
B. *Non-Violent.* LAOS is not regarded as a violent group. Violence among Greek groups has been relegated to other groups in Greece, most notably Golden Dawn. Observed Roushas (2013): "Golden Dawn—in contrast to LAOS—has been explicitly violent throughout its political career." In fact, LAOS offices were attacked in 2009 and 2001 (Michaletos, 2015). Condition: met.
C. *Non anti-Semitic/racist/homophobic.* Multiple sources including the Anti-Defamation League and the *Huffington Post* cite a history of anti-Semitic statements made by leader, Karatzaferis (Tzilivakis 2013; Mionis 2012). *The Jewish Chronicle* (Elgot 2011) reported: "The party has been condemned by the American Jewish Committee ... one party member Adonis Georgiadis, has publicly endorsed a book called *Jews: The Whole Truth* on a television show, on a TV channel owned by the party." The book "has been described by the Central Board of Jewish Communities in Greece as a 'defamatory, anti-Semitic book in which Jews are called "subhuman" and are directly threatened with annihilation'" (Elgot 2011).

   The United States Department of State also reported in Country Reports on Human Rights Practices for 2011 that "LAOS Party leader Georgios Karatzaferis had made numerous anti-Semitic statements in the past, insinuating that Jews planned the September 11 attacks and denying the existence of the Holocaust" (US State Department 2011). Condition: unmet.
D. *Eurosceptic.* Vasilopoulou (2010) contended that the LAOS perspective is "soft Eurosceptic": "LAOS sustains that the future of Greece is linked to a great extent to the European Union. The party supports the incorporation of all the European states into a viable Union, and is in favor enlarging the EU. However, it argues that 'this can only occur within the context of a Confederation where there would be recognition and protection of the historic, cultural and ethnic roots as well as the ethnic characteristics of the European peoples'" (LAOS website as documented in Vasilopoulou 2010).[5] Such identification qualifies LAOS as contingent or qualified Eurosceptic. Condition: met.
E. *Nationalist/Reformist.* Al Jazeera (Bollier 2012) reported that LAOS "describes itself as 'hellenocentric'—opposes illegal immigration, and suggests deporting all undocumented immigrants." Commented party leader Giorgis Karatzaferis: "I don't want them to become a majority" (Bollier 2012). The US State Department (2011) described LAOS as a

"small, extreme right-wing party (that) supports virulent nationalism." Condition: met.

LAOS: ALL CONDITIONS NOT MET

Lega Nord (Northern League-LN), Italy

Lega Nord per l'Indipendenza della Padania is a Italian political party better known as Lega Nord, Lega or Carroccio. The party was founded as a regional party in 1991 by Umberto Bossi. In 1996, Lega Nord declared its full name as the "Independent Republic of Padania" (Brambilla 2012). The party "advocates federalism and transfer of control of resources to regional governments" and is a fierce opponent of immigration (European Election and Referendum Database 2015). LN has an ultimate of realizing the secession of Padania (the northern region of Italy) and creating a new pan-European state that would include northern Italy, Switzerland, Austria, Bavaria and Savoy (Brambilla 2012).

Paxton (2004) observed: "In the parliamentary elections of 1992, the Lega Nord won almost 19 percent of the northern vote (8.6 percent nationally) by playing on northern small businessmen's resentment of the social burden of the Italian south, expressed in terms approaching racism." Lega Nord currently holds 60 seats in parliament (European Election and Referendum Database 2015).

A. *Occurring post-Cold War.* Lega Nord was created in 1989 as a result of a merger of seven regional leagues, including Alleanza Nord, Lega Lombarda and Liga Veneta (Caramani and Mény 2005). It was officially established in February 1991 with Umberto Bossi serving as chairman. Condition: met.
B. *Non-Violent.* LN condemns violence, instead advocating for civil disobedience. As Zaslove (2011) notes, "Lega has not been directly involved in any acts of violence other than small skirmishes and some acts of civil disobedience." Counterpoint (2014) concurred, rating the group as a "low danger" of violence. Condition: met.
C. *Non anti-Semitic/racist/homophobic.* Research from Counterpoint (2014) indicated "little or no evidence—either from the party manifesto or comments by the party leadership—that the party stokes fears of Jews" or that "the party discriminates against people on the basis of race or ethnic group." However, Counterpoint (2014) found "there is mixed evidence—either from the party manifesto or comments by the party leadership—that the party discriminates against gay people." The Democratic Society (4/22/2014) reported that "some of the party's local councils have banned kebab shops 'to preserve real local foods'… . The party is widely

considered to be Italy's most strongly anti-immigrant party. The party has often been labelled as Islamophobic, and has sometimes been accused of racist rhetoric."

In 2014, Lega Nord's Gianluca Buonanno "dirtied his face with makeup to illustrate the point that Italians 'needed to be a little bit darker' if they were going to get welfare benefits. During a discussion in Italy's parliament last year on gay issues, he produced a bulb of fennel—whose name in Italian is a homosexual slur—to taunt two openly gay lawmakers. That particularly nicety came on the heels of a radio interview in which he said that, if confronted by a homosexual, he would 'kick him in the balls'" (Faiola 2014).

Davies (2012) recounted a 2013 incident in which "Roberto Calderoli, a former minister under Silvio Berlusconi and senate vice-president of the Northern League, told a rally in the northern town of Treviglio that Kyenge would be better off working as a minister 'in her country.'" Calderoli also suggested "the country's first black government minister had the features of an orangutan" stating: "I love animals, but when I see her, I can't help but think of an orangutan" (Davies 2013). Calderoli himself claimed that what he had said was a "little joke" and that it was "not racist" (Foot 2013). Foot (2013) opined:

> The Lega has always been a racist party, fanning the flames of ethnic and religious conflict whenever it has been able to. You could compile an encyclopedia of the League's racist comments and activities. There was, for example, the mayor of a major Italian city who argued that immigrants should be dressed as animals and hunted down, or the League politician who recently claimed to be happy on hearing of the death of immigrants trying to arrive by sea. (Foot 2013)

One of the problems is that there is disagreement over what racism actually is. Calderoli thinks that comparing a black woman to an orangutan is a "little joke," or even a "funny joke." When [Italian footballer] Mario Balotelli was depicted as King Kong in a cartoon, many people didn't see any problem at all. (Foot 2013)

Smythe (2013) provided provocative insight: "When you have Italians in the South not considered Italians because of their skin colour or the lack of industry, oblivious to the fact that Italians worldwide have been considered people of colour until only recently. Italy does not need an awareness campaign of the Other. Italy needs first to recognise who the Other is, and it should start with a mirror."

Are these examples of ignorance, insensitivity, or racism? It is best to revisit the original qualifiers/disqualifiers set forth at the beginning of this chapter: mission and vision do not specifically contain anti-Semitic, racist, or homophobic ideology with information gathered from a review of group's mission, vision, official website(s)/publications, and/or media/news reports. In the case of LN, the party was founded with the guiding principle of separatism and creating a distinction between northern Italy and southern Italy. Can one be racist against his/her own race? Could such sentiment be better described as elitism?

In 1993, Putnam acknowledged the long-standing dichotomy between southern and northern Italy, and pointed to the level of civic engagement as an explanation. Putnam (1993) contends that this concept of social capital was largely absent in southern Italy but present in northern Italy and led to the north's prosperity. This disparity is the foundation of LN's argument and the foundation of their separatist ideology.

The final word comes in the form of an opinion rendered by the European Commission against Racism and Intolerance (ECRI). In 2002, the ECRI denounced the party, asserting that "members of Lega Nord made a particularly intense use of racist and xenophobic propaganda." Yet the racist hate speech continued despite the party's 2013 creation of a new "anti-racist committee" to defend Italians from Roma. The 2015 report found that "from January 2013 to March 2015 the ERRC has documented the following in relation to hate speech: 35 cases of hate speech by public figures, including two demonstrations. Most of the hate speech (15 cases) came from the Lega Nord (Northern League), a political party" (ERRC 2015). Condition: unmet.

D. *Eurosceptic.* LN argues that "the European institutions are not close to the European citizens and that integration should mean the respect of the traditions and cultures of the European peoples, which is not currently the case. However, it argues that 'we must construct a Europe that is founded on the respect of national and territorial realities, giving the European Union only a limited degree of sovereignty, delimiting its competences and the fields of its intervention avoiding ambiguities'" (LN website as documented in Vasilopoulou 2010).[6] Further, "as a consequence of Italy's integration in the EMU in 1998, the Lega Nord shifted from a pro-European to a Eurosceptic position. The Lega's Eurosceptic vision combines a strong identification with Europe with a hostile attitude towards the institutions of the EU" (Huysseune 2010). LN's new party secretary, Matteo Salvini, has recently "described the European Union as a 'monster' that needs to be 'slaughtered' and has called the Euro a 'crime against humanity" (Squires 2013). Condition: met.
E. *Nationalist/Reformist.* LN advocates for the creation of a new, independent state that would better serve the people of northern Italy. The Democratic Society (4/22/2014) observed: "The party has wavered between

separatism for the North and a federal Italy. At its most separatist the *Lega* claims that the North of Italy is a forgotten nation called 'Padania'. In the late 1990s the *Lega* went as far as to arrange elections to a 'Padanian parliament', a Padanian football team and even a 'Miss Padania' beauty contest in order to lay claim to a 'Padanian' nationhood."The Democratic Society (April 2014) reported that the group touts a "Padanian nationalist stance and stronger anti-immigrant stances." Condition: met.

LEGA NORD: ALL CONDITIONS NOT MET

National Democratic Party of Germany (Nationaldemokratische Partei Deutschlands-NPD)

An official NPD website states that NPD "is Germany's oldest nationalist party since 1945 and one of the few patriotic organizations not yet banned by the government. It was formed on November 28, 1964, by leading members of the disbanded Deutsche Reichspartei and several smaller patriotic groups" (NPD 2015). The party has been the target of much scrutiny due to alleged ties with neo-Nazism, racism, anti-Semitism, and homophobia. The party website notes that "in 2004 the NPD attained 9,2% of the electorate and won factional strength in state parliament in the southeastern State of Saxony and only two years later 7,3% in the northeastern State of Mecklenburg-Vorpommern where a second faction in a state parliament was established with Udo Pastörs as leader. This was a real shock for the system-parties in Germany. Besides these victories, the NPD also made good progress in municipal and local elections with over 21% of the votes in some districts" (NPD 2015). The party is viewed as extreme right-wing with racist tendencies and there are ongoing attempts to ban the group.

A. *Occurring post-Cold War.* According to the NPD website, beginning at the end of the 1970s then chairman, Martin Mussgnug, "began a restructuring which combined the dropping of much of the early conservative political rhetoric with an emphasis on the ideological education of members. Thereafter the party began concentrating upon building a strong organizational infrastructure, rather than upon short-term electioneering. Consequently, after the partial reunification of Germany in 1990, the NPD was able to gain considerable strength in the eastern part of the country: the former German Democratic Republic" (NPD 2015).

   Thus, despite some waxing and waning, because the party was founded in the 1960s and has held to a similar agenda throughout, the party will not meet the condition of occurring post-Cold War. Condition: unmet.

B. *Non-Violent.* According to the Southern Poverty Law Center (Lee 2015): "The German government asked the country's highest court to ban the

NPD, claiming it has ties to neo-Nazi Skinhead gangs involved in a surge of violent attacks against foreigners and other minorities."

Further, "describing the NPD as the ideological seedbed for neo-Nazi aggression, German officials accuse the party of fomenting racist violence throughout the country. ... [In 1998] NPD candidate Manfred Roeder called for the violent overthrow of the German government" (Lee 2015). Borrud (2015) has noted that many people "have witnessed first-hand the violence that groups like the NPD are able to bring about." Condition: unmet.

C. *Non anti-Semitic/racist/homophobic*. Ralf Jäger, interior minister of North Rhine Westphalia, contended that "the NPD provides the basis for neo-Nazi violence and spreads hatred against foreigners" (Borrud 2015). In the past few years, there have been numerous attempts to have the party banned. *Deutsche Welle* has reported that the primary problem in having the party (or any party) prohibited (Borrud 2015) is mounting sufficient evidence: "Explicit proof that the party not only condones—but also takes an active part in—unconstitutional actions such as the propagation of racism and xenophobia must be successfully demonstrated before the country's leading justices. The case is to be made by the leaders of Germany's 16 federal states, who comprise the Bundesrat, or the upper house of federal parliament." Indeed, following an unsuccessful attempt in 2003 to ban the party, it was determined that NPD executives had provided much of the evidence (Borrud 2015). Additionally, the NPD Party Program states that "homosexual couples are not family and may not be promoted. Children need a mother and father for a healthy development."[7]

As reported by *Reuters* (Chambers 2012): "Germany's domestic intelligence service has described the NPD as 'racist, anti-Semitic and revisionist' and says it aims to abolish democracy." Further, noted Chambers (2012): "The party calls the German constitution a 'diktat' imposed by victorious Western powers after 1945." Condition: unmet.

D. *Eurosceptic*. The NPD Party Program (NPD 2015) explicitly declares: "We reject all 'multicultural' societal models as inhuman, because they alienate both German and non-German community order."[8] The EU Observer reported that "NPD is in favour of a breakup of the eurozone and a return to national currencies, and demands a 'rapid dismantling of the European Stability Mechanism'—the eurozone bailout fund" (Pop 2014). Condition: met.

E. *Nationalist/Reformist*. As proclaimed in the Party Program, NPD is the home of the Social Party of Germans, is committed to human rights and is therefore working consistently for national identity, national sovereignty and national solidarity as a means of livelihood of our people.[9] Condition: met.

NPD: ALL CONDITIONS NOT MET

Party of the Swedes (Svenskarnas parti–SVP), Sweden

The party disbanded in May 2015 following highly disappointing national election results in 2014.

PARTY OF THE SWEDES: N/A

Pegida, Germany

Pegida is far-right radical group which has taken Germany by storm during its short existence. The *Economist* (2/23/2015) reported that "the movement was founded last autumn [2014] in Dresden. … Its first organiser was Lutz Bachmann, an owner of an ad agency who had repeatedly fallen afoul of the law and who once fled to South Africa to avoid going to prison." Germany's *Spiegel* expanded, noting that "on Oct. 10, 2014, Lutz Bachmann posted a video on YouTube showing a Dresden rally in support of Kurdish fighters battling Islamic State. One day later, he founded a Facebook group called 'Peaceful Europeans against the Islamization of the West,' which ultimately turned into Pegida" (Popp and Wassermann 1/12/2015). Explained the *Economist* (2/23/15*):* "Pegida is a German acronym for 'Patriotic Europeans Against the Islamicisation of the Occident.'" *The Economist* (2/23/2015) also observed that "the sudden and spontaneous rise of Pegida has caused much soul-searching in German society and has shaken its political system." The group holds well-attended demonstrations every Monday known as "Monday marches." *Time* magazine (Shuster 2015) noted that a survey taken in December 2014 "found that 30% of respondents had 'full and total' sympathy for Pegida's cause, the same level of support that Merkel's political party got in the German elections to the European Parliament last year."

A. *Occurring post-Cold War.* Pegida was founded in the fall of 2014 by Lutz Bachmann. Condition: met.
B. *Non-Violent.* Shuster (2015) reported in *Time* magazine that Bachmann publicly renounces extremist violence of any kind. In July 2015, a town hall in Freital, Germany, to discuss housing of refugees turned into chaos as opposing sides argued and fights ensued. When *Deutsche Welle* asked Bachmann for comment on the violent nature of the meeting, he replied*:* "In principle we support any protests that are directed against economic migrants. We're behind those. But we do not support protests directly against homes where there are definite war refugees" (Knight 2015).

   Such a comment is thinly veiled support of violence. Condition: unmet.
C. *Non anti-Semitic/racist/homophobic.* The *Economist* (2/23/15) calls Pegida "a German movement with an explicitly anti-Islamist and

implicitly xenophobic message" and perceive Muslims as a threat to German culture. Indeed, Pegida member Siegfried Däbritz has stated, "We want to gather to oppose the advancing Islamization of our country. We don't want terrorist, Islamist powers to fight their religious war on our streets. We are against IS, PKK, al-Qaida and all the others," (Popp and Wassermann 1/12/2015). Further, Bachmann added: "It is clear that people will accuse us of being Nazis. But why should we make it easy for them rather than being clear about where we stand from the beginning: PATRIOTIC and not Nazi!"

In January 2015, Bachmann "abruptly stepped down after pictures of him posing as Hitler on his Facebook page became public. A march on January 19th was cancelled by police after they obtained information concerning a possible plan to assassinate Mr Bachmann" (Economist 2/23/2015). Bachmann, however, reassumed his leadership of Pegida by February 2015.

In a January 2015 interview with YNet News, Christian Mayerhoff, a spokesperson for Pegida, asserted "We are no Nazis. Personally I was active in left-wing human rights movements in my youth during the early 1990s. After 9/11 I started learning about Islam and Islamism and this changed my opinion about multiculturalism and political correctness. In PEGIDA there are leftists, centrists and conservatives. In the city of Kassel our committee includes a Croatian, a Jew and a secularized Muslim."

As with PVV and others, there is a definite prejudice against Islam but prejudice is, arguably, not racism and Islam is a religion not a race. Condition: met.

D. *Eurosceptic.* The *Economist* (2/23/2015) wrote that "supporters seem troubled by the perceived threat to German culture posed by immigrants and asylum-seekers." In January 2015, the group presented a 19-point manifesto with a "six-point plan demanding clear immigration rules, an end to 'absurd' EU controls and direct democracy in Germany through referenda" (Scally 2015). Condition: met.

E. *Nationalist/Reformist.* Pegida presented their six-point highly nationalistic and reformative political platform in January 2015: "First: qualitative rather than quantitative immigration; second: compulsory integration for foreigners; third: no entry visas for jihadis; fourth: referendums; fifth: a good relationship with Russia; sixth: more money for the police" (Schulze 2015).

Thran and Boehnke (2015) analyzed Pegida's nationalist views, noting "the xenophobic logic of Pegida's value-based nationalism." Condition: met.

PEGIDA: ALL CONDITIONS NOT MET

Podemos (We Can), Spain

Frayer (2015) reported that Podemos was founded by Pablo Iglesias (also known as El Coleta "the ponytailed one") and Miguel Urbán of the radical-left party "Izquierda Anticapitalista" in January 2014, with pretensions of breaking the two-party hegemony in Spanish politics. Iglesias (2015) noted that "after the May 2014 elections, Podemos had five MEPs, although it still lacked a formal political leadership and an organized territorial and sectoral structure across regions, as well as formal mechanisms for decision-making." McHugh (2015) observed: "By May 2015, Podemos had swept many local elections, winning important mayoral seats in major cities like Barcelona and destabilizing parties that had held positions since the 1980s."

Noted Duarte and Tadeo (2015): "At the center of the Podemos's platform is a plan to force a restructuring of Spain's 1 trillion euros ($1.1 trillion) of government debt in what would be the biggest sovereign reorganization in history. The proposal has helped Podemos top 10 opinion polls in Spain since November." McHugh (2015) observed that Podemos "built its platform in opposition to the austerity policies adopted by most debt-stricken European nations, which included budget cuts and higher taxes in exchange for debt-relief loans from European lenders." Many people in the political arena voice concern regarding Iglesias' close relationship with Greek SYRIZA leader Tsipras, wondering how it might impact or even steer Podemos.

A. *Occurring post-Cold War.* Iglesias officially announced the creation of Podemos on January 17, 2014, at a small theater in Lavapiés, a district in Madrid (Tremlett 2015). Condition: met.
B. *Non-Violent.* Podemos has virtually no connections with violence though, as noted by Kassam (2014), "Others have taken aim at his words—he has been accused of justifying terrorism at the hands of Eta after he said that the group's violence 'had political explanations' that needed to be understood in order to find democratic solutions."

   Observers note the party's rise based on peaceful demonstrations: Podemos "was forged on the back of the largely peaceful protests held across Spain by the M-15 anti-austerity movement during 2011 and 2012" (Nicholas 2014). Condition: met.
C. *Non anti-Semitic/racist/homophobic.* As outlined in the 2015 Podemos electoral platform, "El Programa del Cambio" (Podemos 2015), Podemos advocated for gay rights, abortion rights, gender equality, and civic liberties (Igualidad), and favored an open and inclusive immigration policy (Migraciones). Zabala (2015) observed: "Contrary to Beppe Grillo's Five Star Movement, which ruined its reputation in Italy by joining Nigel Farage's racist Europe of Freedom and Democracy group, Podemos opted for

the European United Left/Nordic Green Left group, where Israel's occupation of Palestinian territories as well as the CIA's torture programme are often condemned."

Further, the Podemos platform specifically addressed racism: "We will implement a plan to combat racism, xenophobia and other forms of discrimination affecting both people of Spanish origin residing abroad as well as people of foreign origin residing in Spain."[10] Condition: met.

D. *Eurosceptic.* Frayer (2015) noted that "Iglesias argues that Spain's recovery has come at the expense of the Spanish working-class, which continues to suffer from slumping wages and persistently high unemployment—still 23%. He blames ruling conservatives, Germany and the troika of the European Union, European Central Bank and International Monetary Fund—and vows, if elected prime minister, to roll back the austerity measures they support." Iglesias contends one enemy of Spain is "Germany's chancellor Angela Merkel and the unelected officials who oversaw the euro from the European Central Bank in Frankfurt. Iglesias did not want Spain to leave the European Union, but he was not satisfied with it either" (Tremlett 2015). Such views are in line with soft euroscepticism.

Stokes (2015) also pointed out that Podemos "has called for a renegotiation of EU-demanded fiscal austerity measures and a curbing of EU powers." Condition: met.

E. *Nationalist/Reformist.* Above all, Iglesias has stated that "he wanted Spaniards to recover 'sovereignty'" (Tremlett 2015). As noted above in Duarte and Tadeo (2015): Podemos sought "a plan to force a restructuring of Spain's 1 trillion euros ($1.1 trillion) of government debt in what would be the biggest sovereign reorganization in history." The 2015 Podemos platform (Podemos 2015) explicitly states "El nuestro es un programa ciudadano. De la ciudadanía y para la ciudadanía" (Ours is a national program. Of the citizens and for the citizens). Condition: met.

PODEMOS: ALL CONDITIONS MET

Republican People's Party (Cumhuriyet Halk Partisi—CHP), Turkey

The Republican People's Party (CHP) was established in 1923 "and mostly ran a single-party regime for the first quarter century of existence. It transformed Turkey from a mostly pious Sultanate to a westward-looking country: political Islam was banned, women were enfranchised, and a Latin alphabet replaced the old Arabic lexicon" (JamesinTurkey.com 2015).

However, as part of a military coup on September 12, 1980, the National Security Council (MGK), dissolved the parliament and the government, and created adopted a military-inspired constitution that banned political parties

(*Reuters* May 3, 2010). The *Turkey Analyst* (May 2008) noted that "when the ban on pre-1980 political parties was lifted in 1992, Baykal immediately re-established the old CHP."

In February 1995, CHP merged with SHP, then the main left-wing party, with Baykal serving as leader until May 2010 (All About Turkey 2015). Reported All About Turkey (2015):

> Following the general elections of April 1999, CHP—which obtained only 8.7% of the votes—disappeared from the Parliament for the first time in its history. During the elections of 2002, ex-leader Mr. Baykal re-gained his seat and they were able to get 19.39% of the votes, thus became the second and the main opposition party in the parliament.
>
> In 2007 they joined their forces with DSP and got 20.88% of the votes. After the elections, members from DSP have left the party and returned to their original party. In 2011 they got 25.92% of the votes and thus hold 135 seats. In 2015 they got 25.13% of the votes and hold 132 seats.

In 2014, *Today's Zaman* reported that "the main opposition Republican People's Party (CHP) is undergoing a transformation and has, under the leadership of Kemal Kılıçdaroğlu, nominated certain names in local and presidential elections who are affiliated with the political center-right and who embrace a conservative ideology in consecutive elections in an effort to break the party's reputation of only appealing to a limited part of society. The party has also signaled change in its policy direction on the Kurdish problem, which has occupied the agenda of the country for decades" (Üstüntağ 9/6/2014).

A. *Occurring post-Cold War*. Though CHP was formed in 1923, it survived the 1980s ban on political parties to reemerge in a new Turkey in 1992. Through leadership changes and party mergers, the party took various forms though it presented a new ideology in 2014. Caliskan (2014) argued that CHP has experienced three transformations—the first during the 1930s when CHP was the state; the second beginning around 1971 under the leadership of Bülent Ecevit; and the third in the 2000s under Kılıçdaroğlu.

Kılıçdaroğlu promised a fundamental change of course in the party's political practice with an initial goal of bridging the gap between CHP's two ideological wings, the Nationalists and Social Democrats (Caliskan 2014). Following an electoral loss in 2011, Kiliçdarogllu called for a party congress to change the dated party constitution. He pushed for democracy and introduced positive discrimination for women and a 10% youth quota (Caliskan 2014). In 2015, the success of the new party ideology was apparent as CHP garnered 25% of the vote. Condition: met.

B. *Non-Violent.* CHP condemns violence. In 2014, Kılıçdaroğlu stated: "We all need to know that terrorism is a humanity crime" (*Daily Sabah* 10/10/2014). Turkish Weekly (2015) reported that Kılıçdaroğlu has spoken against violence: "Turning our demonstrations into violent acts would only serve the terrorist organization. Let's denounce terrorism, let's march against it with our flags in our hands." Condition: met.
C. *Non anti-Semitic/racist/homophobic.* Kulaoğlu (2015) reported: "Faruk Loğoğlu, deputy chairman of CHP, told Turkey's Zaman that the CHP categorically rejects any manifestation of anti-Semitic behavior and discourse, whether in Turkey or elsewhere." Loğoğlu stated: "We strongly blame Erdoğan and his cohorts for hurting the feelings of our citizens of Jewish origin and for endangering their well-being and safety … no one should forget that that the family of nations views anti-Semitism as a crime against humanity. The CHP stands in solidarity with our citizens of Jewish origin" (Arslan 3/16/2014). Further, CHP has proposed homosexual candidates for elections and has signed on to protect the rights of homosexuals (Kulaoğlu, 2015). Condition: met.
D. *Eurosceptic.* Uzun and Kaleagasi (2015) noted that "CHP has consistently been against censoring of media, for freedom of speech, and for further integration into the European Union." In 2015, "CHP announced plans to build a new mega city called 'Central Turkey' (Merkez Türkiye) to serve as a trade hub between Europe, Asia and other continents" (CHP EU 2015). Condition: unmet.
E. *Nationalist/Reformist.* According to All About Turkey (2015), "CHP's main ideological source has always been Kemalism, which is the modernization paradigm of Turkish Republic … [Kemalism] was meant to preserve the independence of the Republic of Turkey and also to help the Republic's political development. It was a nationalism which respected the right to independence of all other nations."

   CHP is reported to be embracing "soft-nationalism." Mahçupyan (2012) opined that, as embraced by CHP, "nationalism represents a true alternative and is a postmodern form of Kemalism." Condition: met.

   CHP: ALL CONDITIONS NOT MET

Right Sector (Pravy Sektor/ Правий сектор), Ukraine

The Right Sector is a Ukrainian movement led by Dmitry Yarosh. According to the group's official website (http://pravyysektor.info), the movement originated during the early events of Euromaidan in Kiev Square (Maidan) on November 28, 2013, as a union of right-wing organizations and individual activists. Right Sector is considered a far-right, ultra-nationalist, militant group.

A. *Occurring post-Cold War.* The group was formed in 2013, in Kiev. Condition: met.

B. *Non-Violent.* According to the BBC (April 28, 2014), "activists claiming to be Right Sector members were involved in Kiev's Maidan protests from late November, but the group did not attract much attention until violent clashes with police in central Kiev on 19 January, in which it played a leading role. By early February Mr Yarosh was saying the Right Sector had 500 fighters on Independence Square and could mobilise up to 5,000 nationwide." Additionally, the BBC (April 28, 2014) reported that Russia has accused the Right Sector of "involvement in multiple acts of violence" including "against pro-Moscow separatists in eastern Ukraine … . The Right Sector denies this, but maintains a barrage of anti-Russian rhetoric." Indeed, after a "Right Sector activist wounded a number of people in central Kiev in 2014, the group was forced to vacate its city headquarters, leaving all weapons behind" (BBC April 28, 2014).

   Peters (2015) reported that the Right Sector has threatened violence throughout Ukraine, and on July 11, 2015, "the neo-fascist organization engaged in a gun battle in the town of Mukacheve." Condition: unmet.

C. *Non anti-Semitic/racist/homophobic.* Party leader Yarosh has rejected all accusations of racism, asserting that "he regards anyone who fights for Ukraine as a comrade. Right Sector leaders have recently assured the Israeli ambassador that they reject anti-Semitism along with other forms of chauvinism and xenophobia" (BBC April 28, 2014). In April 2014, a representative of Right Sector "travelled to Odessa after vandals defaced a Holocaust monument with Nazi symbols to show solidarity with the local Jewish community" (*International Business Times* 2014). Condition: met.

D. *Eurosceptic.* BBC (April 28, 2014) reported that Right Sector leading figure, Andriy Tarasenko, has stated that the group aimed "not for closer ties with Europe but rather to build a nationalist Ukrainian state and stage a nationalist revolution." Not only is the group adamantly anti-Russia, they are also anti-Europe. The group "regards the EU as an 'oppressor' of European nations" (BBC January 2014). Condition: met.

E. *Nationalist/Reformist.* Right Sector's official website states that it is an organized movement that aims for Ukrainian national liberation from foreign and domestic occupation and nation-building (Pravy Sektor 2015) The website further states that the mission of the movement is gaining and development of an Independent Ukrainian State through a national revolution. The BBC (April 28, 2014) refers to the group as "ultra-nationalist." Condition: met.

   RIGHT SECTOR: ALL CONDITIONS NOT MET

Slovak National Party (Slovenská národná strana-SNS), Slovakia

The Institute for European Policy (2013) noted that the Slovak National Party claimed to be "the oldest Slovak political party, tracing its roots to the nineteenth-century Slovak National Party. However, this historical SNS was rather an honorary party representing all political groups nationally self-defined as Slovak ... there is no traceable continuity among these two subjects from 1938 to 1990." The party in its current form was founded in March 1990. The party has seen multiple leadership changes and mergers/splits. A 1999 splinter of the party led to the creation of Real Slovak National Party though both parties shared a principal ideology and policies (Institute for European Policy 2013). Ultimately, the parties merged in 2003 naming Ján Slota as chairman. By 2006, they had "gained 11% of the votes and became the third biggest parliamentary faction and, after eight years, also part of the ruling coalition" (Institute for European Policy 2013). In July 2011, "SNS signed a memorandum of understanding with the Austrian Freedom Party to oppose Turkeys bid for EU membership" (Lansford 2015). The SNS is a member of the EP group "Europe of Freedom and Democracy."

A. *Occurring post-Cold War.* The current iteration of SNS was established in March 1990. Condition: met.
B. *Non-Violent.* No associations with violence were identified in conjunction with SNS. Any accusations lobbied against SNS in regards to violence related to their agenda inciting violent behavior in others. Counterpoint (2014) concurs, discovering "no evidence of violence within the party leadership." Condition: met.
C. *Non anti-Semitic/racist/homophobic.* The group is perceived as racist and xenophobic, but is perception reality? In its manifesto for the general elections of 2010, SNS "defined the nation in terms of values and culture" (Institute for European Policy 2013). It included ethnic minorities into the definition of national culture rather than speaking about helping this community [Roma minority], the manifesto calls for control of this ethnic group" (Institute for European Policy 2013). In the 2006 general election SNS manifesto, the party acknowledged that "the nation was understood as the primary value of reference. However the nation is not defined by race or blood but rather by culture, shared history and most importantly by language and values" (Institute for European Policy 2013).

    However, Slota, the party's former leader (Slota was removed as leader in 2013), "made many controversial statements, including threatening to role tanks into Budapest, referred to medieval Hungarians as 'Mongoloid types with crooked legs and even more disgusting horses' suggesting that they were 'civilised' by Slovaks. He has referred to Hungarians as a 'tumour in the body of the Slovakian nation'. He stated that 70% of Roma were criminals and suggested the best policy for dealing with them was a 'long whip in a small yard'" (Democratic Society 2014).

A 2009 report on Slovakia prepared by the ECRI and published in May 2009 by the Council of Europe (Ivo.sk 2015), pointed out the "worrying increase … in racist political discourse mainly against the Hungarian minority as well as against, inter alia, Roma and Jewish people" since the coalition government comprising the Slovak National Party took power in 2006 (ECRI 2009). However, blaming an entire coalition's behavior on one member seems quite a stretch. Indeed as discussed by Mesežnikov (2009), "The SNS may be described as the most relevant factor of radical (though not anti-system) nationalism in Slovakia. The party currently enjoys a strong position within the power system thanks to its ability to capitalize on xenophobic and anti-minority (i.e., anti-Hungarian) sentiments of certain population segments and due to coalition strategies applied by other populist parties."

Ultimately, UK's Counterpoint (2014) summarized it most succinctly: "There is mixed evidence from the party's history that the party promoted (or promotes) values directly opposed to democracy and human rights … the roots of the Slovak National Party (SNS) are in the campaign for Slovakian independence in the 1990s. It has had a chequered past, with a number of splits and changes in approach. But the SNS has claimed continuity with the historical Slovak National Party, which in turn had members connected to the Nazi regime in Slovakia, and the party shown support for fascist leader Jozef Tiso."

Counterpoint (2014) rated the SNS as a high danger for racism and homophobia, arguing that there is "clear evidence—either from the party manifesto or comments by the party leadership—that the party discriminates against people on the basis of race or ethnic group" and that the party discriminates against gay people. Condition: unmet.

D. *Eurosceptic.* According to the SNS manifesto, the party "advocated for a Europe of sovereign nation states and criticized the bureaucracy of the European institution" (Institute for European Policy 2013). The "party explicitly refuses the liberal immigrant policy produced by the EU. …The EU is defined as an institution importing liberal policy such as multiculturalism; but in fact, the EU misuses Slovakia while ignoring national sovereignty and serving TNCs and global capitalism" (Institute for European Policy 2013). Condition: met.

E. *Nationalist/Reformist.* The primary objective of SNS, as stated repeatedly in their 2010 manifesto, was "to establish a government composed only of Slovak political parties, meaning without any party representing ethic minority interests … . The creation of this so called 'Slovak government' was necessary, according to SNS, because Slovak national interests were in grave danger" (Institute for European Policy 2013).

Further, "SNS strongly condemns the secession of Kosovo from Serbia and rejects any possibility to recognize Kosovo as a sovereign state. The nation is more than simply a summary of the citizens—it is an entity with its own, distinctive identity." Condition: met.

SNS: ALL CONDITIONS NOT MET

Svoboda (Всеукраїнське об'єднання «Свобода), Ukraine

As detailed on the Svoboda website (Svoboda 2015), "the Svoboda Party—formerly the Social National Party of Ukraine (SNPU)—was formed as a merger of several groups including: the Varta Rukhu (Rukh's Guards), the Studentske Bratstvo (Students' Brotherhood), the Spadshchyna (Heritage) and the Ukrainian Veterans of Afghanistan." They note that "on 29 September 1991, a coordinating group session was held in Lviv, followed by a founding Convention on 13 October 1991 which announced the creation of the SNPU" (Svoboda 2015). "At the 9th SNPU Convention on 14 February 2004, a new name was adopted for the party—the 'All-Ukrainian Svoboda Union,' and elected Oleh Tiahnybok as Svoboda's leader" (Svoboda.org 2015).

The BBC (4/28/2014) reported that "the nationalist Svoboda party—also a significant player in the Maidan protests—now has three powerful posts in the interim government: acting chief prosecutor, deputy prime minister and chairman of the National Security Council." In the 2012 parliamentary election, 10.44% voted for Svoboda, lading the party to claim 37 parliamentary seats. However, 2014 would be a resounding disappointment. Svoboda failed to earn a seat in Parliament "falling only 0.3% short of the required minimum of 5%" (Ishchenko 2014). However, the *Guardian* also noted that "infamous extreme right politician from the Svoboda party Yuriy Mykhalchyshyn, who once promoted Joseph Goebbels' A Little ABC of National Socialism and the 25-point NSDAP Program, will head up propaganda and analysis in the Security Service of Ukraine" (Ishchenko 2014).

A. *Occurring post-Cold War.* SNPU was formed in 1991 and the name change to Svoboda occurred in 2004. Condition: met.
B. *Non-Violent.* Yahoo News (8/31/2015) reported that "the Ukrainian ultranationalist party Svoboda, blamed for clashes that killed one person and injured dozens more outside parliament on Monday, has a long-established reputation for violent confrontation." The August 2015 incident outside Parliament involved an admitted member of Svoboda and the Sich battalion who tossed a grenade at police officers and journalists—its shrapnel killing a 24-year-old member of the National Guard.

Additionally, "Svoboda lawmakers have been known to engage in physical confrontations with pro-Russian parliamentarians" (Yahoo News 8/31/2015). On its website, Svoboda has noted that 19 of its members have died in fighting with pro-Russian separatists since April 2014 (Yahoo News 8/31/2015). Condition: unmet.

C. *Non anti-Semitic/racist/homophobic.* Olszański (2011) noted that "the party advocated the social nationalist ideology by combining radical nationalism with equally radical social rhetoric. Among the canons of its ideology there was: a vision of the nation as a natural community, the primacy of the nation's rights over human rights, the urge to build an 'ethnic economy', but also an openly racist rhetoric concerning white supremacy."

Andrew Srulevitch, director of European Affairs for the Anti-Defamation League, said: "Svoboda has been disciplined in its messaging regarding Jews since the Maidan demonstrations started in November, but they have a history of anti-Semitic statements to overcome, and a clear political program of ethnic nationalism that makes Jews nervous" (Zawadzki, Hosenball, and Grey 2014).

However, in 2004, concurring with the party name change to Svoboda, "the radical neo-Nazi and racist groups were pushed out from the party" (Olszański 2011). Ivan Katchanovski, an expert in comparative politics, contended that "Svoboda is currently best described as a radical nationalist party, and not as fascist or neo-Nazi. … It is now not overtly anti-Semitic" (Zawadzki, Hosenball, and Grey 2014). Additionally, Zawadzki, Hosenball and Grey (2014) reported that a senior US official observed that "since entering the Ukrainian Parliament in October 2012, the Svoboda leadership has been working to take their party in a more moderate direction and to become a modern, European mainstream political party. … The leadership has been much more vigilant about expelling or otherwise punishing individual members who engage in xenophobic behavior or rhetoric." Yahoo News (8/31/2015) noted that "Svoboda has continued to adopt hugely controversial positions, staunchly opposing gay pride parades and annual pilgrimages to the country by Hassidic Jews."

This variable is difficult to call. However, news reports indicate strong past (and potentially ongoing) connections with anti-Semitism and note "efforts" to change. "Efforts" in this case are not strong enough on their own merit to overcome strong anti-Semitic connections, particularly when they are unaccompanied by party leadership's promotion of Jews. Condition: unmet.

D. *Eurosceptic.* In the 2008 Svoboda party manifesto, the party sought to "terminate agreement with the EU on readmission. Conclude with other states, from territories where illegal immigrants come to Ukraine, readmission agreements (return of illegal immigrants) on favorable conditions for Ukraine" (Svoboda 2015).

Noted Olszański (2011), "The strategic direction of the state is to be 'European Ukraine-centrism' which should guarantee Ukraine's status as 'not only geographical, but also a geopolitical centre of Europe'. Ukraine is to leave the Commonwealth of Independent States (CIS) and other post-Soviet structures, demand an explicit guarantee of accession to NATO within a set period of time, and to once again become a possessor of tactical nuclear weapons. The European Union is not even mentioned in the programme." Indeed, the BBC reported in 2014 that Svoboda "supports EU integration—an exception among Europe's far right" (March 7, 2014). Condition: unmet.

E. *Nationalist/Reformist.* Katchanovski has said that "Svoboda is currently best described as a radical nationalist party" (Zawadzki, Hosenball, and Grey 2014). In fact, Svoboda's party manifesto contained an entire section devoted to its nationalist posture. On their website, Svoboda (2015) described in the "program for the Protection of Ukrainians" their desire to: adopt a new Citizenship Act, under which citizenship will be given only to those persons who were born in Ukraine or are ethnically Ukrainian, who returned from abroad for permanent living and working in Ukraine. Allow people born in Ukraine from foreigners or stateless persons to acquire Ukrainian citizenship upon reaching age of majority only under the conditions of Ukrainian language fluency, knowledge of Ukrainian history and content of the Constitution of Ukraine (Svoboda 2015). Condition: met.

SVOBODA: ALL CONDITIONS NOT MET

Swedish Democrats (Sverigedemokraterna-SD), Sweden

The Swedish Democrats were founded in 1988 "to preserve Swedish values and to reducing immigration to Sweden. Initially, the party was led by a number of people linked to Nazi and right-wing extremist groups" (Radio Sweden 2014). *Foreign Policy* (September 16, 2014), reported that the national elections resulted in "the Sweden Democrats, which has turned xenophobia and anti-immigrant posturing into a political growth industry, captured 12.9 percent of the vote. The election marks the end of the eight-year rule of the Moderate Party, which saw a huge number of its voters jump ship and vote for a group that has been roundly denounced by Sweden's political class as a racist movement that has no place in the country's politics." Party MEPs joined the Europe of Freedom and Direct Democracy group.

A. *Occurring post-Cold War.* The party was founded in 1988. Noted Bengtsson (2014), "the party lived in the political shadows and scored a few tenths of a percentage point in the general elections. But in 2010 the party, after polishing its act for a considerable time, entered parliament with 6% of the vote." Condition: met.

B. *Non-Violent.* The SD is widely reported and considered to condemn violence. *Reuters* (Johnson 2014) reported that SD "rejects violence." Indeed, the group is often the target of violence. "A 2012 police study found that nearly half of the party's politicians reported threats or assaults in 2011. Some had been beaten with iron bars, some had bombs detonated in their cars, and some had cans of tear gas emptied into their mouths in front of their children" (Teitelbaum 2014). Condition: met.

C. *Non anti-Semitic/racist/homophobic.* The BBC (2014) reported that one local "party candidate stood down after a picture emerged of her wearing a swastika armband" while another "was highlighted for posting racist and anti-immigrant comments online." Party leader Akesson has stated that "Islamism is the Nazism and communism of our time. It has to be met with disgust and much stronger resistance than has so far been the case."

   The Independent (Sims 2015) reported that "while the party has sought to distance itself from associations with Nazis, some of its founders were linked with Nazi groups and its secretary said in 2014 that Jews were not Swedish unless they abandoned their ethnic identity."

   Al Jazeera (Bengtsson 2014), commented that although other parties have related manifestos, "the Sweden Democrats' extremist roots, as well as its single-track obsession with migration policy, makes it different. … The main reason why the Sweden Democrats stand out in this context is probably due to the strong consensus behind the country's policy on immigration by the other Swedish political parties and the fact that Sweden has a long tradition of viewing immigration favourably."

   Interestingly, the SD organized a gay-pride parade in July 2015, though their motivations were called into question because the parade route passed through a Muslim neighborhood. One commenter on PoliticsForum.org (2015) responded that "since Islam holds that gays should be executed, something like this is obviously an attack on Muslims."

   The SD manifesto is certainly anti-immigrant but there are no racist, anti-Semitic, or homophobic declarations nor are there directives or statements from leadership indicating such leanings. Condition: met.

D. *Eurosceptic.* Radio Sweden (2014) reported that "immigration and asylum policy are the core issues for the Sweden Democrats. This election [2014], the party is pushing for a ninety percent reduction in immigration." Tommy Nilsson, southern Sweden's party manager, told the *Telegrap*h in 2015 that "there's too much immigration and too many beggars from eastern Europe" (Orange 2015). Condition: met.

E. *Nationalist/Reformist.* Akesson has "identified himself as a nationalist but called for his party to show they were 'broad and inclusive'" (BBC 2014). Radio Sweden (2014) noted that "the Sweden Democrats are a socially conservative party with a nationalist foundation, who want to preserve Swedish traditions, increase punishments for criminals and to invest more in care for the elderly." Condition: met.

SD: ALL CONDITIONS MET

Swiss People's Party (Schweizerische Volkspartei, SVP), Switzerland

The Swiss People's Party was "originally founded in 1971 by the merger of the Farmers, Artisans, and Citizens' Party—generally known as the Agrarian Party—with the Democratic Party" (Encyclopedia Britannica 2015). The party adopted "a more populist agenda in the 1990s, particularly on immigration and social welfare," and made "substantial gains." "In the 1999 elections it won the largest vote share and the second greatest number of seats in the lower house of the parliament" (Encyclopaedia Britannica 2015). One writer for the London School of Economics has contended that "the Swiss People's Party (SVP) has established itself as the most powerful radical right-wing party in Western Europe" (Stockemer 2012).

A. *Occurring post-Cold War.* Stockemer (2012) reports: "Coinciding with the rise of the party's charismatic leader Christoph Blocher in the 1990s, the SVP began to embrace initiatives to halt immigration, engaged in historical revisionism and spread anxiety about globalization and Switzerland's possible entry into the European Union." The party also "expanded enormously in the 1990s, increasing the number of cantonal sections from fourteen to twenty-six. … The 1992 vote was also the starting point for the electoral and political success of the SVP, which, with Christoph Blocher as a wealthy and sedulous populist leader, had been the driving force in the campaign against EEA membership" (Skenderovic 2013).

Rejection of membership in the European Economic Area (EEA) is one example of the reformed ideology embraced by the new SVP, as is "the SVP's new 'winning formula' which consists of linking nationalist and exclusionist demands in immigration and foreign policy with neo-liberal and anti-state positions in economic and taxation policy" (Skenderovic 2013).

The party does, however, consciously draw on its agrarian beginnings. Observed Skenderovic (2013): "The party continues to refer in its narratives and political iconography to peasantry and agrarian life. At party meetings, in public speeches and political campaigns, the party likes to evoke the rural world and farmers as steadfast representations of national authenticity and as a highly symbolic, historically tested bulkhead in the fight against any kinds of foreign influence."

Ultimately, though the party was originally founded in the 1970s, its well-documented and publicized philosophical facelift, which addresses and focuses on post–Cold War issues, will be determined to have met the threshold for an ideological change so great as to render it a "new" group. Condition: met.

B. *Non-Violent.* Political violence in Switzerland is considered "exceptionally rare" according to the *Switzerland Business Law Handbook* (2012). Indeed, violent acts involving SVP appear to be not only rare, but incidental and in one case SVP members were on the receiving end. This was the case in a 2009 incident concerning the ban of minarets when the "black bloc" damaged property at locations used by the SVP (Switzerland Business Law Handbook 2012). Condition: met.

C. *Non anti-Semitic/racist/homophobic.* SVP is often labeled "racist" due to its tough stance on immigration. In an October 2003 speech, SVP was accused of "xenophobic appeals, including running a newspaper advertisement blaming 'black Africans' for crime" (Piano 2005). SVP countered by noting that it "had nothing against legal immigrants and was merely opposed to illegal immigration and abuse of the asylum policy" (Piano 2005). Further, following a 2010 interview with Lesbenorganisation Schweiz—LOS, the Council of Europe reported that a Swiss parliamentarian group for LGB persons was been established within the SVP.

In 2007, the group was accused of racism after using campaign posters which depicted three white sheep booting a black sheep out of the country (Swiss Info 2007). Roman Jäggi, spokesman for the Swiss People's Party, described the poster campaign as "completely fair," and it had nothing to do with race, asserting that "It is not racist … . We have a big problem with violence and in particular youth violence, and foreign criminals are a big factor," (Swiss Info 2007). Condition: met.

D. *Eurosceptic.* The party "opposed Swiss membership in international bodies such as the United Nations (which Switzerland joined in 2002) and the European Union" (Britannica 2015). The SVP firmly supports imposing strict immigration quotas. "We identified this [immigration] problem before the others and the citizens know it," asserted SVP vice president Claude-Alain Voiblet (RT.com June 25, 2015). Condition: met.

E. *Nationalist/Reformist.* The Swiss People's Party electoral platform for the term 2015–2019 was expressed in the motto "SVP—the party for Switzerland" (SVP 2015). Further, the group declared: "Our country must no longer be insidiously integrated into international structures such as the EU" (SVP 2015). In 2014, the party authored a referendum against mass-immigration. SVP head Toni Brunner stated: "We have created the initiative because it's really become excessive" (Bleiker 2014). Skenderovic (2013) also observed that SVP voters are primarily attracted to "its identity politics on questions of preserving Swiss traditions and national sovereignty." Condition: met.

SVP: ALL CONDITIONS MET

SYRIZA—Συνασπισμός Ριζοσπαστικής Αριστεράς Synaspismós Rizospastikís Aristerás (The Conference of the Coalition of the Radical Left), Greece

SYRIZA is an acronym meaning the "Radical Coalition of the Left." The BBC (1/29/2015) reported that SYRIZA, "formed in 2004, is an umbrella group, with the party Synaspismos—the Coalition of the Left of Movements and Ecology—as the key component." Comprised of 16 "ideologically diverse" left-wing parties, SYRIZA includes "social democrats, radical ecologists, radical socialists, Trotskyists, and even anarchists," according to SYRIZA supporter Matthaios Tsimitakis, also an editor of the *Greek Left Review* (Bollier 2012). The party is led by Alexis Tsipras, and boasts the motto: "Always struggling for unity among the Left, the now united SYRIZA asserts a government of the Left with a new, broad and strong social majority that will allow for the people's interests to be served" (Πρίφτη 2015).

BBC reporter Paul Mason (2012) noted that, "under Tsipras' leadership, SYRIZA grew the far left's vote from 3.3% to 5.6% in the 2007 election—giving it 14 MPs … [by 2012] SYRIZA massively scooped up the votes of leftist, progressive, socially liberal young people, as well as the trade union voters, not specifically aligned with the Communist Party, to gain 52 seats." By 2015, claimed approximately "36% of the vote, an eight-percentage-point lead over the New Democracy party of Antonis Samaras, the outgoing prime minister. SYRIZA's support leapt by nine percentage points compared with the 2012 election result; … SYRIZA fell just short of an absolute majority, winning 149 seats in the 300-seat parliament" (*The Economist* 1/25/15). In 2015, *Time* magazine named Tsipras one of the 100 Most Influential People (Iglesias 2015b).

A. *Occurring post-Cold War*. SYRIZA was founded in 2004 when Greek left-wing political forces united. Condition: met.
B. *Non-Violent.* Though SYRIZA has been accused of violence and is oft-considered a violent party, the SYRIZA manifesto lists its adherence to "the principle of the peaceful settlement of disputes" (SYRIZA 2015). In 2013, SYRIZA's primary opponent, the New Democratic Conservatives, released a video that appeared to show "SYRIZA Member of Parliament

Vangelis Diamantopoulos delivering a speech in which he is seen to suggest that Greeks taking up guns is a justifiable response to the country's crushing economic crisis" (Dabilis 2013). However, "SYRIZA said New Democracy was guilty of 'forgery and a disgusting provocation' because they had used a heavily edited version that took comments out of context" (Dabilis 2013).

Spiegel (2015) noted concerns that the party, though perhaps not partaking in violence itself, did not distance or disassociate itself from groups that did advocate for violence. Speaking of the 2008 street riots that resulted in the death of a teenager at the hands of police, Nikos Voutsis, a leading SYRIZA MP, commented: "Nobody [in the party] was ever arrested for smashing up a shop, but there was a social upheaval and we heard the voices ... we're not in favour of violence, but we like having people in the street protesting" (Spiegel 2015).

In 2013, SYRIZA "refused to vote for a motion by the Parliament's ethics committee that condemned violence, arguing that the text should refer to 'racist violence' and not just 'violence'" (van Versendaal 2013). A few months later, in response to the bail-out agreement with the EU and the International Monetary Fund in 2013, Tsipras asserted: "We condemn violence but we understand the frustration of those who react violently to the violence of the memorandum," (van Versendaal 2013).

Due to insipid and open-ended statements made by party leadership, SYRIZA has certainly not disentangled itself from violent acts for the cause committed by the hands of others. Ultimately, though the party seems to be comfortable with allowing others to do their "dirty work," it does not officially condone violence nor has leadership been personally involved in violent acts. Condition: met.

C. *Non anti-Semitic/racist/homophobic*. The symbol of the party is "the five-pointed star, a symbol of unity, along with three flags: a red one for the classic left, a Greek one for the ecological movement and a purple one that represents other social movements that SYRIZA embraces, such as feminism, migrant rights and gay rights" (Πρίφτη 2015).

As stated in SYRIZA's 2013 political resolutions: "We combat racist and homophobic violence, all discriminations based on racial or national origin, religion, color of the skin, disability, age, sexual orientation or gender identity, which are endemic in many aspects of social life and we guarantee the change of the legislative framework that legalizes, directly or indirectly, such discriminations. In this context, we fully support the right to self-determination in terms of sexual orientation and gender choice, homosexual civil marriage with full and equal rights, and recognition of gender identity" (SYRIZA 2015). Condition: met.

D. *Eurosceptic.* In their *Political Resolution of the 1st Congress of SYRIZA* (July 2013), SYRIZA (2015) claimed:

> In Greece, very harsh measures that lead large parts of the population to a humanitarian crisis are implemented by the troika of the European Union, IMF, and European Central Bank, with Germany playing a dominant role in the European strategy. National resources, public goods and companies are put under privatization/sell-off. Production collapses, tens of thousands of small and medium-sized companies close down, public services dismantle, the welfare state is constantly shrinking, and large parts of the population are deprived of health, education, pension, and social security. (SYRIZA 2015)

Bollier (2012) observed that "SYRIZA ultimately supports Greece's membership in the European Union, but rejects the austerity measures required by the memorandum." Lesniak (2014) pointed to one of SYRIZA's main points their manifesto *The Exit from the Crisis Is on the Left*: "The capitulation of our foreign policy to the desires of the U.S. and the powerful states of the European Union endangers the country's independence, peace, and security." Condition: met.

E. *Nationalist/Reformist.* An article in *Foreign Policy* (Papadogiannis 2015) noted the nationalist rhetoric employed by Tsipras. "Radical left-wing nationalism has been both an enduring and a multifaceted phenomenon, and Syriza's trajectory serves as the most recent reminder. Riding on a wave of opposition to bailout packages and the austerity measures that accompanied them, SYRIZA stressed the need to bring back hope and defend the dignity of the Greek people. This rendered the party as an attractive choice to more than a third of the voters this past January" (Papadogiannis 2015). Lesniak (2014) wrote that Tsipras believed the party's win in 2014 sent "a clear message against the budget-cutting austerity measures tied to Greece's 240 billion euro ($327 billion) bailout from the euro area and International Monetary Fund," noting he immediately called for national elections. Condition: met.

SYRIZA: ALL CONDITIONS MET

UKIP (England)

UKIP, or the UK Independence Party, was "founded on 3 September 1993 at the London School of Economics by members of the Anti-Federalist League, which was founded by Dr. Alan Sked in November 1991, with the aim of running candidates opposed to the Maastricht Treaty in the 1992 general election" (BBC Nov 21, 2014).

The party has seen a surge in popularity the past decade. The BBC reported: "The party's initial successes were all in the proportional representation elections for the European Parliament—winning its first three seats in 1999 with 7% of the vote. It built on that in 2004, winning 12 seats and pushing the Lib Dems into fourth place. The 2009 poll saw its total grow to 13 seats, pushing Labour into third place with 16% of the vote. And in 2014's European election the party lived up to its confident promise to top the vote, getting 27.5% of all those cast" (BBC Nov 21, 2014). The 2014 success was likely due in part to shift in rhetoric, courtesy of party leader Nigel Farage. In March of 2014, Farage stated that his "party has got rid of 'old UKIP' and now has a 'huge' opportunity to take votes from Labour in future elections" (BBC March 16, 2014). Farage added: "New UKIP is a lot more professional, a lot more smiley, a lot less angry, and it's going places" (BBC March 16, 2014). UKIP led the charge in the 2016 cross-party Leave campaign, which sought (successfully) Britain's exit from the EU. Farage served as the party's leader until July 2016—long enough to see his vision of a sovereign Britain become a reality.

A. *Occurring post-Cold War.* UKIP was founded in 1993 (UKIP 2015). Condition: met.
B. *Non-Violent.* UKIP has found itself the target of accusations of violence, which the group repeatedly denies. *News Channel 4* reported that, following a May 2015 incident involving a campaigner who said he was punched in the face by a man who appeared to be one of the party's supporters, a UKIP spokesman categorically stated: "We condemn any intimidation or violence towards anybody, whether involved in this election or otherwise."

   In 2012, West observed that "not all movements that occupy the far right-wing are the same: whereas some, such as the British National Party (BNP), are associated more strongly with ideological extremism, criminality and violence, other movements, such as the more moderate UK Independence Party (UKIP), advocate similar policies in many areas but would strongly reject any association with extremism and violence." In terms of likely engagement in violence, Counterpoint (2014) classified UKIP as low risk.

   Condition: met.
C. *Non anti-Semitic/racist/homophobic.* News headlines often obscure the real story, as in the case of one headline that proclaimed "*UKIP is a Racist Party.*" The article explained that "Lord Heseltine, who advises the Coalition on economic growth, told the BBC: 'Of course it's racist, who doubts that? Farage isn't racist but his party is very attractive to a racist agenda'" (Hope 2013). The quote tells a different story.

Party leader Farage has made it perfectly clear that UKIP was strengthened as a result of "reforms … getting rid of 'old UKIP'" (BBC March 16, 2014). He further acknowledged that "aspiring UKIP candidates now have to declare that they have 'never engaged in, advocated or condoned racist, violent, criminal or anti-democratic activity' and that there are no 'skeletons in my cupboard' that may cause me or UKIP embarrassment" (BBC March 16, 2014).

Counterpoint (2014) rated UKIP a moderate threat for racism and homophobia noting that "there is mixed evidence—either from the party manifesto or comments by the party leadership—that the party discriminates against people on the basis of race or ethnic group" or sexual orientation. Condition: met.

D. *Eurosceptic.* Quite simply, "the UK Independence Party has, as its name implies, one key policy—to leave the European Union" (BBC Nov 21, 2014). Further, the UKIP Manifesto states, "We can never control immigration while we continue to be members of the European Union. Until we leave, we are forced to abide by the EU's founding, unshakable principle of the 'free movement of people,' meaning we cannot prevent the flow of citizens from all EU member states into Britain" (UKIP 2015). It also details exit strategies and legal options for leaving the EU.

Lesniak (2014) explained that "UKIP advocates leaving the European Union, resulting in stopping payments to the EU and withdrawal from EU treaties, while maintaining trading ties with other European countries." In 2016, Farage was a critical component of "Vote Leave," the cross-party comprised of members of Parliament from Conservatives, Labour, and UKIP who sought "Brexit"—Britain's exit from the EU. Among the arguments extended by the "Vote Leave" campaign was the belief that "Britain was being held back by the EU, which they said imposed too many rules" and the desire for "Britain to take back full control of its borders and reduce the number of people coming here to live and/or work. … The Leave campaign also objected to the idea of 'ever closer union' between EU member states and what they see as moves towards the creation of a 'United States of Europe'" (Wheeler and Hunt 2016). The successful campaign was the crowning moment for UKIP leader Farage who would resign soon after the referendum. Condition: met.

E. *Nationalist/Reformist.* UKIP's 2015 Manifesto states "immigration has driven down wages and led to job losses for British workers. … The sheer weight of numbers, combined with rising birth rates (particularly to immigrant mothers) and an ageing population, is pushing public services to breaking point. Our current immigration rules ignore the wishes of the British people. They discriminate in favour of EU citizens and against the rest of the world. The system is failing so badly that we cannot even properly identify how many people enter and leave our country" (UKIP 2015).

UKIP's nationalist policies pervade almost every aspect of its 2015 Manifesto, with numerous references to returning Britain to its people. The *Guardian* noted "UKIP is a 'civic' nationalist party, rejects 'blood and soil' nationalism and claims to be 'open and inclusive' to anyone who wishes to identify with Britain, regardless of ethnic or religious background" (April 14, 2014). Condition: met.

UKIP: ALL CONDITIONS MET

Vlaams Belang (Flemish Interest), Belgium

According to the *Brussels Journal*, the Vlaams Belang (Flemish Interest) is Belgium's largest party with a goal of an independent Flanders (Belien 2007). Until 2004, the Vlaams Belang was called the Vlaams Blok; the name change came as a result of the party's reformation following the government's decision to force the party to disband following their conviction as a criminal organization (Belien 2007). Its party slogan was "Our own people first" (Belien 2007). Belien (2007) observed that it had not lost a single election in 25 years (through 2007), "growing slowly but continuously from 3% of the vote in 1987, to 10.3% in 1991, 12.3% in 1995, 15,8% in 1999, 18.2% in 2003 to 24.1% in 2004," and is "the most successful of all the so-called 'Euro-nationalist' parties" (Belien 2007). However, the party has seen its popularity begin to decline. In the 2014 Parliamentary elections in Belgium, the party, now chaired by Gerolf Annemans, only garnered 3.69% of the vote and three seats (down nine) (Fondation Robert Schuman 2014).

A. *Occurring post-Cold War.* Belien (2007) reported: "Originally founded in 1977 as a radical Flemish-secessionist break-away of the Flemish-nationalist party, in the late 1980s the party transformed itself into a mainstream conservative party." Observed Coffé (2005): "While the far-right party had cut a radical profile in its first years, throughout the 1990s its appeal was populist, as it presented itself ever more as a right-conservative people's party." In 2004, following a government-ordered disbandment, Vlaams Blok reemerged with a "new handle" as Vlaams Belang (Coffé 2005). "With its new statement of principles and platform, the Vlaams Belang—at least on paper—has [had] cut the ties with its unsavoury past" (Coffé 2005). Condition: met.
B. *Non-Violent.* Counterpoint (2014) found no evidence of violence, positing that there was "no evidence of violence within the party leadership." Media reports point, ironically, to an incident in 2007 in which Vlaams

Belang several members were assaulted at a 9/11 tribute (Flemish Republic 2009). Condition: met.

C. *Non anti-Semitic/racist/homophobic*. In 2004, Vlaams Blok (as Vlaams Belang was then known) was declared a criminal organization by the Supreme Court in Brussels. According to Belien (2007):

> In the 1990s in an effort to kill the party the Belgian Parliament changed the Constitution and voted a series of new laws, including an Anti-Racism Act and an Anti-Discrimination Act, which define "discrimination" so broadly that anyone and everyone is vulnerable to hate-crime prosecutions. These new laws were used against the Vlaams Blok... .
>
> The party was convicted on the basis of an anthology of as few as 16 texts published by various local Vlaams Blok chapters between 1996 and 2000. Though many of these texts simply quoted official statistics on crime rates and social welfare expenditure the court posited that they had been published with "an intention to contribute to a campaign of hatred."

As part of its current (2015) manifesto, the party asserted: "Inspired by its concern to defend and protect the cultural identity of the Flemish people, the Vlaams Belang rejects the tenets of the multicultural ideology" (Flemish Republic 2015). This verbiage supports the party's strong anti-immigrant platform but does not necessarily correlate to racism or anti-Semitism.

The party manifesto also noted that "the traditional family is at the heart of a humane society. Its merit is acknowledged and safeguarded in the marriage between a man and a woman. Policymakers should recognize the central role of families with children in society. Their task is to protect the family instead of attempting to usurp its functions. This is the only approach which can provide solutions for the urgent problem of the birth dearth" (Flemish Republic 2015). Because Vlaams Belang promotes family and children and does not present a pro-gay or pro-gay marriage stance, it does not necessarily follow that they are anti-gay or homophobic.

In 2005, the Vlaams Belang approved a Holocaust resolution, strongly indicating that "it will not be equated in absolutely any circumstances with Holocaust advocates and holocaust deniers of all kinds" (DeWinter 2005). Counterpoint (2014) found that "there is little or no evidence—either from the party manifesto or comments by the party leadership—that the party stokes fears of Jews, though there is mixed evidence—either from the party manifesto or comments by the party leadership—that the party discriminates against people on the basis of race or ethnic group" or sexual orientation. Condition: met.

D. *Eurosceptic.* "The Vlaams Belang is also the only Eurosceptic party in Belgium and the only one that rejects the official state ideology of multiculturalism" asserted Belien (2007). "Vlaams Belang opposes Brussels and does not really differentiate between Brussels as the capital of Belgium and Brussels as the capital of Europe. It sees both Belgium and Europe—in other words Brussels and Brussels—as enemies of Flanders and of the Flemish people, whose national identity these enemies want to subvert and destroy" (Belien 2007). Condition: met.
E. *Nationalist/Reformist.* "The Vlaams Belang strives for the secession of Flanders from the artificial Belgian state. Our aim is to dissolve Belgium and establish an independent Flemish state" (Flemish Republic 2015). Erk (2005) noted that as part of the group's name change, the party sought to rebrand "itself as a Flemish nationalist party on the political right." Condition: met.

VLAAMS BELANG: ALL CONDITIONS MET

In Sum

In accordance with our description of MF as a post–Cold War political philosophy founded on a non-violent, non-anti-Semitic/racist/homophobic ideology that embodies euroscepticism and the promotion of nationalism and reform, and following analysis and qualification, the following groups have met all criteria for categorization as a Millennial Fascist Group:

- Alternative for Germany (Alternative für Deutschland-AfD)
- Danish People's Party (Dansk Folkeparti-DF)
- Dutch Freedom Party (Partij voor de Vrijheid-PVV)
- Front National
- True FINNS Party
- Freedom Party of Austria (Freiheitliche Partei Österreich-FPÖ)
- Podemos
- Swiss People's Party, SVP
- Swedish Democrats
- SYRIZA
- UKIP
- Vlaams Belang

Table 5.1 provides a summary of the results. These 12 MFGs will now serve as our subjects as we next turn to the task of determining the common elements that have facilitated their startling rise and success.

Table 5.1 MFG Qualification Results

Groups	Variables: Post-Cold War	Non-violent	Non anti-Semitic/ racist/ homophobic	Eurosceptic	Nationalist/ Reformist	MFG?
Alternative for Germany-AfD (Germany)	☑	☑	☑	☑	☑	YES
ATAKA (Bulgaria)	☑	☑	☒	☑	☑	
Congress of the New Right (Poland)	☑	☒	☒	☑	☑	
Danish People's Party –DF (Denmark)	☑	☑	☑	☑	☑	YES
Dutch Freedom Party-PVV (Netherlands)	☑	☑	☑	☑	☑	YES
EDL (England)	☑	☒	☑	☒	☑	
Fascism and Freedom Movement-National Socialist Party (Italy)	☑	☑	☒	☑	☑	
Finns Party (formerly True Finns)-PS (Finland)	☑	☑	☑	☑	☑	YES
Freedom Party of Austria -FPÖ	☑	☑	☑	☑	☑	YES
Front National (France)	☑	☑	☑	☑	☑	YES
Golden Dawn (Greece)	☑	☒	☒	☑	☑	
Jobbik (Hungary)	☑	☑	☒	☑	☑	
LAOS (Greece)	☑	☑	☒	☑	☑	
Lega Nord (Italy)	☑	☑	☒	☑	☑	
National Democratic Party of Germany (NPD)	☒	☒	☒	☑	☑	
Party of the Swedes (Sweden)	☒	☒	☒	☒	☒	
Pegida (Germany)	☑	☒	☑	☑	☑	
Podemos (Spain)	☑	☑	☑	☑	☑	YES
Republican People's Party-CHP (Turkey)	☑	☑	☑	☒	☑	
Right Sector (Ukraine)	☑	☒	☑	☑	☑	
Slovak National Party-SNS (Slovakia)	☑	☑	☒	☑	☑	
Svoboda (Ukraine)	☑	☒	☒	☒	☑	
Swedish Democrats (Sweden)	☑	☑	☑	☑	☑	YES
Swiss People's Party (Switzerland)	☑	☑	☑	☑	☑	YES
SYRIZA (Greece)	☑	☑	☑	☑	☑	YES
UKIP (England)	☑	☑	☑	☑	☑	YES
Vlaams Belang (Belgium)	☑	☑	☑	☑	☑	YES

Each of the groups tested is indicated along with each of the six variables serving as criteria. The final column indicates where a group qualified as a MFG. (Ramswell 2017).

NOTES

1. Original German text, translation is my own: "Ich verurteile das nicht, es gibt Menschen, die leben anders als man selbst oder als man es gewohnt ist. Darum geht es nicht. Es geht um das staatliche Leitbild" from "Die Gesellschaft kann nicht das leisten, was eine Familie leistet" Interview mit Beatrix von Storch, Vorsitzende der Zivilen Koalition e. V. (Von Storch Interview 2011).

2. Original Italian text: "Il MFL-PSN privilegia l'adesione agli ideali del Fascismo al colore della pelle, alla nazionalità ed al credo religioso: per noi un Fascista di colore ed islamico vale mille volte più di un antifascista bianco e cattolico."

3. The original Italian text is as follows: "Tuttavia MFL-PSN sa bene che il nemico non è il profugo o il clandestino o l'immigrato (chiamiamolo come vogliamo) bensì il SISTEMA che permette allo straniero di entrare in Italia indisturbato ... In realtà il sistema che favorisce l'immigrazione selvaggia (così come l'introduzione del matrimonio gay, la teoria del gender e il Jobs Act) è un sistema capitalista" (http://fascismoeliberta.info/page/2/).

4. The original Italian text is as follows: "Riteniamo che il Fascismo sia, nei suoi propositi essenziali e fondamentali (difesa dell'identità, esaltazione del concetto di sovranità nazionale, socializzazione delle imprese, difesa della collettività con una grande attenzione al sociale e ai ceti più deboli della popolazione) la soluzione ai problemi che affliggono un'Italia la quale, grazie a questa classe di politici è diventata solo più povera, più insicura, più debole economicamente, socialmente e nei rapporti con gli altri Stati" (http://fascismoeliberta.info/page/2/).

5. Original document no longer online. Original Greek text per Vasilopoulou: "θεωρούμε όμως ότι κάτι τέτοιο είναι δυνατόν να επιτευχθεί μόνο στα πλαίσια μιας Συνομοσπονδίας όπου θα αναγνωρίζονται και θα προστατεύονται οι ιστορικές τόσο οι πολιτισμικές και οι εθνικές ρίζες όσο και τα ιδιαίτερα εθνικά χαρακτηριστικά των Ευρωπαϊκών λαών."

6. Original document no longer online. Original Italian text per Vasilopoulou (2010): "si deve cercare di costruire un'Europa fondata sul rispetto delle realtà nazionali e territoriali, cedendo all'Unione Europea solo una limitata parte di sovranità,delimitando chiaramente le proprie competenze; vanno delimitati con precisione gli ambiti di intervento dell'Unione Europea, evitando norme ambigue ed indefinite."

7. Original German text, translation my own: "Homosexuelle Lebenspartnerschaften bilden keine Familie und dürfen nicht gefördert werden. Kinder brauchen Mutter und Vater für eine gesunde Entwicklung."

8. Original German text, translation my own: "Wir lehnen alle 'multikulturellen" Gesellschaftsmodelle als unmenschlich ab, weil sie Deutsche und Nichtdeutsche gleichermaßen der nationalen Gemeinschaftsordnung entfremden."

9. Original German text, translation is my own: "Die Nationaldemokratische Partei Deutschlands ist die soziale Heimatpartei der Deutschen, bekennt sich zu einem lebensrichtigen Menschenbild und setzt sich deshalb konsequent für nationale Identität, nationale Souveränität und nationale Solidarität als Lebensgrundlagen unseres Volkes ein."

10. Original Spanish text (translation my own): "Pondremos en marcha un plan de lucha contra el racismo, la xenofobia y cualquier otra forma de discriminación que afecte tanto a las personas de origen español que residen en el exterior como a las personas de origen extranjero residentes en España" (Podemos 2015).

Chapter 6

The Rise of MFGs

Theoretical Justification and Selection of Causal Conditions

With the qualification and selection process completed, attention may now be directed to the isolation and identification of the factors that have led to the emergence and success of MFGs. There is appallingly little research on these groups as a body, as well as in the area of Euroscepticism. As Sorenson noted in 2008 (6), "No coherent theory exists that details *what* euroscepticism is, or *why*, *when* and *how* it occurs and develops." That statement remains true today, a decade later.

As previously noted, identifying the factors that have led to the rise of MFGs is important for many reasons. Of primary importance is understanding and explaining the profound impact these groups are having on European politics and society. They have served to create a new European political landscape, and led the charge for Brexit. Further, many of these groups have established connections with an increasingly complex Russia. Discovering the factors and conditions that have allowed for MF and MFGs to emerge is, thus, vitally important in terms of international relations and political stability.

The surge of twenty-first-century fascism has not gone unnoticed; in fact, it has become impossible to ignore. Efforts to explain this rise, however, have presented more of a challenge. The broad nature of these groups' goals, capabilities, abilities, and tactics belies a quite simplistic commonality: achieving change. The methods these groups employ to seek change vary as greatly as their goals, though there are several traditional theories of social mobilization which are typically utilized to explain a movement's rise. Are the elements that have served to catapult MFGs to the forefront of the political scene based in classic or modern theory? A hybrid? Something completely different?

The process of selecting variables should begin with a look into the most pertinent theories and their most significant factors. The classic theorists offer insight into fascism, certainly, with varying threads of relevancy to euroscepticism and populism. Max Weber and Karl Marx agreed that economic factors are integral to understanding a social system, though Weber believed that Marx's reductionist concept of a single economic cause was too simplistic. In the case of euroscepticism, Weber's perspective is the more germane as euroscepticism is a product of various strains both within and apart from the economic realm. The concept of alienation and anomie was a focal point in Marx, Weber, and Emile Durkheim's work. The three theorists shared the notion of man's disconnection to society and the natural state. However, Marx viewed this disconnect as a result of class struggle, Durkheim as a loss of touch to society leading to a loss of values (anomie), and Weber as the iron cage created by the bureaucracy. In classic Marxist theory, competition between workers alienated them from one another (as well as from the means of production) as they had no say in its operation. This is an excellent parallel to the nations of the EU who believe they no longer have any say in or control over their own governance. Though each perspective offers insight into the current political environment in Europe, Weber's idea of an iron cage that limits individual human potential is perhaps most applicable when juxtaposed with the confines of the European system in which Eurosceptic groups have found themselves imprisoned. Quite astutely, Weber (1904/1930) observed: "No one knows who will live in this cage in the future, or whether at the end of tremendous development entirely new prophets will arise, or there will be a great rebirth of old ideas and ideals or, if neither." Ultimately, it appears as if alienation should be considered to some degree, perhaps as motivation.

Modern social movement theory also appears to provide some basis of explanation. In particular, the concepts within the political opportunity framework, resource mobilization theory, protest cycles, and the political process model contain plausible rationales. Doug McAdam's 1982 conception of the political process model (PP) utilized in his work on black insurgency and civil rights. McAdam's version of PP stemmed from Political Process Theory (PPT), the political process framework considered an umbrella which incorporates the ideas of political opportunity and protest among other concepts such as resource mobilization (RM). PP asserts that social movements are established as a result of shared ideas (cognitive liberation) and develop as a result of the strength of its members and the structure they have created (indigenous organizational strength). Continued development is facilitated by a favorable political environment (expanding political opportunities) (McAdam 1982).

Tarrow (1998) asserted that many of the elements of PPT occur as a result of one another or in concert with one another. As an example, contentious politics "is produced when political opportunities broaden, when they demonstrate the potential for alliances, and when they reveal the opponents' vulnerability" (Tarrow 1998). Tarrow declared:

> Contention crystallizes into a social movement when it taps embedded social networks and connective structures and produces collective action frames and supportive identities able to sustain contention with powerful opponents. By mounting familiar forms of contention, movements become the focal points that transform external opportunities into resources. Repertoires of contention, social networks, and cultural frames lower the costs of bringing people into collective action, induce confidence that they are not alone, and give broader meaning to their claims. Together, these factors trigger the dynamic processes that have made social movements historically central to political and social change. (Tarrow 1998)

The concept of seizing opportunity is highly relevant in explaining MF. As a framework, PPT seems to hold significant explanatory power though its elements and principles can be so broadly applied it appears more difficult to prove a lack of correlation.

RM emphasizes the importance of resources in developing a successful social movement or political party. Resources include money, labor, knowledge, solidarity, legitimacy, and internal/external support from the "power elite"—those people in a society considered to hold the most power and influence. The key concept of RM is the ability of people with shared grievances to mobilize sufficient resources to enable action. Cragun, et al. (2006) observed that this emphasis on resources offered an explanation as to why some aggrieved individuals are able to organize while others are not. A core tenet of RM posits that the availability of resources and the ability to assemble and coordinate them for use (mobilization), influences the likelihood of social movements forming and their outcomes. Two key elements of RM, state capacity and state crisis, are also critical components of political process theory and political opportunity structures.

In 1973, Eisinger presented the first conceptualized use of the Political Opportunity framework in his research on rioting during the 1960s. Eisinger focused on the open versus closed nature of government and its reception to public input. Meyer (2004) noted that the "approach implicitly assumed constant pressures across urban America and treated the most proximate institutional arrangements as the key factors influencing the way political dissent emerged." Political opportunity focuses on exogenous factors and the role played by the strategies, protest tactics, and resources of non-elite groups for the sustained expansion of social movements (Ayres 1996). Meyer (2004) observed that changes in demography, repression, migration, and political economy contribute to a climate conducive to organizing collective action, and issues would be more readily received by at least some governmental institutions (Meyer 2004). Meyer and Minkoff (2004) highlight the basic premise that "exogenous factors enhance or inhibit prospects for mobilization, for particular sorts of claims to be advanced rather than others, for particular strategies of influence to be exercised, and for movements to affect mainstream institutional politics and policy."

Tarrow posited that opportunities are associated not only with state crisis but also with state capacity. Indeed, Tarrow (1998) contended that revolution occurs when the state collapses. He believed that a state's threshold for enduring challenges could actually serve as "a double-edged sword," depriving challengers of the opportunity to confront hostile authorities and to play upon the sympathies of the larger public audience (Tarrow 1998).

The concept of protest cycles is another theory which should be considered. Tarrow (1989) defined protest cycles as "a phase of heightened conflict across the social system" with "intensified interactions between challengers and authorities which can end in reform, repression and sometimes revolution." Many scholars suggest that repertoires develop during times of societal crisis, when innovation is a product of struggle (McAdam, Tilly, and Wood 2001; Tarrow 1995; and Tilly 1995). Tarrow (1995, 286) ascribed such formation as a part of the cyclic model in which "new forms of collective action develop within the experimental context of cycles of protest." The most "successful, transferable tactics" are then adopted as part of a movement's repertoire for use during what Tarrow referred to as the "quieter times" (Tarrow 1995). In the case of MF, the 1970s would have served as an example of Tarrow's "quieter" times since they encompassed periods of time between war and protest, a relative lull between heightened periods of activity.

In 1991, Tarrow remarked: "If cycles of protest are such watersheds of social and political change, then why is it that … we have so few studies of such cycles?" Is this not true of the current environment, the one that gave birth to Millennial Fascism? Frank and Fuentes (1992) keenly observed that Tarrow was able to answer his own question when he noted that "because they are a moving target, they interweave with institutions," and "there are problems with the way they have been conceived and studied" (Tarrow 1991). Indeed, many scholars now incorporate the concept of protest cycles into Political Process Theory (PPT) as one of its components. Tarrow's political process approach traced a "cycle of protest," by considering institutional politics along with social protest and disorder (Tarrow 1989).

Tarrow prophetically observed that there was a transnational opportunity structure: "a triangular structure of relations among states, non-state actors, and international institutions" (Tarrow 2000). He contended that "states created international practices, regimes and institutions to solve their collective action problems and monitor one another's behavior. But, once formed, new norms, identities and interests developed around these venues, attracting the attention of groups of states, non-state actors, and other international actors" (Tarrow 2005).

In 2014, Almeida made the observation that cycles of protest occurred "when multiple social movements or social groups engage in sustained protest, clustered in time and span, across a wide geographical boundary." He recognized that during cycles of protest, multiple segments of society would participate and employ increasingly confrontational tactics (Almeida 2014).

These observations are particularly relevant in considering the rise and success of euroscepticism. Indeed, the concept of protest cycles as a whole superficially appears to provide exceptional explanatory power for the rise and emergence of what will, in this study, be termed *Millennial Fascism*, and the euroscepticism embodying it. The idea of waves of activity in conjunction with a strategic seizure of opportunities goes far in explaining this turn-of-the-century timeframe flurry of activity from so many fascist groups.

The emergence and rise of MFGs superficially appear to be connected to the political, economic and social environment. A deeper examination into which aspects within the environment are shared elements among MFGs is expected to reveal a significant relationship with opportunity and timing. In researching euroscepticism and Eurosceptic groups, the modern theories of resource mobilization, political opportunity, protest cycles, and political process possess elements that seem most relevant, although alienation appears to play a significant role as well.

What conditions allowed for the emergence and success of MF? It is believed that the elements of the PP model (political opportunities, indigenous organizational strength, and cognitive liberation) lead to the success of MFGs in Europe but cannot stand alone. Additional elements incorporating dynamic factors are necessary to account for emergence and long-term success.

To test this theory, analysis will focus on two sets of variables. The first test set will focus on a strict interpretation of McAdam's PP model and utilize political opportunities, indigenous organizational strength, cognitive liberation as the causal conditions which led to the emergence and success of MFGs in Europe. Political opportunities will be measured as "openness of the government;" indigenous organizational strength will be determined by membership size; and cognitive liberation will be measured in terms of euroscepticism and nationalism.

The second test set will be a looser, more dynamic interpretation of PP and PPT elements with a focus on opportunity and organizational strength referred to as Organizational/Opportunity Theory (OO Theory). OO utilizes organizational elements from Modern Structural Organizational Theory. Observed Shafritz, Ott, and Jang (2011): "Organizations are rational institutions whose primary purpose is to accomplish established objectives; rational organizational behavior is achieved best through systems of defined rules and formal authority." It also incorporates elements of opportunity from PPT; it specifically utilizes four aspects of opportunity, as identified by Tarrow (1991): "The openness or closedness of the polity, stability or instability of political alignments, presence or absence of allies or support groups, divisions within the elite and its tolerance or intolerance of protest. Optimum opportunity exists in conditions of openness, stability, presence of allies/support groups, and tolerance of protest."

It was Doug McAdam and William Sewell Jr. (2001) who stressed the importance of "crucial junctures" in the timing and frequency of contentious politics. They noted the possibility of specific events or phases in EU development that triggered peaks in European protest as well as the likelihood of more incremental and linear development of European contention (McAdam and Sewell 2001). Observed Tarrow (2005): "We have seen that, at least through the late 1990s, there was a long-term trend toward more Europe-directed collective action. But the more erratic inflections … suggest that both processes were at work. A critical juncture marked the mid-to-late 1990s."

The introduction of OO was not intended to imply fault with PP. Indeed, such an introduction should not imply a belief that PP fails to offer explanatory power. Rather, this research posits that PP is too easily applicable. A strength and a weakness of PP is its macro-level approach which lends itself to wider application, allowing it to explain many things. Whelan (2008) observed that Goodwin and Jasper (1999) and Morris (2000) presented sound critiques of the "overly structural bias and neglect of strategic analysis of much political process theory." Gamson (2011) noted that "with cognitive liberation, the basic problem is that the concept tends to conflate and blur different simultaneous but at least partially independent processes." Nepstad (1997) concurred, arguing that the concept of cognitive liberation tends to emphasize a state of consciousness rather than a process or set of processes. "It conveys *what* people believe but not *how* they change their beliefs" (Nepstad 1997).

OO solves this problem by digging deeper into strategic analysis and better isolating the variables determined to be causal conditions. Its isolation of two elements, narrowed in scope, place focus on pivotal and essential components. Specifically, OO focuses on *opportunity* created by a trigger event and *organizational aptitude*. In 2004, Meyer defined political opportunity as an event in an ongoing cycle of resource mobilization. This concept is similar to the idea broached in this study, though here it is conceived as the genesis rather than part of the cycle.

As previously discussed, the element of opportunity in this model is exogenous and spurred by a trigger event. This event must be large-scale and significant, meaning it must be impactful and life-changing to a large population. The event leads to a change in population dynamics and results in cultural change which, in turn, creates social-political opportunity. The other essential element is organizational aptitude. While the aspect of opportunity is based on exogenous factors, organizational aptitude is internal. An organization's indigenous strength stems from elements within its realm of control such as efficacy and consistency in leadership, ideology, public outreach, and marketing.

For data compilation and analysis of the OO model, internal organizational efficacy and capacity will be measured in terms of consistent leadership and ideology, public outreach, and marketing presence. Examination of these causal conditions will provide insight into the elements of greatest importance and allow for additional, more focused study into the reasons why some parties succeed and some do not.

Chapter 7

The Rise of MFGs

Analysis of Causal Conditions

The selection process in chapter 5 resulted in a subject group of 12 MFGs: Alternative for Germany "Alternative für Deutschland" (AfD-Germany); Danish People's Party "Dansk Folkeparti" (DF-Denmark); True FINNS Party "Finns" (Finland); Freedom Party of Austria "Freiheitliche Partei Österreich" (FPÖ-Austria); Front National (FN-France); Podemos (Spain); Dutch Freedom Party "Partij voor de Vrijheid" (PVV-Netherlands); Swiss People's Party (SVP-Switzerland); Swedish Democrats (Sweden); SYRIZA (Greece); UKIP (England); and Vlaams Belang (Belgium). Scrutiny of these groups and their commonalities will determine whether the elements of the Political Process (PP) model or the Organizational/Opportunity (OO) theory best account for their emergence and success.

The unprecedented increase, emergence, and success of non-traditional parties in Europe served as the genesis of Millennial Fascism (MF). In an effort to explain this trajectory, we will first examine the causal conditions of the PP model, followed by study into the causal conditions of the proposed OO theory (OO). Causal condition measurement will utilize data compiled from various sources including Eurobarometer[1] and the Open Government Index. Following the compilation of data, analysis will utilize Fuzzy Set Qualitative Comparative Analysis (fsQCA) designed by Rihoux and Ragin (2009).

CAUSAL CONDITION DATA COMPILATION

Data compilation will be a two-step process. The first test set will focus on data necessary to examine political opportunities, indigenous organizational strength (aptitude), and cognitive liberation as established in the PP model. The second test set will concentrate on the collection of data for the causal conditions of opportunity and organizational strength referred to in the OO model.

PP MODEL DATA COMPILATION

The casual conditions of this model are political opportunity, indigenous organizational strength (aptitude), and cognitive liberation. Let us now take a look at each of these conditions to isolate the variables for analysis.

Political Opportunity

The significance of opportunity in the MF realm has not gone unnoticed. According to Jens Rydgren (2004), some of the following political opportunities need to be present for radical right-wing populist parties to emerge:

1. A niche, or a gap, between the voters' opinions and their perceived position of the parties.
2. Decreased trust in (established) political parties.
3. Politicization of new issues, preferably immigration.
4. A high degree of convergence among the established parties.
5. An open political system, where new parties have a good chance to enter.
6. Allying with established parties might render credibility, but being controversial might also do the same.
7. The state's capacity and propensity for repression.
8. A potent master frame (Rydgren 2004).

Accordingly, Gifford (2014) contended that from 2010 to 2013, "a constellation of forces created the opportunities for a significant Eurosceptic challenge to the UK's Coalition Government's European strategy." Gifford (2014) believed that the failure of the Conservative party to win a clear victory in the 2010 election weakened the Cameron leadership coupled with the crisis in the Eurozone and the pro-integrationist response of European leaders served to create a unique synthesis of opportunity.

Eisinger (1973) and Koopmans (1996) focused on the "openness" of government as the key factor in opportunity. This research utilized the concept of openness of government as the means of measurement of political opportunity by utilizing data from the 2015 Index of Economic Freedom. The Index measured economic freedom based on 10 quantitative and qualitative factors, grouped into four broad categories, or "pillars," of economic freedom:

1. Rule of Law (property rights, freedom from corruption);
2. Limited Government (fiscal freedom, government spending);
3. Regulatory Efficiency (business freedom, labor freedom, monetary freedom); and

4. Open Markets (trade freedom, investment freedom, financial freedom) (Index of Economic Freedom 2015).

The 2015 data covers the timeframe of the second half of 2013 through the first half of 2014 (Index of Economic Freedom 2015). Each of the ten economic freedoms within these categories was graded on a scale of 0 to 100. The "Freedom from Corruption" percentages from the "Rule of Law" category were used as the data representing political opportunity (Table 7.1) and will be scaled between 0 and 1 for fsQCA.

Data

These are the results for each group:

Alternative for Germany (Alternative für Deutschland-AfD)- Germany 73.8
Danish People's Party (Dansk Folkeparti-DF)-Denmark 76.3
Freedom Party of Austria (Freiheitliche Partei Österreich-FPÖ)-Austria 71.2
Front National-France 62.5
Podemos-Spain 67.6
Dutch Freedom Party (Partij voor de Vrijheid-PVV)-Netherlands 73.7
Swiss People's Party, SVP-Switzerland 80.5
Swedish Democrats-Sweden 72.7
SYRIZA-Greece 54.0
True FINNS-Finland 73.4
UKIP-England-United Kingdom 75.8
Vlaams Belang-Belgium 68.8

Table 7.1 Freedom from Corruption

Country	*Percentage*
Austria	69.1
Belgium	75.0
Denmark	91.0
Finland	89.0
France	71.0
Germany	78.0
Greece	40.0
The Netherlands	83.0
Spain	59.0
Sweden	89.0
Switzerland	85.0
Unted Kingdom	76.0

Source: Rule of Law category from the 2015 Index of Economic Freedom.
Freedom from Corruption Data. This figure shows the Economic Freedom data in 12 categories for each of the 12 countries represented by our MPEGs. Data compiled from: Index of Economic Freedom 2015.

Indigenous Organizational Strength

Indigenous organizational strength, as explained by Kropczynski (2013), refers to the resources that allow a marginalized population to exploit opportunities afforded to them by changes in the political opportunity structure. Examples of these resources include members who can be recruited as a group, respected leaders, a communications network, and individual connections (Kropczynski 2013). McAdam (1982) believed that the more organized a group, the greater the capacity of its members to act, and the more likely it was to be successful. Oberschall (1973) concurred, assigning paramount importance to the degree of organization within the group and its creation of strong networks. The topic of structural strength and its importance was also recognized by Griffin (Griffin 1991). In his study of the success and failure of 53 social movement organizations in the United States between 1800 and 1945, Gamson (1990) found that a formalized structure increases a movement's chance of success, and Cress and Snow (2000) found the same in their study of homeless movement organizations in 12 cities. In a 2012 study on party organizational strength, Tavits (2012) found that "strong organization helps parties increase their vote share significantly and steadily, and that organizational strength played a significant independent role in helping parties succeed electorally." For this study, indigenous organizational strength will be measured in terms of a group's network—its resources—in the form of members. A six-value fuzzy set will be utilized: Place/Score: 1st=1.; 2nd–3rd =.9; 4th =.6; 5th–6th =.4; 7th–8th=.1; ≥ 9th=0.

Groups were ranked according to the size of their group as compared to other parties in their respective country. Results are listed below by group with their rank, source, and fsQCA corresponding score in parentheses.

Membership Size

Alternative for Germany (Alternative für Deutschland-AfD): 7th (Fischer 2015); (.1)

Danish People's Party (Dansk Folkeparti-DF): 3rd (Foght 2014); (.75)

Finns Party: 5th (Politiikka 2013); (.4)

Freedom Party of Austria (Freiheitliche Partei Österreich-FPÖ): 3rd (Briggs 2015); (.9)

Front National: 3rd (Clavel 2014); (.9)

Podemos: 2nd (Garcia 2014); (.9)

Dutch Freedom Party (Partij voor de Vrijheid-PVV): The Hague (2013) noted that the PVV "does not have any members, but consists solely of delegates who represent the party in local, provincial and national parliaments." Because there are no membership numbers to compare, data for this variable utilized Eurbarometer 71.1 survey results asking respondents to name the party to which they felt an attachment: 7th (Eurobarometer 71.1): (.1)

Swiss People's Party, SVP: 3rd (Swiss Confederation 2010); (.9)

Swedish Democrats: 4th (Holmqvist 2014; Sverigedemokraterna 2015); (.6)

SYRIZA: 4th (no membership numbers located—see PVV above; Eurobarometer 71.1); (.6)

UKIP: 5th in 2014 (Nardelli 2014); (.4)

Vlaams Belang: 5th in 2014 (Paelinck 2014); (.4)

Cognitive Liberation

McAdam (1982) posited: "Mediating between opportunity and action are people and the subjective meanings they attach to their situations." Such meanings are the basis of cognitive liberation or shared ideas developed from an "injustice frame." McAdam (1982) suggested that cognitive liberation comes first from the subjective interpretation of political opportunities or *macro-level events* (see Phase II for expansion on the concept of macro-level study as it relates to this research).

In his study, Wessels (2007) found that "41 per cent of citizens across the EU-25 are neutral or negative with respect to European identity, of whom a third can be described as hard-core Eurosceptics." He concluded that "Euroscepticism has the potential to become system-threatening" (Hooghe 2007). The impact of euroscepticism has only increased since Wessels' study.

Brown (2009) suggested that cognitive liberation is based upon grounded knowledge and social trust: as corruption and lawlessness increased in the post-transition years, people's sense of efficacy decreased. It was also Brown (2009) whom asserted that nationalism was "arguably the most important of these subterranean movements, bearing the standard of environmental activism (Dawson 1996; Pryde 1991; Weiner 1999). Many of the break-away Soviet Republics were as concerned with the Russian influence meddling in their native homeland as they were with the rivers and forests themselves" (Brown 2009). Such perspective served as a guide in determining how to best measure cognitive liberation. In this study, cognitive liberation was characterized in terms of nationalism and euroscepticism.

Cognitive Liberation: Euroscepticism

The data utilized for euroscepticism was compiled from Eurobarometer 83.3 (2015). For purposes of this research, euroscepticism was measured in terms of tendency to trust the EU. Eurobarometer results were based on the query "if you tend to trust it or tend not to trust it" with regards to the specific entity

Table 7.2 Trust in the European Union

	Tend to Trust	*Tend Not to Trust*	*Don't Know*
Belgium	48%	45%	7%
Denmark	57%	32%	11%
Germany	39%	48%	13%
Greece	26%	73%	1%
Spain	35%	54%	11%
France	32%	51%	17%
The Netherlands	47%	42%	11%
Austria	32%	59%	9%
Finland	58%	30%	12%
Sweden	48%	41%	11%
UK	29%	55%	16%

Trust in the European Union. Trust in the EU is depicted for each of the 12 countries represented by the MPEGs. Data source: Eurobarometer 83.3; May 2015.

European Union. Table 7.2 indicates the results of each of the 12 subject groups' countries with the exception of Switzerland, whose data was not included in Eurobarometer. As a result, data for Switzerland (Swiss People's Party-SVP) was compiled from the World Values Survey (2015).

Five of the 11 countries had greater than a 50% response indicating a tendency NOT to trust the EU. Greece scored the highest in this regard with 73% of respondents tending to not trust the EU. Finland had the highest response rate of those who trusted the EU (58%). This survey question also had a significant number of "don't know" responses. In France, 17%, and in the UK, 16%, of respondents replied they didn't know if they could trust the EU.

For Switzerland, data was compiled from the World Values Survey (2015) question: "I am going to name a number of organizations. For each one, could you tell me how much confidence you have in them: is it a great deal of confidence, quite a lot of confidence, not very much confidence or none at all? The European Union." Data from wave five, covering the years from 2005 to 2009, was utilized. Figures 7.1 and 7.2 reveal that 59.6% in wave five had none to "not very much" confidence in the EU. The percentages for "tendency not to trust" and "not very much" and "none at all" will be used for statistical analysis purposes in QCA.

Cognitive Liberation: Nationalism

The data for the element of nationalism followed the above utilized methodology for Euroscepticism, with data from Switzerland gathered separately from the World Values Survey. The dataset for determining nationalism was based on the query "Please tell me how attached you feel to … [OUR COUNTRY]." Table 7.3 offers a visual of the results gathered from Eurobarometer 77.3 (May 2012).

V146_00.- Confidence: The European Union

Cross by

-- None selected --

	Number of cases	%/Total
A great deal	43	3.4%
Quite a lot	414	33.3%
Not very much	544	43.9%
None at all	195	15.7%
No answer	14	1.1%
Don´t know	32	2.6%
(N)	(1,241)	100%

Selected sample: Switzerland 2007 (1241)

Figure 7.1 Confidence in the EU-Switzerland. Date from Wave Five (2005–2009) indicates the amount of confidence in the EU as reported by Swiss respondents. WORLD VALUES SURVEY Wave 5 2005–2008 OFFICIAL AGGREGATE v.20140429. World Values Survey Association. (www.worldvaluessurvey.org). AggreSwiss respondents.gate File Producer: Asep/JDS, Madrid SPAIN.

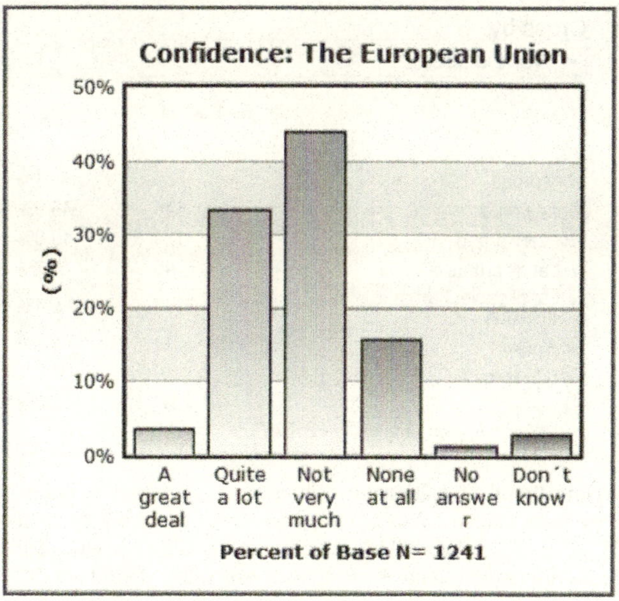

Figure 7.2 Bar Graph of Confidence in the EU-Switzerland. Date from Wave Five (2005–2009) indicates the amount of confidence in the EU as reported by Swiss respondents. WORLD VALUES SURVEY Wave 5 2005–2008 OFFICIAL AGGREGATE v.20140429. World Values Survey Association. (www.worldvaluessurvey.org). AggreSwiss respondents. gate File Producer: Asep/JDS, Madrid SPAIN.

Table 7.3 Attachment to Country

Country/sample ID (Series standard)	*Very Attached*	*Fairly Attached*	*Not Very Attached*	*Not at All Attached*	*Total*	*N=*
FR - France	91.2	8.8	0	0	100	147
BE - Belgium	77.6	18.6	2.5	1.2	100	161
NL - The Netherlands	69.6	26.8	1.8	1.8	100	56
DE-W - Germany - West	82	16.9	1.1	0	100	89
DK - Denmark	88	10.7	0	1.3	100	75
GB-GBN - Great Britain	83.3	–	4.2	0	100	24
GR - Greece	93.7	6.3	0	0	100	63
ES -Spain	82.2	11.9	3	3	100	101
DE-E- Germany - East	89.2	8.1	2.7	0	100	37
FI - Finland	88.6	11.4	0	0	100	35
SE - Sweden	85	12.5	2.5	0	100	40
AT - Austria	86.2	12.3	1.5	0	100	65
TOTAL	86.5	10.1	2.4	1	100	2,929

Note: Data compiled using Eurobarometer 77.3 (May 2012) Europe 2020, the Financial and Economic Crisis, European Citizenship and European Values (Ramswell 2017).

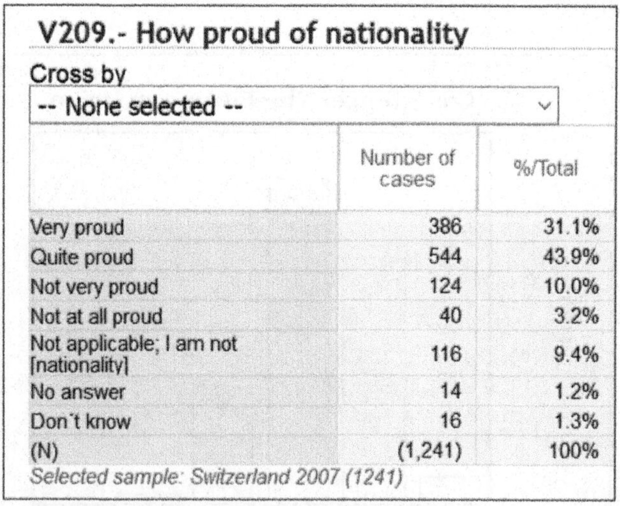

V209.- How proud of nationality

Cross by

-- None selected --

	Number of cases	%/Total
Very proud	386	31.1%
Quite proud	544	43.9%
Not very proud	124	10.0%
Not at all proud	40	3.2%
Not applicable; I am not [nationality]	116	9.4%
No answer	14	1.2%
Don´t know	16	1.3%
(N)	(1,241)	100%

Selected sample: Switzerland 2007 (1241)

Figure 7.3 How Proud of Nationality. Chart indicating level of pride in nationality experienced by Swiss citizens. WORLD VALUES SURVEY Wave 5 2005–2008 OFFICIAL AGGREGATE v.20140429. World Values Survey Association. (www.worldvaluessurvey.org). AggreSwiss respondents.gate File Producer: Asep/JDS, Madrid SPAIN.

France (91.2%) and Greece (93.7%) returned the highest percentages of people "very attached" to their respective country. The Netherlands returned the lowest percentage at 69.6%. Because data from Germany was separated into east/west, the percentages were averaged resulting in a percentage of 85.6% for Germany as a whole.

For Swiss data, results were utilized from the most recent wave including Switzerland: Wave Five 2005–2009 (Figure 7.3). The question asked was "How proud are you to be [nationality]?" Data indicated 31.1% were "very proud" of the Swiss nationality, and another 43.9% were "quite proud."

For QCA analysis, the percentages for "Very attached" and "Very proud" will be used for membership degree data.

OO MODEL DATA COMPILATION

This model is built on the concept of organizational aptitude and capacity existing concurrently with external opportunities, set into motion as a result of a specific event. It is comprised of two essential elements: opportunity borne from exogenous factors triggered by a large-scale event leading to cultural change, and internal organizational elements. Let us now take a look at each of these causal conditions to isolate the variables for analysis.

Opportunity

Azmanova (2004, 18) observed that a "realignment is taking place between centre and periphery between, on one hand, the centre-left and centre-right midpoint and, on the other hand, the circumference of far-right and radical-left parties. In this new alignment, the new centre … becomes one of the poles in the political axis, embracing the 'opportunity' side of the dilemma, while the farright and radical-left constitute the opposite pole responding to societal fears of the hazards of the new economy of increased competition and open borders." In this vein, H1 asserts that the elements of opportunity created an environment allowing for H2. OO posits that a trigger event, in this case the end of the Cold War, symbolized by the removal of the Berlin Wall (referred to as "the Fall of the Wall"), led to a new cultural norm that created a political and social environment conducive to the formation of MFGs in Europe. These elements are held to be necessary preconditions considered necessary for the rise and success of MFGs (H2).

Fall of the Wall

The Fall of the Wall (FOTW) concept is built on the premise of a trigger event serving as the impetus for wide-scale change or reform. Examples of such events are the onset/end of war; a catastrophic event such as 9/11; or a sociopolitical event of international proportion like the fall of the Berlin Wall.

As an example, the signing of the Treaty of Versailles in 1919 marked the end of World War I, but it also signaled the beginning of Hitler's rise to power. Within the Treaty was an article (Article 231—now referred to as the *War Guilt Clause*), which not only blamed Germany for World War I, but punished them for it as well. Hitler leveraged and utilized the growing frustration and anger felt by the Germans over the conditions of the Treaty, calling for its abrogation in his 1920 Nazi Program (Yale University 2008). The signing of the Treaty of Versailles served as a trigger event for the rise of Hitler and the Nazi regime—a regime that would orchestrate one of the world's most horrific and notorious events—the Holocaust.

Additionally, the September 11, 2001 attacks in the United States by Al Qaeda offer another example of a trigger event. The attacks, carried out that morning, led to the formation of a "War Cabinet" by 9:30pm and a declaration of a "War on Terror" by 11:00 pm, the same day (Chossudovsky 2011). The effects of 9/11 continue to impact the world today, culturally and politically, leading to altered way of life, a new bureaucratic structure, a new international alliance known as the "Global War on Terror." Perspectives changed to mindsets of "us vs. them" and illustrated Samuel Huntington's titular prophecy of a "Clash of Civilizations."

This research's symbolic event, the fall of the Berlin Wall in November 1989, and subsequent end of the Cold War in December 1991, led to significant changes throughout Europe, specifically culture change and new-found freedom. Indeed, Mudde (2007) identified the 1992 signing of the Maastricht Treaty as the "turning point" for radical right parties in terms of both their position on European integration and the salience of the issue in their agenda. Although the EU existed before the Maastricht Treaty, it was formally established under its current name following the signing of the Treaty in 1993 with 12 member countries. Since that time, the EU has more than doubled in size. In 1995, Austria, Finland, and Sweden were admitted. In 2004, the largest enlargement of the EU occurred with the addition of ten countries: Czech Republic, Estonia, Cyprus, Latvia, Lithuania, Hungary, Malta, Poland, Slovakia, and Slovenia. Romania and Bulgaria joined in 2007, and Croatia in 2013, bringing the total number of member countries to 28 (European Commission 2015). Such rapid expansion, coupled with the launch of the euro as the single currency and austerity issues, has led to significant backlash against the status quo in the form of euroscepticism, in addition to altering life for its citizens. Malone (2014) noted that "in the years immediately following World War II, right-wing populist parties virtually ceased to exist across Europe, as their brand had become toxic." In fact, statistics reflect a waxing and waning of fascist groups that will coincide with the end of war. Halla, et al. (2014) observed that from "the 1970s until the mid-1980s, hardly any ERW [extreme right-wing party] had gained more than five percent in a general election. Fifteen years later, ERW parties received between ten and twenty-five percent in these votes."

In 2011, Nora Langenbacher and Britta Schellenberg presented a project at the Forum Berlin on behalf of the Friedrich-Ebert-Stiftung titled "Combating right-wing extremism." The project analyzed election data of radical right-wing parties in selected EU countries between 1980 and 2009. The data, presented in five-year increments showed that from 1980 to1984, the average percentage of the vote received by radical right-wing groups was 2.8%, with about half above 4%. Between 1985 and 1989, the number grew to 6%, with more than half greater than 6%. By 2005 and 2009, the average had reached 12.7% with more than half of the groups earning 14% or greater. The highest percentage was Switzerland with 30%, followed by Austria with 28.2% (Langenbacher, 2011).

Langenbacher (2011) opined that "present-day European right-wing radicalism is a modern phenomenon that has undergone several phases of renewal. These phases were either visible as the consequence of modernisation spurts in postwar Western societies, or appeared as newly constituted forms in the wake of the regime changes in Eastern Europe." In 2004, Paxton noted that "all the eastern European successor states have contained radical right movements since 1989, but most of these have remained gratifyingly weak" (Paxton 2004). Such perspectives support the argument of the FOTW as the trigger event for MF, but also provide support for the theory that a subsequent trigger event within a short timeframe—9/11—could serve to strengthen resolve and offer additional opportunity for groups in transition or on the verge of formation. In fact, groups such as ATAKA (2004), Jobbik (2003), and SYRIZA (2004) were all formed within 2 to 3 years of 9/11.

These examples support the claim that a single event can dramatically change and impact life. The chain of events each set into motion evidences the influence possible from one single event. In the case of MF, the FOTW as a trigger event served as the impetus for socio-cultural change: the variable examined in the next section.

Cultural Change

It was Geertz (1973) who observed that symbols derive their meaning not from their relationships with one another, but rather from the various roles they play in people's lives, and the Berlin Wall was one powerful symbol. With its demise, literal and figurative borders were opened providing opportunity and freedom—often where none before existed. In an interview with *Foreign Policy*, Volen Siderov, leader of the Bulgarian ATAKA party, discussed the hopes and expectations shared by those against the communist regime that were borne from the FOTW:

> People … believed that with the fall of the communist regime, things would settle down in a democratic fashion along the lines of the freedoms that were missing—the freedom of expression, the freedom of speech—as well as in terms of lifestyle, because back then we were frustrated from an economic point of view … we were too naïve. (Feffer 2013)

Interestingly, Siderov even referenced Huntington when discussing the effects of the FOTW:

> Ideologically, I realized that there was a clash between the model of globalization and the model of national identity. This is not the clash of civilizations offered by Samuel Huntington, the clash between Islam and Christianity. The true clash is between the globalization model and the well-developed national sovereign state that has a well-preserved identity, economy, middle class, and social system. (Feffer 2013)

In 2004, Paxton observed that "the most successful of a number of antiliberal, anti-Western, anti-Semitic parties in Russia was Vladimir Zhirinovsky's badly misnamed Liberal Democratic Party (LDP), founded at the end of 1989, with a program of national revival and unification under strong authority combined with wild-eyed proposals for the reconquest of Russia's lost territories."

Indeed, theorists tend to view culture change from one of two schools of thought: one views traditional values as declining due to modernization while the other views traditional values as persisting in spite of modernization (Inglehart and Baker 2000).

Accordingly, Griffin's concept of palingenesis—a rebirth—is acutely appropriate. Such rebirth captures traditional values bringing them to the forefront. His idea of palingenetic ultra-nationalism (1991) mirrors the surge in post-war nationalism seen in Japan. Surges in post-war nationalism are more common than not lending more plausibility to the idea of social and culture change following a trigger event. Examples include the United States following the War of 1812, Germany after World War I (in which Hitler embraced symbols), and Africa following World War II. The surge in nationalism in Europe following the FOTW, however, had unintended consequences and led to a nationalism collision rather than unification and, ultimately, euroscepticism. As noted by Langenbacher (2011): "More than sixty years after the end of World War II, with Europe largely reunited, radical-right-wing, ultra-nationalist and xenophobic movements and parties have become part of the normal political scene."

Snow, et al. (2004) observed that two conceptual shifts have occurred. First, the political opportunity structure in Europe is conceived as multilevel. Scale shift has become part of the social movement repertoire. When problems implicate several levels of government but political opportunities across these governments vary, strategic actors can be expected to exploit the opportunities that are available. Tarrow (2001) opined that "the European Union … is at the same time cross-territorial, intergovernmental, and multilevel, which opens opportunities for coalitions of actors and states to formulate common positions and overcome their diversity and dispersion to exploit its political opportunities."

Harmsen and Spiering (2004) acknowledged the relevance of culture and the pervasive role it plays. They noted that the term euroscepticism "assumes a meaning which must be understood relative to the different national political traditions and experiences of European integration which frame those debates" (Harmsen and Spiering 2004). This is particularly critical in times of transition when values and norms can be challenged and even targeted.

Many Europeans point to demographic changes as a primary cause of socio-cultural change in the 90s. Allievi (2005) noted that "the presence of ever-increasing numbers of immigrants in the European social landscape it is not merely a quantitative fact with different consequences for many social and cultural dynamics. Changes in the quantitative levels of so many different indicators (economic, social, cultural, political, religious) not only produce quantitative change, they alter the scenario completely." Azmanova (2004) focused on political change, noting that "the nature of political centrism itself has undergone a change in the nineties, and thus given rise to new political cultures. At the root of this change are the deep socio-economic transformations in Europe." In fact, a 2015 Pew Research Study revealed that 50% or greater of people surveyed now view non-traditional parties positively. Langenbacher (2011) offered additional support for the argument of a cultural shift: "Various studies show that from the 1980s up to the present day, the framework conditions have shifted towards a higher rather than a lower degree of tolerance."

In 1961, Maurice Bardéche wrote that "fascism is, by its essence, nationalist, and while it originates as the reaction to a crisis, all fascist reaction is resurrection" (Griffin 1991). This dissertation argues that Bardéche's 'resurrection' is Griffin's palingenetic ulltranationalism; it is the manifestation of coveted traditional values embraced by MFGs and materializing in the form of nationalism and euroscepticism as a result of the culture change in Europe triggered by the FOTW.

Organizational Aptitude

Organizational aptitude will be defined as the internal elements of an organization that have contributed to solidifying its presence. The OO model argues that leadership and ideological consistency, marketing presence, and public outreach are essential components of a successful group.

Success in this study will be considered as a group having a member in the EP. Scores are coded using the six-value fuzzy set: ≥25%=1; 15–24%=.9; 9–14%=.6; 4–8%=.25; 1–3%=.1; and 0=0. Table 7.4 details the scoring process. Testing of H2 consisted of data from sources including the World Values Survey and the Eurobarometer. Data was analyzed using fsQCA.

Table 7.4 MFG Success as of January 2016

Party	*MEP*	*%*	*Score*
Alternative für Deutschland (AfD)	2 of 96	2.083	.1
Finns Party-Perussuomalaiset	2 of 13	15.384	.9
Freiheitliche Partei Österreich (FPÖ)	4 of 18	22.222	.9
Front National (FN)	23 of 74	31.081	1
Podemos-Spain	5 of 54	9.259	.6
Partij voor de Vrijheid (PVV)	4 of 26	15.384	.9
Swiss People's Party (SVP)	2 of 7*	28.571	1
Swedish Democrats (SD)	2 of 20	10.00	.6
SYRIZA-Greece	4 of 21	19.047	.9
UKIP-England	22 of 73	30.136	1
Vlaams Belang-Belgium	1 of 12	8.333	.25

Note: Scores: ≥25%=1; 15–24%=.9; 9–14%=.6; 4–8%=.25; 1–3%=.1; 0=0. As Switzerland is not part of the EU, party success was measured as a seat on the Federal Council (Ramswell 2017).

Consistency: Leadership and Ideology

In their article on elements of social movement organizations, Benford and Snow (2000) discussed the importance of consistency in framing collective action, noting that it "refers to the congruency between an SMO's articulated beliefs, claims, and actions." Further, the National Democratic Institute (NDI) specified that "clearly defined political identity serves to strengthen political parties through its contribution to consistent policies based on common values" (NDI 2008).

The link between consistency and political parties has become increasingly significant. A 2014 survey by the Pew Research Center revealed that "as ideological consistency has become more common, it has become increasingly aligned with partisanship." In their survey on American ideological partisanship, Pew found that "70% of the politically engaged now [2014] take positions that are mostly or consistently in line with the ideological bent of their party. By comparison, the equivalent positions were held by 58% of Republicans and 35% of Democrats in 1994 and 40% of Republicans and 59% of Democrats in 2004" (Pew Research Center 2014).

For this research, consistency was examined as it related to a group's leadership, mission, and ideology. Though leadership can and often does change, it was held that when a group's central focus and ideology remained consistent, its status and level of success would not falter. MIT (April 2014) underscored the importance of leadership consistency, noting that "consistent, replicable behavior of leaders plays a crucial role to create organizational trust." Though leadership is certainly believed to be important, change in leadership is surmountable as long as the group's underlying mission and goals remain consistent. An examination of the DF revealed a positive result when leadership was replaced by consistent ideology was maintained: "DF's broader appeal among the voting public has also increased significantly since the polarizing Pia Kjærsgaard stepped down in 2012 and was replaced by the younger and more rhetorically restrained Kristian Thulesen Dahl" (Jensen 2015).

In this study, consistency was measured in terms of ideology and of leadership. Some of the information for this dataset utilized data compiled in the qualification of MFGs. Leadership and ideology scores will again be based on a six-value fuzzy set with a scoring system as detailed in Table 7.5.

Alternative for Germany (Alternative für Deutschland-AfD). AfD has had two leaders in as many years. However, it has remained solidly nationalist, populist, and right-wing with a firm anti-Euro/anti-EU stance. Leadership: .9; Ideology: 1

Danish People's Party (Dansk Folkeparti-DF). In more than 10 years of existence DF has seen one leadership change in 2012. It has remained a right-wing populist group since its inception with strong anti-immigration policies. Leadership: .9; Ideology: 1

True FINNS Party. The True Finns have had the same leader, Timo Soini, since 1997. The party was founded as and remains socially conservative, populist, and nationalist. Leadership: 1; Ideology: 1

Table 7.5 Leadership and Ideology Scoring

Score	*Leadership*	*Ideology*
1 (fully in)	same leader since founding	same ideology since founding
0.9 (mostly but not fully in)	two leaders total in 10+ years	same ideology though softer or harsher stance
0.6 (more or less in)	three leaders total in 10+ years	same ideology but shift in primary focus
0.4 (more or less out)	three leaders in less than 10 years	one change in primary ideology OR two shifts in focus
0.1 (mostly but not fully out)	more than four leaders in 10 years	more than one change in primary ideology in 10 years
0 (fully out)	ALL OTHERS	more than one change in primary ideology in 10 years

Scores were based on a six-value fuzzy set as described by Ragin 2008 (Ramswell 2017).

Freedom Party of Austria (Freiheitliche Partei Österreich-FPÖ). FPÖ has had two leaders as well as coalition government rule since the 90s. However, it has remained fervently right-wing, nationalist, and anti-immigration since its reinvention in the 90s. Leadership: .6; Ideology: 1

Front National. Led by a Le Pen since 1972; Founded by Jean-Marie Le Pen and assumed by daughter Marine Le Pen in 2011. The party has been consistently right-wing and nationalist with increasing focus on immigration. Leadership: .9; Ideology: .9

Podemos. As a new party, Podemos has only seen one national election and one leader. Its platform continues to evolve though it is left-wing and focused on economic recovery. Leadership: 1; Ideology: 1

Dutch Freedom Party (Partij voor de Vrijheid-PVV). Party leader Wilders has remained at the helm since the party was founded in 2006. It is staunchly right-wing, populist, and Eurosceptic. Leadership: 1; Ideology: 1

Swiss People's Party, SVP. Since it was reinvented in the 90s, the SVP has had three leaders with their current leader serving since 2008. The party has refined its goals and policies several times, presenting a new manifesto in 2010. It remains firm is its rejection of EU membership and is right-wing populist. Leadership: .6; Ideology: .4

Swedish Democrats. The party has had several leadership changes, though current leader Akesson has been at the helm since 2005. The party has maintained a right-wing-populist, nationalist, and anti-immigration focus since Akesson assumed leadership. Leadership: .6; Ideology: .4

SYRIZA. SYRIZA was founded and remains a left-wing, populist, and nationalist party. Its leader, Tsipras, has served as chairman since 2009, sitting out a little more than a month following a party splinter in 2015. This led to Tsipras' loss of the majority in parliament, so he stepped down as prime minister and called for a new election, which SYRIZA ultimately won. Leadership: 1; Ideology: 1

UKIP. Nigel Farage has served as party leader from 2006 to 2009 and again from 2010 to present (2016). Since 2006, UKIP has had Roger Knapman, the Lord Pearson of Rannoch, Jeffrey Titford and Farage at the helm. UKIP is firmly populist, right-wing, and Eurosceptic. It was founded as a Eurosceptic party. Leadership: .1; Ideology: 1

Vlaams Belang. Vlaams Belang has remained an anti-immigrant, right-wing nationalist party seeking an independent Flemish republic. The party has had four leaders since 2004, with Frank Vanhecke, Bruno Valkeniers, Gerolf Annemans, and Tom Van Grieken serving as chairman since 2008. Leadership: .1; Ideology: 1

Online Marketing Presence

As explored in Phase I testing of PP, McAdams's idea of cognitive liberation was a powerful and important concept. However, one must consider how these shared ideas are developed and imparted. This study holds that messaging/marketing is the method of delivering and establishing these shared ideas and beliefs.

One of Adolf Hitler's legacies was his adept usage of propaganda. The London Jewish Cultural Centre (2011) noted that Hitler chose to appoint Josef Goebbels as minister of propaganda to propel his efforts: "Goebbels developed extremely successful campaigns using simple slogans and images repeated over and again in order to win public support for the party. The Nazis spent huge sums on newspapers, leaflets and poster campaigns." Hitler had Goebbels depict Germany as a country "with traditional values and with Hitler as the beloved Führer. The promotion of Nazi racial policy was at the very centre of Goebbels's message. The re-writing of school books and the production of antisemitic books, films and exhibitions supported this policy" (London Jewish Cultural Centre 2011). This early manifestation of a marketing campaign was telltale of the potential impact possible through a strategic marketing effort.

A marketing campaign can take many forms and involve many different aspects. Social media and traditional media are now the two primary outlets. In 2012, Ramalingam determined that "in recent years, the far right's use of social media has expanded. The extreme right capitalises on relationship-building mechanisms online, and the emergence of new social media and other such tools has become far more important than static websites, particularly to build a sense of comradeship as well as ownership over the movement." De Vreese (2007) highlighted the role of the media in shaping citizen's attitudes toward European integration, concluding that "Euroscepticism is, at least partially, a function of the diet of information that citizens consume about European affairs. News media coverage of EU-issues and events, such as Council meetings, can cause changes in the level of cynicism about European integration."

Another important aspect of marketing is branding and messaging, that is, how a group presents itself and the words and methods it uses to represents its ideology and goals. Word use is particularly important—in this case semantics are everything. Word choice paints a clear picture of a group's meaning and/or intention; for example, opting to use the word "demand" rather than "ask for" conveys a particular tone and meaning. In an article for the BBC, Williamson (2014) reported: "In the past three years, Marine Le Pen has put a lot of effort into 'detoxifying' her party—ridding it of the racist stigma and neo-Nazi links it attracted under her father's leadership." Le Pen stated that "the devil's cloak that we were forced to wear has been removed … the

French are beginning to see us as we really are. Our party was never racist. None of our proposals are based on race or religion. We are patriots: we welcome and work with all who are French" (Williamson 2014). It is important to note Le Pen's emphasis on and, perhaps, misdirection evidenced by the choice of the word "patriot."

As a whole, the method and manner of spreading the word about one's organization takes a new form in the twenty-first century. The number of people using the internet as their primary source of news has continued to climb, while the number of traditional print news readers declines. Observed Sheppard (2015): "Industry focused research reiterates the popularity of online news consumption in comparison to the fading traditional print formats. Accessing news online is favoured over print in France, Germany, Italy, Denmark, United Kingdom, Spain and Finland."

It is therefore not surprising to recognize the utility, reach, and growing need to focus marketing and publicity campaigns online. In this study, marketing will be measured in terms of online presence. Each party in our study will be analyzed to determine whether it has a website and, if so, what social media links they have included. Any icon links/feeds displayed on the party's homepage will be noted.

Scoring was based on the number of social media links found on a party's main/home page on its website, if applicable (Table 7.6). The party's own website counted as one point. One additional point was given if a website offered any additional languages. An additional point was also given for a group exceeding more than 100,000 page likes on Facebook, 50,000 followers or 5,000 tweets on Twitter, and 10,000 YouTube subscribers. Thus, a maximum of 15 points was possible. The tallied points corresponded to a score which was then utilized for fsQCA. For consistency, the English versions of online media were utilized for data compilation. For example, Facebook was utilized instead of the Dutch version "Hyves." An online presence chart (Table 7.7) shows the information compiled.

Alternative for Germany (Alternative für Deutschland-AfD)

- http://www.alternativefuer.de/ (1)
- Four social media links: Google +, Facebook, Twitter, YouTube (4)

Table 7.6 Social Media Scoring

# of social media links plus bonus points	10+	9	8	7	6	5	4	3	2	1
Corresponding Score	1	.9	.8	.7	.6	.5	.4	.3	.2	.1

Scoring for each group was based on the number of social media links found on the party's main/home page on its official website (Ramswell 2017).

Table 7.7 Millennial Fascist Groups—Online Presence as of January 2016

Online Presence/ Group	*Facebook*	*Twitter*	*Google +*	*You Tube*	*Instagram*	*Pinterest*	*RSS*	*Flickr*	*Other*
Alternative für Deutschland AfD - Germany www. alternativefuer.de	alternativefuer.de 27,063 People Talking About This 180,270 Total Page Likes	@AfD_Bund Tweets 3,908 Following 333 Followers 14.3k Likes 96 Lists 1	+Alternativefuer Deutschland 1,536 followers 2,461,801 views	wahlalternative 2013 2,398 subscribers					Online Shop
Dansk Folkeparti- DFDenmark www. danskfolkeparti. dk	Dansk- Folkeparti/5204493 47983427 2,011 People Talking About This 63,026 Total Page Likes	@DanskDf1995 Tweets 286 Following 354 Followers 4,915 Likes 82 Lists 1	+Dansk Folkeparti Official 20 followers 4,170 views	Dansk FolkepartiUCi Di10- eqJ2Sv0w YW-RoS9g 41 Subscribers				dfkolding	
Perussuomalaiset True FINNS Party www. perussuomalaiset. fi	Perussuomalaiset 6,856 People Talking About This 30,446 Total Page Likes	@VerkkomediaPS Tweets 2,809 Following 414 Followers 2,077 Likes 74		Psverkkomedia 303 Subscribers				perussuom alaiset	blogit.perussuo malaiset.fi
Freiheitliche Partei Österreich FPÖ– Austria www. fpoe.at/	HCStrache 85,143 People Talking About This 303,107 Total Page Likes	@HCStracheFP Tweets 15.4K Following 15 Followers 8,879	+11705239601 9063368226 21,914 views	FPOETVonline 12,938 Subscribers					

Table 7.7 Millennial Fascist Groups—Online Presence as of January 2016 (*continued*)

Online Presence/ Group	*Facebook*	*Twitter*	*Google +*	*You Tube*	*Instagram*	*Pinterest*	*RSS*	*Flickr*	*Other*
Front National-France www.frontnational.com/	FN.officiel 15,206 People Talking About This 337,574 Total Page Likes	@FN_officiel Tweets 18.2K Following 500 Followers 106K Likes 104	+frontnational 1,519 followers 557,431 views	fnofficiel 15,089 Subscribers	marine_lepen/ 90 posts 5,509 followers 219 following		www.frontnational.com/feed		•iTunes • Google Play •Daily Motion MarineLePen 1.6M views 1,009 followers 239 videos 1 playlist
Podemos- Spain unpaiscontigo.es/	Ahorapodemos 349,292 People Talking About This 1,044,750 Total Page Likes	@ahorapodemos Tweets 52.1K Following 1,386 Followers 881K Likes 1,002 Lists 2		Circulos Podemos 64,961 Subscribers				podemos 167 Followers 8 Following	Reddit-/podemos
Partij voor de Vrijheid- PVV Netherlands www.pvv.nl/	Partijvoor devrijheid 1,071 People Talking About This 19,543 Total Page Likes	@geertwilderspvv Tweets 3,807 Followers 657K Likes 1	+1106126 96216819 000000 No posts				www.pvv.nl/index.php		
Swiss People's Party, SVP www.svp.ch/	SVPch 611 People Talking About This 16,165 Total Page Likes	@SVPch and @UDCch Tweets 542 /233 Following 134 /72 Followers 4,937 /679 Likes 35 Lists 1		svpch 1278 subscribers	SVPch/ 39 posts 431 followers 84 following		www.svp.ch/rss/home/		

Swedish Democrats sd.se	Sverigedemo kraterna 13,610 People Talking About This 106,317 Total Page Likes	@sdriks Tweets 1364 Following 34 Followers 36K Likes 381 Lists 1	Sverigedemo kraterna 105 followers 130,281 views	Sverigedemo kraterna 8,551 Subscribers				
SYRIZA- Greece www.syriza.gr/	syrizaofficial 1,128 People Talking About This 112,696 Total Page Likes	@syriza_gr Tweets 3,591 Following 591 Followers 68.4K Likes 46 Lists 2	+officialsyriza 130 followers 191,865 views	officialsyriza and UCx8UP CwjLXbnMAz K845mckw 681 subscribers		www.syriza.gr/ rss.php	Syrizaofficial 5 Followers 3 Following	
UKIP-England www. ukip.org	UKIP 22,920 People Talking About This 518,174 Total Page Likes	@UKIP Tweets 24.5K Following 4,851 Followers 113K Likes 1 Lists 1		UKIP MEPs UC3iZz Ce7M5nLM Pjm5Yh91hw 12,628 Subscribers			1598582@ N24 6 Members 37 Photos 1 Discussions	Online Donations- Paypal UKIP Store
Vlaams Belang- Belgium www. vlaamsbelang.org	Vlbelang 7,089 People Talking About This 34,494 Total Page Likes	@vlbelang Tweets 8,050 Following 1,549 Followers 6,272 Likes 727 Lists 1	+vlaamsbelang 88 followers 45,009 views	VlaamsBelangIn Beeld 1202 Subscribers	Vlaamsbelang 2 Boards 4 Pins 3 Followers 5 Following	vlaamsbelang. org/rss/index. php		•E-magazine •FEC• •Magazine •Uitgeverij Egmont

Ramswell (2017).

- Offers English as a language (1)
- Facebook likes >100,000K (1)
  TOTAL: 7 (.7)

Danish People's Party (Dansk Folkeparti-DF)

- http://www.danskfolkeparti.dk/ (1)
- One social media link to Facebook (1)
- Also has links to the FB pages of several members/leaders
  TOTAL: 2 (.2)

Finns Party-Perussuomalaiset

- https://www.perussuomalaiset.fi/ (1)
- Has four social media links: Facebook, Twitter, Flickr, Blog (4)
- Offers English (1)
  TOTAL: 6 (.6)

Freedom Party of Austria (Freiheitliche Partei Österreich-FPÖ)

- http://www.fpoe.at/ (1)
- Has three social media links to YouTube, Facebook and Twitter (3)
- Also has link to party leader Stroche's website and the FPÖ -TV site
- Facebook >100,000 likes (1)
- YouTube subscribers >10,000 (1)
- Twitter >5,000 tweets (1)
  TOTAL: 7 (.7)

Front National-France

- http://www.frontnational.com/ (1)
- Lists seven social media links on their website (7)
- Lists two audio/video links (iTunes and Google play)
- Live Twitter feed with >5,000 tweets and >50,000 followers (1)
- Facebook >100,000 likes (1)
- YouTube >10,000 subscribers (1)
  TOTAL: 11 (1)

Podemos-Spain

- http://unpaiscontigo.es and podemos.info (1)
- Has social media links to Facebook, Twitter, YouTube, and Flickr (4)
- Lists hashtags for use in English and Spanish #TOGETHERPODEMOS #UnPaísContigo

- Offers five language choices (1)
- Twitter >5,000 tweets and >50,000 followers (1)
- Facebook >100,000 likes (1)
- YouTube >10,000 subscribers (1)

  TOTAL: 9 (.9)

Dutch Freedom Party (Partij voor de Vrijheid-PVV)

- http://www.pvv.nl/ (1)
- Has links to RSS feed and party leader Geert Wilders' Twitter (2)
- Twitter >50,000 followers (1)

  TOTAL: 4 (.4)

Swiss People's Party, SVP

- http://www.svp.ch/ (1)
- Has social media links to YouTube, Twitter, Facebook, and Instagram (4)
- Offers French or German (1)

  TOTAL: 6 (.6)

Swedish Democrats

- http://sd.se (1)
- Has social media links to Twitter and Facebook (2)
- Facebook >100,000 likes (1)

  TOTAL: 4 (.4)

SYRIZA-Greece

- http://www.syriza.gr/ (1)
- Has social media links to Twitter, Facebook, YouTube, Flickr, RSS feed (5)
- Offers international option for other languages (1)
- Twitter >50,000 followers (1)
- Facebook >100,000 likes (1)

  TOTAL: 9 (.9)

UKIP-England

- http://www.ukip.org/ (1)
- Has links to Twitter, Facebook and YouTube (3)
- Has live Twitter and Facebook feed
- Twitter >50,000 followers (1)
- Facebook >100,000 likes (1)

- YouTube >10,000 YouTube subscribers (1)
  TOTAL: 7 (.7)

Vlaams Belang-Belgium

- http://www.vlaamsbelang.org/ (1)
- Has social media links to Facebook, Twitter, Google+, Pinterest, YouTube, and RSS feed (6)
- Live feed/video links Twitter, Facebook, Google+
- Twitter >5,000 tweets (1)
  TOTAL: 8 (.8)

Public Outreach

In 2005, the European Commission found that "access to decision-makers is more difficult for the Eurosceptics than for supporters of the integration process. In other words, we expected the strong EU opponents to rely more heavily on public-related strategies than the EU supporters." They further observed that "eurosceptics are obliged to rely more heavily on public-related strategies, because they find it difficult to get access to decision-makers at the national or the EU-level" (European Commission, 2005).

Such insight is central to the proposed variable of grassroots activism. Public appeal and involvement is a critical component of most campaigns, but especially so with MFGs. Evans and Butt demonstrated that "public opinion increasingly cues political parties rather than the reverse," and that "Euroscepticism in Britain has become less driven by economic insecurity and moreso by concerns about British (or English) identity" (Hooghe and Marks, 2007).

MFGs have sought to change the status quo; to do so they must involve and call upon the masses to gain voters and, subsequently, seats. Groups seek to inspire and mobilize the public, encouraging them to engage and demand change on behalf of their cause. From these efforts emerge voters—like-minded and patriotic citizens responding to a call to action.

Websites and social media are now considered agents of mobilization. They allow politicians and parties to interact and engage with constituents and members as well as serve to broadcast a call to action. Indeed, Bartlett, et al. (2013) observed that "The M5S Movement in Italy has evolved rapidly to become a significant political player by using social media to engage like-minded people in virtual and real life political action." Indeed, traditional outreach efforts may not have disappeared from the choice of tools in the toolbox, but they have been forced to make ample space for millennial grassroots activism such as online marketing and targeting.

As a practical example, Podemos is widely considered to have created one of the best social media and marketing campaigns in Europe. Miguel Arana

Catania, co-founder of Laboratorio Democratico, noted that "the use of social media has been a major success for Podemos" (Sangsari 2015). Sangsari (2015) reported that "Podemos's social currency reaches close to one million Facebook fans and 557,000 Twitter followers. To put that in perspective, the four largest federal parties in Canada have a combined total of 270,000 Facebook likes and 370,000 Twitter followers." Troncoso (2014) described how "Podemos' unprecedented tactics and organizational methods can reinvigorate the New Left in Europe." Accordingly, Ken Loach, co-founder of the UK party Left Unity, told Troncoso: "I think we can emulate [*Podemos*] in the organising in the grassroots, drawing people in, speaking to the 90%, using social media when necessary" (Troncoso 2014).

The Podemos website not only proudly recruits members and volunteers, it encourages public involvement and engagement. Their efforts include online do-it-yourself door hangers, bicycle tags, and campaign cards. They also involve visitors by encouraging them to take "selfies" and videos and post them with a Podemos hashtag. Podemos even goes the extra mile when it comes to online fundraising, offering microcredit, and crowdfunding options in addition to more traditional methods. Further, Podemos uses Reddit to enable their political candidates to debate with citizens.

A MFG's level of public outreach was tabulated utilizing a scale of 0–2 points for each of five categories:

1. info availability (news, manifesto, events)
2. face-to-face efforts (canvassing, leafleting, contacting voters)
3. public events (demonstrations, protests, rallies)
4. encouragement of youth involvement
5. media mentions

Table 7.8 provides the compiled results. Info availability focused on ease of access (via the group's website) to news, manifesto, vision, goals, and events. Face-to-face efforts reflected the extent of personal contact with voters via methods such as canvassing, leafleting, and door-knocking. Results were obtained by searching the group's website and via open-source google searches using the MFG name and the terms (and variations thereof) "canvassing," "leafleting," and "door-knocking." Public events were opportunities for the party to address the public and for the public to gather in support of and to promote the group. These include rallies, demonstrations, and protests. The same method was used as was for face-to-face, utilizing search terms/variations of "demonstrations," "protests," and "rallies." Encouragement of youth involvement reflected whether a group had a youth wing and how interactive, embedded, and involved the MFG was with them. The MFG's website was examined for links to a youth group and google was used to search for

Table 7.8 Scoring for Media Mentions in 2015 (highest percentage if from a year prior to 2015)

MFG	*Percentage*	*Score*
AfD	.01 (.02 in 2016)	1
DF	.01 (.03 in 2016)	1
Finns Party	.0 (.02 in 2016)	1
FPÖ	.0 (.01 in 2000)	0
Front National	.01 (.03 in 2016)	1
PVV	.0	0
Podemos	.14	2
Swedish Democrats	.0	0
SVP	.0 (.01 in 2014)	0
SYRIZA	.32	2
UKIP	.04	1
Vlaams	.0	0

Scores for each MFG were calibrated based on a conversion of the percentage of mentions received (Ramswell 2017).

the MFG and "youth wing." Open-source news reports were searched using google and the same terms to determine any news items involving the group and youth. A "0" will reflect a below average result in that category, "1" will indicate an average result, and a "2" will reflect an above average result.

Media mentions revealed the number of times a group made the news. Media mentions data was compiled utilizing the *New York Times* visualization tool "Chronicle" (Figure 7.4). The Chronicle tool is described as "visualizing language usage in *New York Times* news coverage throughout its history" (NYTlabs 2015). Though the *New York Times* is a US-based newspaper, it amasses and prints news from around the world. The tool is considered a method of visualizing "a historic corpus of news coverage" (NYTlabs

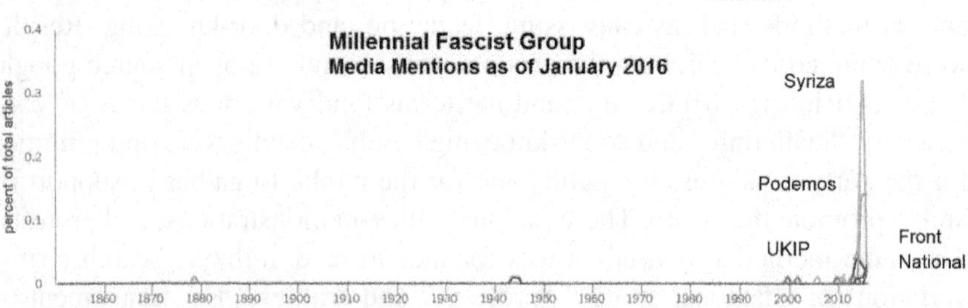

Figure 7.4 Media Mentions. Media mentions of each MFG are indicated by color-coded waves. Data was compiled using the *New York Times* Chronicle Visualization Tool. Created by the author.

2015). Similarly, because none of the MFGs are US based, the groups are equally disparate and any mentions would be equally impartial and based on widespread European media coverage. Note that searches were performed using MFG native language spelling and English language spelling (e.g., Alternative für Deutschland vs Alternative for Germany). In all cases, the native language search returned fewer or no results, most likely because the *New York Times* is US based and, therefore, would present the group's name in English. Table 7.9 provides the calibrated score for each MFG.

Highest percentages were used as media mentions fluctuate with peaks typically occurring during election years (which vary per country). Based on the results using Chronicle, percentages above .10 earned a "2" representing an above average result; percentages of .02-.09 were assigned an average score of "1"; and percentages less than or equal to .01 were assigned a below average score of "0." With five categories and a maximum score of "2" for each, the greatest total score possible was a "10" which corresponded, for fsQCA purposes, to a "1." A total score of "5" equaled a ".5," and so on.

All MFGs had fairly comprehensive websites that included their program/manifesto. Some had extensive news reports and even included news and

Table 7.9 MFG Public Outreach Scores. The 12 MFGs in this study are shown with their respective scores in each of five public outreach categories. (Ramswell 2017)

MFG Public Outreach	*info Availability (News, Manifesto, Events)*	*face-to-face Efforts (Canvassing, Leafleting, Contacting Coters)*	*Public Events (Demonstrations, Protests, Rallies)*	*Promoting Youth Involvement*	*Media Mentions*	*Total*
Alternative für Deutschland (AfD)	1	1*	1	1	1	**5**
Dansk Folkeparti (DF)	1	2	1	2	1	**7**
Finns Party-Perussuomalaiset	2	2	2	2	1	**9**
Freiheitliche Partei Österreich (FPÖ)	1	2	2	2	0	**7**
Front National (FN)	2	2	2	2	1	**9**
Podemos-Spain	1	2	2	2	2	**9**
Partij voor de Vrijheid (PVV)	1	1	1	0	0	**3**
Swiss People's Party (SVP)	2	1	1	2	0	**6**
Swedish Democrats (SD)	1	2	1	0**	0	**4**
SYRIZA-Greece	2	2	2	2	2	**10**
UKIP-England	1	2	2	1	1	**7**
Vlaams Belang-Belgium	2	2	2	2	0	**8**

0=Below Average, 1=Typical, 2=Above Average
*the "door-to-door" campaign is considered an unacceptable invasion of privacy of Germany;
**The Swedish Democrats' engagement with youth league is spotty; ties were severed in 2015.

social media feeds (Front National, SVP). A few were difficult to navigate and/or information was buried/difficult to locate (PVV, FPÖ). In some cases, a party had few events listed on their primary website but a google search led to a local branch of the group which had posted additional events in that location (e.g., AfD vs http://afd-bw.de/termine-veranstaltungen/). Others had extensive schedules listed on their primary site (Finns Party, SVP). Some parties had less events noted, but extensive details such as the food to be served and how to carpool or take the bus to attend (DF). Others had full schedules during the election year but few to none other years (SD). Podemos relied heavily on social media for advertising events. This strategy is excellent for cutting costs and targeting younger, tech-savvy voters but overlooks those accustomed to and expecting traditional notification methods.

As depicted in Figure 7.4, results for media mentions indicated that SYRIZA and Podemos had significantly greater results than any other group. UKIP, Front National, and DF had the next three highest scores, while PVV, Swedish Democrats, and Vlaams Belang had negligible results.

Overall public outreach scores revealed that PVV had the lowest total score for public outreach—ostensibly because as a one-man party Wilders simply cannot do everything a traditional party with members can do. SYRIZA had the highest and only perfect score of 10.

CAUSAL CONDITION ANALYSIS

Utilizing the causal condition data, our next step is a determination of the causal conditions. This analysis will be done utilizing a method known as QCA. QCA is an analytic technique pioneered by Charles Ragin that uses Boolean algebra, crisp/fuzzy sets, and multi-variates to implement principles of comparison. QCA permits a researcher to assess causation that is very complex, involving different combinations of causal conditions capable of generating the same outcome. Ragin (2008) notes that QCA is grounded in the analysis of set relations rather than correlations. Further, because social theory is largely verbal and verbal formulations are largely theoretical in nature, QCA provides a closer link to theory than is possible using conventional quantitative methods. QCA evolved to utilize fuzzy numbers leading to a variation known as Fuzzy Set QCA, or fsQCA. This also led to the use of the term csQCA (Crisp Set QCA) in order to distinguish between methods.

Data is presented in the form of a matrix referred to as a "truth table." QCA then minimizes the data "making multiple comparisons of configurations—through computer algorithms. The goal of the logical minimization is to represent—in a shorthand manner—the information in the truth table regarding the different combinations of conditions that produce a specific outcome" (Rihoux and Ragin 2009).

Fuzzy sets allow cases to have varying degrees of membership via assigned membership scores ranging from 0.0 to 1.0. As an example, a country could potentially have only partial membership in the set of democratic countries depending on the perceived extent of democracy (Ragin 2000). For our purposes, data sets required a determination of degree of membership based on a scale of 0–1: zero ("0") corresponded with .00% and "1" equated with 100% or 10, depending on data format. Each variable's value was considered to be its degree of membership. A "1" indicated "full membership" in the data set and a "0" was indicative of "full non-membership." FsQCA analysis will indicate the strength of the relationship between causal conditions and the outcome, allowing for a determination of the conditions which might be sufficient, necessary, or both.

The MFG data consisted of four variables representing its causal conditions of PP: political opportunity, cognitive liberation (two variables), and indigenous organizational strength. The variables utilized for testing PP were: *Political Opportunity (polopp), Indigenous Organizational Strength (indorgst), Cognitive Liberation-Euroscepticism (coglibeur), and Cognitive Liberation-Nationalism (coglibnat).*

OO model testing also had four variables derived from its causal conditions: consistency (two variables), marketing presence, and public outreach. The variables utilized for testing OO were: *Consistent Leadership (consldr), Consistent Ideology (considea), Marketing Presence (markpres),* and *Public Outreach (pubout).* The outcome was *success* for both models. Figure 7.5 provides the variables by MFG that were entered into fsQCA.

In fsQCA, analysis is based on relationships between and among sets rather than correlations. The truth table is the starting point and is essentially a data spreadsheet that displays the causal conditions (independent variables),

	success	polopp	indorgst	coglibeur	coglibnat	consldr	considea	markpres	pubout
AfD	0.1	0.7	0.1	0.5	0.9	0.9	1.0	0.7	0.5
DF	1.0	0.8	0.8	0.3	0.9	0.9	1.0	0.2	0.7
Finns	0.9	0.7	0.4	0.3	0.9	1.0	1.0	0.6	0.9
FPO	0.9	0.7	0.9	0.6	0.9	0.6	1.0	0.7	0.7
FN	1.0	0.6	0.9	0.5	0.9	0.9	0.9	1.0	0.9
Podemos	0.6	0.7	0.9	0.5	0.8	1.0	1.0	0.9	0.9
PVV	0.9	0.7	0.1	0.4	0.7	1.0	1.0	0.4	0.3
SVP	1.0	0.8	0.9	0.6	0.3	0.6	0.4	0.6	0.6
SD	0.6	0.7	0.6	0.4	0.9	0.6	0.4	0.4	0.4
Syriza	0.9	0.5	0.6	0.7	0.9	0.8	1.0	1.0	1.0
UKIP	1.0	0.8	0.4	0.6	0.8	0.9	1.0	1.0	0.7
VB	0.3	0.7	0.4	0.5	0.8	0.4	1.0	1.0	0.8

Figure 7.5 Variables by MFG. The eight independent variables and the dependent variable are identified by group, calibrated according to fsQCA requirements. Created by the author.

the outcome (dependent variable), and the degree of membership of each. It provides consistency scores based on various relationships and allows for the researcher to input an outcome value based on data and theoretical information.

The researcher then determines a frequency threshold and a consistency threshold in order to establish whether a result is relevant. FsQCA can then analyze causal combinations to determine those which are sufficient and/or necessary for the outcome.

PHASE I: TESTING OF PP MODEL

To determine the degree to which PP explains rise and success, the combination of causal conditions specific to this model were evaluated: *polopp, indorgst, coglbeur*, and *coglibnat*. Analysis began with subset/superset analysis. Testing for Necessary Conditions and Coincidence was also performed. Success was considered to be a group having a member in European Parliament.

Subset and superset analysis offers insight into potential relationships and causal conditions of interest. It examines all variables and provides coverage and consistency scores which are considered parameters of fit. Consistency scores below .75 indicate substantial inconsistency, while scores greater than 90% tend to indicate those variables which are potentially necessary conditions. Subset/superset analysis (Figure 7.6) identified *indorgst* as the causal condition having the highest combined score as well as the highest consistency score of .81.

Truth Table Analysis

In order to interpret the results, it is essential to understand the components used in analysis. Ragin (2008) defined coverage as the measurement of how much of the outcome is explained (or covered) by each solution term and by the solution as a whole. Consistency reflects the degree to which solution terms and the solution as a whole are subsets of the outcome. Another way of explaining consistency is that it determines whether the causal path regularly produces the outcome.

It is important to recognize that fsQCA stresses equifinality—the idea that there is more than one combination of conditions associated with the same outcome. Truth table results report several paths to the outcome. Explained Schneider and Wagemann (2010): "The *empirical* significance of a path, measured by the degree of coverage of the outcome to be explained, is not equivalent to its *theoretical* significance. Some paths with a high coverage can be theoretically uninteresting or even trivial. Likewise, researchers

****
SUBSET/SUPERSET ANALYSIS
****

Outcome: success

	consistency	raw coverage
polopp*indorgst*coglibeur*coglibnat	0.834108	0.509595
indorgst*coglibeur*coglibnat	0.836280	0.517703
polopp*coglibeur*coglibnat	0.782328	0.573108
polopp*indorgst*coglibeur	0.843945	0.548108
polopp*indorgst*coglibnat	0.808370	0.613378
coglibeur*coglibnat	0.766530	0.581216
indorgst*coglibeur	0.845869	0.556216
indorgst*coglibnat	0.804518	0.678514
polopp*coglibeur	0.793200	0.611622
polopp*coglibnat	0.703978	0.758108
polopp*indorgst	0.823866	0.680135
coglibeur	0.777815	0.619730
coglibnat	0.654330	0.850541
indorgst	0.812950	0.763514
polopp	0.717780	0.824865

Figure 7.6 PP Model Subset/Superset Analysis. fsQCA data report showing consistency and coverage scores for the four variables of the PP model. Shaded indicates potential important relationships. Created by the author.

should not focus on any minimum value of consistency and hide those cases that deviate from broad patterns."

Truth Table Results

Truth table analysis (Table 7.10) yielded two configurations (or paths) leading to success in the complex and intermediate solutions: *coglibnat*polopp* and *coglibeur*indorgst*polopp*. There was no parsimonious (most minimized) solution because causal conditions were evaluated based on their presence rather than absence. The complex and intermediate solutions indicate that political opportunity and cognitive liberation-nationalism cover 73% of the instances of success. Twenty-five percent of the instances of success in MFGs are uniquely explained by political opportunity and cognitive liberation-nationalism. The consistency score of .84 indicated that 84% of this configuration is supported by the empirical evidence or, that this causal combination will lead to the outcome in approximately 84% of cases.

The second path in both the complex and intermediate solutions reveals that cognitive liberation-euroscepticism, political opportunity, and indigenous organizational strength cover 51% of the instances of MFG success.

Table 7.10 PP Model Truth Table Analysis

Testing Parameters *Frequency Cutoff: 1.000000* *consistency cutoff: 0.820896*	*Raw Coverage*	*Unique Coverage*	*Consistency*
COMPLEX			
polopp*coglibnat	0.731148	0.253443	0.839503
polopp*indorgst*coglibeur	0.508852	0.031148	0.968789
		solution coverage: 0.762295	
		solution consistency: 0.845045	
INTERMEDIATE			
coglibnat*polopp	0.731148	0.253443	0.839503
coglibeur*indorgst*polopp	0.508852	0.031148	0.968789
		solution coverage: 0.762295	
		solution consistency: 0.845045	

Ramswell (2017).

Three percent of the instances of success in MFGs are uniquely explained by the cognitive liberation-euroscepticism, political opportunity, and indigenous organizational. The consistency score of .97 indicated that 97% of this configuration is supported by the empirical evidence and that this combination will almost always lead to the outcome of *success*.

The overall solution coverage score of 0.76 indicates the proportion of memberships in the outcome *success* that was explained by the complete solution, while the solution consistency score of 0.84 indicates the degree to which membership in the solution (the set of solution terms) was a subset of membership in the outcome.

According to Tomasino (2015), a necessary condition occurs when "the relevant causal condition is present in all instances of an outcome. In contrast, sufficient conditions represent causal complexity because they exist only in combinations with other conditions" (Tomasino 2015). Ragin (2008) asserted that "when utilizing fsQCA, analysis conditions considered potentially sufficient for an outcome typically have consistencies greater than .8" (Tomasino 2015).

This truth table analysis returns the causal condition *polopp* in both paths to the outcome *success*. As such, in this model, *polopp* is considered a necessary condition for a MFG to achieve *success,* though it is not sufficient because it does not produce the outcome on its own. The two paths indicate they are sufficient combinations of conditions.

Analysis of Necessary Conditions

Beginning with the assumption that the union of all causal conditions is a necessary condition, the variables are separated into singles and pairs in an effort to reduce and determine the fewest number of necessary factors. FsQCA returns a consistency and a coverage score for each condition/

condition union tested with the outcome variable. Consistency scores greater than 90% with coverage scores greater than 50% indicate potentially necessary and/or sufficient conditions. In this analysis, no single conditions met the threshold for necessary, although *indorgs*t had the highest coverage score of .94 and *coglibnat* returned the highest consistency score of .86. This was an interesting result since *polopp* was determined to be a necessary condition in truth table analysis. Two of the six pairs, and the entire union of causal conditions, met the threshold. The combined condition of *polopp+coglibnat* and *indorgst+coglibnat* met the threshold, as did the union of all four variables. The union of *polopp* and *coglibnat* was consistent with the truth table findings and indicated it was a potentially necessary combination to achieve *success.*

Coincidence

Set coincidence measured the number of cases found in the intersection of variables. In essence, it measured the degree to which the sets overlapped. Scores should be closer to zero than one, as this provides for greater diversity in explaining the outcome. Scores close to one indicate conditions that could be capturing the same phenomenon. Analysis of the causal conditions for PP indicated the greatest overlap in cases existed between the variables *polopp* and *coglibnat* with a score of .78. The combination with the least overlap was *coglibeur and coglibnat* with .57. The overlap for all four causal conditions was .44. Political opportunity data was derived from freedom of corruption. Cognitive liberation in the form of nationalism derived from national pride scores. An overlap could be suggested, based on pride for one's country stemming from opportunity. This seems to be quite a reach, however, as one does not require opportunity in order feel pride. An alternate analysis provides the observation that nations experiencing greater freedom from corruption would be exhibit more pride in their country, though the opposite could be true as well. Pride could increase as a demonstration of solidarity to spite existing corruption. For greater perspective, consider whether it seems logical that a country with high levels of corruption would also exhibit high levels of pride. The response is most likely a "probably not." As a result, it is prudent to consider that an overlap between *polopp* and *coglibnat* is possible.

Extending the Analysis: Visual Representations

The XY plot provides a visualization of the relationships between variables. Plots returning cases above the diagonal indicated the X-axis variable was a subset of Y, thus supporting the contention that X was sufficient for Y. If cases were on or below the diagonal, a superset was indicated supporting the contention that X was necessary for Y. The fuzzy set XY plot examines bivariate relationships between conditions. Figures 7.7 and 7.8 examined the

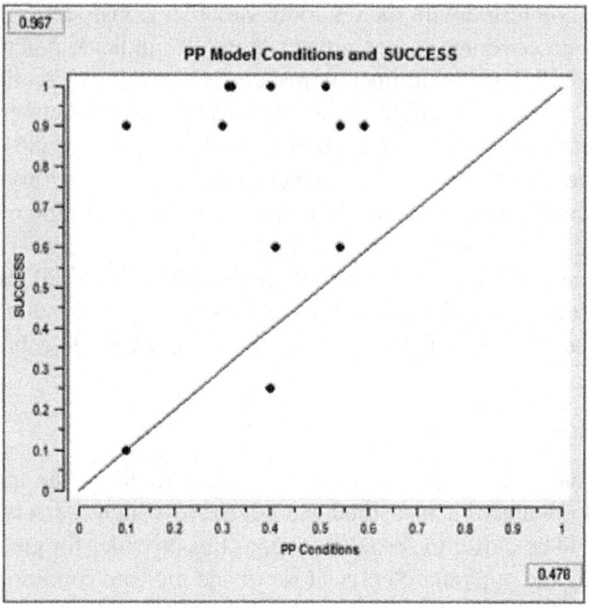

Figure 7.7 PP Model Conditions Leading to Success. The plot indicates that PP model conditions are a potentially sufficient condition for success. Created by the author.

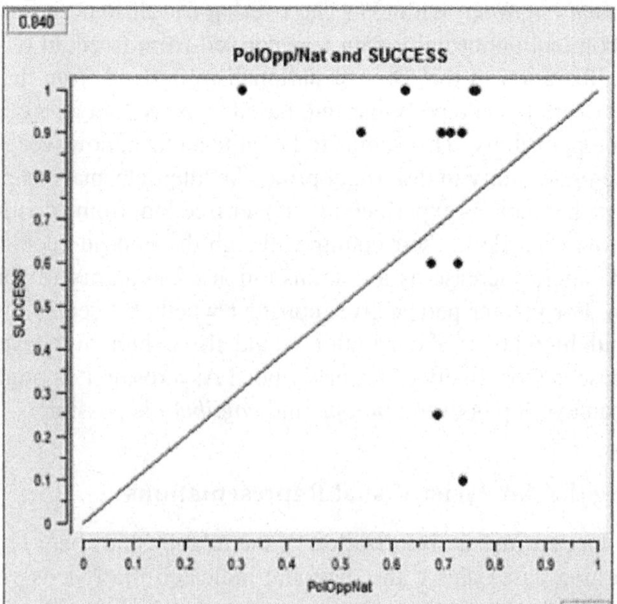

Figure 7.8 PP Model Conditions Leading to Success. The plot indicates lack of necessity and sufficiency in *polopp* and *coglibnat* for success. Created by the author.

union of the four PP model causal conditions against the outcome variable *success*. It indicated all but one case above the diagonal, with Vlaams Belang serving as the outlier. The plot indicates that the combined four causal conditions of the PP model are a potentially sufficient condition for *success* from a complex causality perspective. The union of *polopp,coglibnat* yielded contradictory results. It was expected to reveal necessity or sufficiency but returned neither. Interestingly, *indorgst* showed a strong relationship with only two outliers: VB and Podemos.

PHASE II: TESTING OF OO MODEL

To determine the degree to which OO explains rise and success, the combination of causal conditions specific to this model was evaluated: *consldr, considea, markpres,* and *pubout*. As in Phase I, analysis began with the creation of the truth table, followed by appropriate evaluation and deletion/coding, causal condition selection, and finally, evaluation. Again, as in testing of the PP model, success in this study was considered as a group having a member in the European Parliament.

In this analysis, no OO causal conditions returned scores greater than the threshold of .85. The highest consistency score was found in *consldr*markpres*pubout,* which returned a score of .75.

Truth Table Analysis

In this model, data was run with causal conditions present as well as with causal conditions present or absent. Results (Table 7.11) were more reliable when run with conditions "present or absent." Truth Table analysis indicated four paths in the complex and intermediate solutions leading to success: *~pubout*~markpres*consldr, pubout*markpres*consldr, ~markpres*considea*consldr, and pubout*considea*consldr.* The parsimonious solution indicated that *consldr* alone caused *success*. This finding indicated *consldr* was a sufficient condition to produce the outcome *success*.

The first path *~pubout*~markpres*consldr* indicated that the absence of both public outreach and marketing combined with consistent leadership covered 27% of the instances of success. Two percent of the instances of success in MFGs were uniquely explained by these conditions. The consistency score of .93 indicated that 93% of this configuration was supported by the empirical evidence and that this combination will almost always lead to the outcome of *success*.

The second path *pubout*markpres*consldr* indicated that the presence of public outreach, marketing presence, and consistent leadership covered 66% of the instances of success. Two percent of the instances of success in MFGs were

Table 7.11 OO Model Truth Table Analysis

Testing Parameters *frequency cutoff: 1.000000* *consistency cutoff: 0.873134*	*Raw Coverage*	*Unique Coverage*	*Consistency*
COMPLEX			
consldr*~markpres*~pubout	0.273224	0.021858	0.925926
consldr*markpres*pubout	0.661202	0.021858	0.876812
consldr*considea*~markpres	0.338798	0.010929	0.939394
consldr*considea*pubout	0.726776	0.032787	0.886667
		solution coverage: 0.814208	
		solution consistency: 0.897590	
PARSIMONIOUS			
consldr	0.879781	0.879781	0.838542
		solution coverage: 0.879781	
		solution consistency: 0.838542	
INTERMEDIATE			
pubout*~markpres*consldr	0.273224	0.021858	0.925926
pubout*markpres*consldr	0.661202	0.021858	0.876812
~markpres*considea*consldr	0.338798	0.010929	0.939394
pubout*considea*consldr	0.726776	0.032787	0.886667
		solution coverage: 0.814208	
		solution consistency: 0.897590	
coglibnat*polopp	0.731148	0.253443	0.839503
coglibeur*indorgst*polopp	0.508852	0.031148	0.968789

Ramswell (2017).

uniquely explained by these causal conditions. The consistency score of .88 indicated that 88% of this configuration was supported by the empirical evidence. In other words, this combination will lead to success 88% of the time.

The third path *~markpres*considea*consldr* indicated that the absence of marketing, consistent leadership, and consistent ideology covered 34% of the instances of success. One percent of the instances of success in MFGs were uniquely explained by these conditions. The consistency score of .94 indicated that 94% of this configuration was supported by the empirical evidence and almost always will lead to *success.*

The fourth path *pubout*considea*consldr* indicated that the presence of public outreach, consistent ideology, and consistent leadership covered 73% of the instances of success. Three percent of the instances of success in MFGs were uniquely explained by political opportunity and cognitive liberation-nationalism. The consistency score of .89 indicated that 89% of this configuration was supported by the empirical evidence. This combination provided the strongest path to *success* because it resulted in the highest consistency and highest coverage scores.

The overall solution coverage score of .81 indicated the proportion of memberships in the outcome *success* that was explained by the complete solution, while the solution consistency score of .90 indicated the degree to which membership in the solution was a subset of membership in the outcome. Because *consldr* appeared in all four paths to the solution and as a single condition leading to success, it is considered necessary and sufficient. The four combined causal conditions were sufficient to cause *success*.

Analysis of Necessary Conditions

In an analysis of necessary conditions, consistency scores of .90 and coverage greater than .50 warrant closer scrutiny. One of the four variables (*considea*) and five of the six pair combinations, as well as the combination containing all four causal conditions, returned scores meeting this threshold, indicating potential necessary conditions. It should be noted that some studies include consistency scores of .85 or greater. In this research, using that threshold leads to the inclusion of another singleton, *consldr*. When comparing these results to the truth table analysis, it becomes important to recognize that a high coverage score is most important but that it must also be accompanied by a high consistency score.

Coincidence

The four variables (*consldr, considea, markpres, pubout)* tested in the OO model indicate that the greatest potential for overlap in cases was between *considea* and *consldr* with a score of .83. *Markpres* and *pubout* also had a high probability scoring a .82. The least overlap occurred between *consldr* and *markpres* with a score of .69. The overlap between all four causal conditions was .60. The higher the score, the more potential for overlap. High scores indicate a need for examination so as to ensure they are not capturing the same phenomena.

The two highest combinations for coincidence were *consldr,considea* (.83) and *markpres* and *pubout* (.82). *Considea* measured the vision, mission, and ideology of a group, while *consldr* measured consistency in a group's leadership. *Pubout* measured a group's public contact and interaction, while *markpres* focused on a group's online presence.

On reflection, consistency in ideology and consistency in leadership could certainly capture the same elements. Consider that a leader often remains in power embracing the same ideology for decades. However, other variances are equally true. A leader can change his/her ideology and different leaders can employ the same ideology. Of course, different leaders often bring different ideologies, and the same leader can try different strategies. Ultimately, this combination is one in which analysis of coincidence rightfully indicates a warning to beware of overlap.

The other pair, *markpres* and *pubout,* measured a group's presence online via social media marketing and public outreach, respectively. At first glance, this combination also seemed likely to potentially capture the same phenomenon. In fact, it now becomes obvious that *markpres* could be a subset of *pubout* since social media activity was certainly a component of public outreach. In this case, the primary objective of the variable public outreach was capturing a group's personal contact with voters, the "reach out and touch someone" phenomenon. However, a review of the indicators within the data collection of *pubout* revealed that the categories "info availability" and "media mentions" did not contain the personal contact the variable sought to capture. They were included as ways of reaching and arming the public with information in order to engage and involve them and gauging how well the information was spread to the public.

Removing these two indicators could result in better measurement of public contact/personal interaction. Further, because *markpres* focused on social media activity there is no direct overlap. However, social media in many cases is exclusively and/or primarily used as a means of public outreach. Technology has greatly reduced the amount of face-to-face interaction people have with one another. Though in-person connections remain valuable they are perhaps not as necessary as they were in in years past. Ultimately, though the two variables were designed to capture different phenomena, in the new millennium these phenomena are no longer distinct.

Extending the Analysis: Visual Representations

An XY plot of the OO model's four causal conditions on the x-axis and the outcome *success* on the y-axis indicated all but three cases in the upper triangle leading to a consistency score of (.87) on sufficiency. This indicated OO causal conditions were a potentially sufficient condition for success from a complex causality perspective. AfD returned a score higher in causal condition membership (.5) than the outcome (.1), as did Podemos (.9, .6) and VB (.4, 25). These three cases can be construed as outliers because they undermine the strength of the argument for an explicit relationship between X and Y.

With data compilation and fsQCA analysis complete, a comparison of the results and closer examination into their meaning is necessary. The next chapter will examine the results to determine those causal conditions which were determined to be a factor in the success of MFGs.

NOTE

1. Results from Eurobarometer are obtained in polling "waves." Countries are separated into groups (or "waves") and are surveyed on a rotating basis. The Eurobarometer data used in this study utilized the most recent wave to include that country and specific question examined.

Chapter 8

The Elements Leading to the Rise of MFGs

Analysis and Discussion of Results

Analysis of the causal conditions suspected to lead to the rise and success of MFGs revealed some surprising insight and results. It was anticipated that data would reflect a stronger relationship between the Organizational/ Opportunity model (OO) and successful MFGs rather than the causal conditions associated with McAdam's Political Process model (PP). Results corroborated the assumption that OO causal conditions would show a greater relationship to success (at least in terms of a couple of conditions), but did not necessarily reveal one model as superior to another.

POLITICAL PROCESS (PP) MODEL

Testing of the causal conditions of the PP model revealed that the union of political opportunity and nationalism (*polopp*coglibnat),* and the union of political opportunity, indigenous organizational strength, and euroscepticism (*polopp*indorgst*coglibeur*) resulted in the greatest causality. In fact, these unions proved sufficient in leading to an MFG's success. The latter union accounted for a greater than .5 membership in 11 of the 12 cases (SVP was the exception). Seven cases had membership in this union of >.7. The former combination contained five of the 12 cases and accounted for greater than .5 membership, though all had membership scores around .5. As political opportunity was present in both paths leading to success, it is considered a necessary condition and, therefore, a factor which bears perhaps the greatest need for further examination in the studies of MFGs.

Data was run again using a higher consistency threshold of .966. This threshold embraced the natural gap in the data and yielded results nearly identical to those at the lower threshold. The difference in the results was the disappearance of the combination of political opportunity and nationalism (*polopp*coglibnat)* and the addition of nationalism, indigenous organizational strength, and political opportunity (*coglibnat*indorgst*polopp).* With a coverage of nearly 60% and a consistency of 96%, this combination was stronger than the other triad of political opportunity, indigenous organizational strength, and euroscepticism (*polopp*indorgst*coglibeur).*

coglibnat*indorgst*polopp 0.588962 0.111257 0.959751
coglibeur*indorgst*polopp 0.508852 0.031148 0.968789

These results revealed a potential overlap in political opportunity and nationalism, so the data was run again, this time omitting the causal condition of nationalism (*coglibnat*). These results revealed only one path leading to success: the union of indigenous organizational strength and political opportunity (*indorgst*polopp).* The parsimonious result (the most minimized result) revealed indigenous organizational strength as a necessary condition. When presented in combination with political opportunity, consistency increased. This finding signified that the addition of political opportunity to an existing condition of indigenous organizational strength had the rather substantial effect of increasing the consistency of the solution (Figure 8.1). Put another way, the pair are stronger together and lead to success more frequently than each variable on its own. This corroborates the underlying premise of this study that it is the union of several conditions that leads to the emergence and success of MFGs.

Data was also reevaluated with the omission of the variable political opportunity in order to gauge any changes. These results nearly mirrored those found above in which nationalism was omitted. Two paths to success were indicated, both of which included indigenous organizational strength, rendering it a necessary causal condition.

coglibeur*indorgst 0.515410 0.031148 0.969174
coglibnat*indorgst 0.641639 0.157377 0.940715

The parsimonious result was identical, also revealing indigenous organizational strength as necessary. These results indicate that in the absence of nationalism, indigenous organizational strength becomes stronger. Results also reveal that political opportunity and nationalism are each stronger when both are present, and weaker when one is absent. If these two variables were capturing the same phenomena, one would expect results to show each supplanting the other.

Due to the unanticipated rise of indigenous organizational strength, the original data was run once again, this time utilizing the natural gap in raw

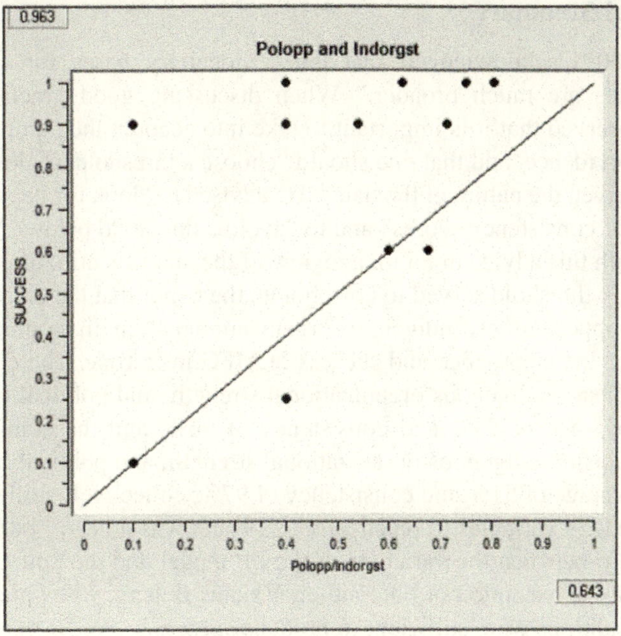

Figure 8.1 This plot revealed that Political Opportunity and Indigenous Organizational Strength were sufficient to produce success. The two outliers were Podemos and VB. Created by the author.

consistency, which occurred between .96 and .84, as a threshold. When compared to the original results, testing revealed indigenous organizational strength emerging as a causal condition in both the intermediate and complex paths, and its appearance as the sole condition in the parsimonious solution.

coglibnat*indorgst*polopp	0.588962	0.111257	0.959751
coglibeur*indorgst*polopp	0.508852	0.031148	0.968789
indorgst	0.710383	0.710383	0.935252

Thus, when consistency was increased, political opportunity became less important and indigenous organizational strength became more important. These findings indicate that, though political opportunity is capable of producing *success* when part of a combination, it does not serve as reliable causal condition on its own. Conversely, indigenous organizational strength proved a reliable charactertistic on its own, as its presence became more important the greater the consistency threshold. These results explain the findings in which the combination of political opportunity and nationalism (*polopp*coglibnat)* failed to show sufficiency, and the somewhat surprising strength of indigenous organizational strength.

PP Model Summary

Ragin (2009) acknowledged that the "evidentiary bases for consistency assessments are much broader." When discussing good practices, Ragin (2009) observed that it is important to take into account the nature and quality of the evidence, and that one should "choose a threshold as close to 1.0 as feasible, given the nature of the data." He advised to "look for gaps in the distribution of consistency scores" and to "avoid a threshold below .75" (Ragin, 2009). With this advice in mind, a review of the analysis utilizing the highest consistency threshold served to corroborate the belief that the elements of PP (political opportunities, indigenous organizational strength, cognitive liberation) led to the emergence and success of MFG in Europe. The combination of nationalism, indigenous organizational strength, and political opportunity with a coverage of 59% and consistency of 96%, and the combination of euroscepticism, indigenous organizational strength, and political opportunity with a coverage of 51% and consistency of 97%, collectively utilized all four of the model's variables to reach *success*. There was a nearly perfect subset relationship between the variables of the PP model and the outcome of *success*. With the exception of one outlier, Vlaams Belang, when present, these causal conditions were sufficient to produce *success*.

ORGANIZATIONAL/OPPORTUNITY (OO) MODEL

As noted above, the underlying premise of this study was the idea that no single condition would produce MFG success, rather it was a combination of causal conditions. Testing of the OO model yielded corroborating results.

Testing of the causal conditions associated with OO revealed that it was indeed the interplay among variables that led to success. The combination of consistent leadership, marketing presence, and public outreach *(consldr*markpres*pubout)*, and the combination of consistent leadership, consistent ideology, and public outreach *(consldr*considea*pubout)*, were most significant, revealing high degrees of both coverage and consistency. Consistent leadership was determined to be a necessary and sufficient condition, returning scores of 0.879781, 0.879781, 0.838542. However, in both combinations to the solution, consistency increased four and 5% when other conditions joined with consistent leadership. This substantiated the argument that it was the combination of causal conditions that provided the strongest path(s) to the solution.

Running the data again and excluding the variable of consistent leadership led to exceptionally low coverage scores of .39 and less, underscoring the necessity of this condition. The removal of consistent ideology led to the rise of consistent leadership as a single causal condition for success in the parsimonious and intermediate analyses, and in two combinations.

consldr*~markpres 0.360656 0.065574 0.942857
consldr*pubout 0.748634 0.453552 0.889610
consldr 0.879781 0.879781 0.838542

The addition of the variable of public outreach resulted in consistency increasing 5%. Interestingly, the absence of marketing presence with the presence of consistent leadership, caused consistency to rise to 94%, although it also reduced coverage to 36%. The low coverage was sufficient cause to rule out this combination.

Exclusion of public outreach also yielded detrimental results as all coverage scores dropped below 36%. Removal of marketing presence as a causal condition resulted in only one path to success in all three analyses: consistent leadership. This finding reinforced the strength of consistent leadership and a determination of it as both a necessary and sufficient characteristic to cause *success*. It is important to recognize that the presence of other conditions only increases its explanatory power.

Changing consistency thresholds for truth table analysis did not substantially alter the results in this model, nor did altering the conditions "Present or Absent." Consistent leadership remained a necessary causal condition because it remained a part of all paths to the solution. What proved interesting was the impact of the absence of two variables when the consistency threshold was increased to .92:

~markpres 0.360656 0.251366 0.942857
~considea 0.142077 0.032787 1.000000

These results indicated that the absence of marketing presence led to success 94% of the time. This seemed counterintuitive, but when viewed in conjunction with the coincidence analysis it was more plausible. The absence of marketing presence would not be impactful in the presence of public outreach if both conditions captured the same phenomena.

OO Model Summary

Results of OO testing were surprising in that there were a number of causal combinations containing the absence, rather than the presence, of specific variables. Adjusting the consistency threshold accomplished little more than adding more combinations containing the "absence of" particular variables. Ultimately, the most reliable threshold was .87.

The strongest combination to the solution was consistent leadership, consistent ideology, and public outreach *(consldr*considea*pubout)* which provided for 73% coverage and 89% consistency. The other strong combination was consistent leadership, marketing presence, and public outreach *(consldr*markpres*pubout),* which had a coverage of 66% and consistency of 88%. With the exception of three outliers, Vlaams Belang (also an outlier in the PP model), AfD and Podemos, when present, these causal conditions were sufficient to produce *success*.

Combinations ultimately provided the strongest paths to success, which supported the idea that MFG success was a result of internal organizational efficacy and capacity (consistent leadership and ideology, public outreach, and marketing presence). In other words, it is the interplay among the four variables that leads to *success.*

PP AND OO MODELS TESTED JOINTLY

Data was analyzed one final time to include all causal condition from both models. Results were somewhat surprising (Table 8.1). Consistent leadership was no longer the standout condition. Rather, indigenous organizational strength proved to be the one causal condition, in the presence of all others, strong enough to cause success on its own. Its coverage of 71% and consistency of 94% *considerably surpassed* any other condition or combination. The next strongest combination was consistent leadership, nationalism, indigenous organizational strength, and political opportunity *(consldr*coglibnat*indorgst*polopp),* with a coverage of 58% and consistency of 96%.

There were several options when running the data with all eight variables. The consistency level could occur at first gap (<.965), second gap (<.896), third gap (<.843), or less than .828, the last of which would code all cases as a "1." The option for coding all cases "1" was dismissed, as even though this met recommended consistency levels of 80%, the results were very complex and contained multiple combinations of seven and eight variables which were not compelling.

Running the data with various consistency thresholds resulted in several observations. Indigenous organizational strength emerged during the highest consistency threshold (first gap) of .96. It was the only causal condition leading to *success* in the parsimonious solution.

At this high level of consistency, the intermediate solution returned the highest scores for the combination containing all eight variables. It scored .46 for coverage and .97 for consistency.

Utilization of the second gap with a consistency threshold of .896, also resulted in the emergence of indigenous organizational strength as a minimum formula of the parsimonious solution. When utilizing the consistency

Table 8.1 OO Model Truth Table Analysis

Testing Parameters *Frequency cutoff: 1.000000* *Consistency cutoff: 0.896373*	*Raw Coverage*	*Unique Coverage*	*Consistency*
COMPLEX			
polopp*indorgst*~coglibeur*coglibnat*consldr*~considea*~markpres*~pubout	0.098470	0.020765	1.000000
polopp*~indorgst*~coglibeur*coglibnat*consldr*considea*~markpres*~pubout	0.189071	0.052459	0.896373
polopp*indorgst*~coglibeur*coglibnat*consldr*considea*~markpres*pubout	0.261312	0.057924	1.000000
polopp*indorgst*coglibeur*~coglibnat*consldr*~considea*markpres*pubout	0.091366	0.031148	1.000000
polopp*indorgst*coglibeur*coglibnat*consldr*considea*markpres*pubout	0.463497	0.255738	0.965839
		solution coverage:	0.631257
		solution consistency:	0.942866
PARSIMONIOUS			
indorgst	0.710383	0.344262	0.935252
~pubout	0.349727	0.010929	0.888889
~markpres	0.360656	0.005464	0.942857
		solution coverage:	0.781421
		solution consistency:	0.893750
INTERMEDIATE			
consldr*coglibnat*indorgst*polopp	0.576721	0.042186	0.958932
~markpres*considea*consldr*coglibnat*polopp	0.325027	0.001421	0.936988
~pubout*considea*consldr*coglibnat*polopp	0.317705	0.010492	0.879044
pubout*markpres*consldr*coglibeur*indorgst*polopp	0.494645	0.031148	0.967921
		solution coverage:	0.674426
		solution consistency:	0.907901

Ramswell 2017.

threshold of the third gap (.843), indigenous organizational strength was replaced by consistent leadership as the single causal condition of the minimum formula. As in the other consistency thresholds including all cases, the combinations leading to *success* were expansive and included no less than seven variables. Overall, there were no combinations of 2–3 variables which would have indicated an opportunity to combine variables from each model to achieve *success*.

PP and OO Models Summary

During the PP model retest, indigenous organizational strength returned scores of 71% coverage and 94% consistency. The two strongest combinations nationalism, indigenous organizational strength, and political opportunity; and euroscepticism, indigenous organizational strength, and political opportunity had coverages and consistencies of 59% and 96%, and 51% and 97%, respectively.

The OO model parsimonious result yielded the causal condition of consistent leadership with scores of 88% coverage and 84% consistency. Its two strongest combinations—consistent leadership, marketing presence, and public outreach; and consistent leadership, consistent ideology, and public outreach—indicated scores of 66% and 88%, and 73% and 89% respectively.

Though the consistency scores in the OO model were not as high as those in the PP model, its coverages were higher. In the second OO model combination (consistent leadership, marketing presence, and public outreach; and consistent leadership, consistent ideology, and public outreach), the difference in coverage was 13% when compared to the PP model's combination with the highest coverage score (nationalism, indigenous organizational strength, and political opportunity). Similarly, a comparison of the consistencies of each model revealed that the PP model had scores seven to 8% greater than the OO model configurations.

CONCLUSION

To summarize (Table 8.2), when consistency was set to greater than or equal to .896, indigenous organizational strength emerged as a necessary condition. For consistency thresholds less than .896, consistent leadership emerged as the necessary condition. With the consistency threshold set at .92, consistent leadership only appeared in combinations (with additional variables serving to increase its consistency), and indigenous organizational strength remained absent because of the presence of other contributing variables.

Setting consistency too high can compromise coverage and lead to the exclusion of important causal conditions. As acknowledged by Ragin (2009) and others, determining that fine line can be tricky. In following the guidance from Ragin (who was consulted via email for this study), the results from the highest thresholds should serve as the ultimate guide in determining the efficacy of the two models. Because sufficiency in fsQCA focuses on the degree of membership rather than a full-in or full-out (as in csQCA), "assessment of each combination of conditions is ultimately based on the 'pattern observed across all cases'" (Ragin, 2009). This was the reason why various consistency thresholds were tested. As discussed, these additional analyses served to eliminate possibilities and obtain a better understanding of the interplay among the causal conditions and the significance of consistency.

Table 8.2 Comparison of PP and OO Model Causal Paths

Causal Path	*Coverage*	*Consistency*
OO Model Combination 1	**66**	**88**
consistent leadership, marketing presence, public outreach		
OO Model Combination 2	**73**	**89**
consistent leadership, consistent ideology, public outreach		
PP Model Combination 1	**59**	**96**
nationalism, indigenous organizational strength, political opportunity		
PP Model Combination 2	**51**	**97**
euroscepticism,indigenous organizational strength, political opportunity		

Ramswell 2017.

Although the results of both models ultimately corroborated expected results, the OO model combinations were determined to be the stronger paths to *success*, if only slightly. This determination was based on the much higher coverage scores in both of its strongest configurations, and consistency scores which were only 7 to 8% lower than those of the PP model. Though lower than the PP model scores, these consistency scores were far above 75%, which is considered inconsistent. At the risk of repetition, it should again be noted that researchers must strike a balance in determining the most effective levels of coverage and consistency, armed with the awareness that as consistency increases, coverage decreases.

Chapter 9

The Rising Threat of Millennial Fascism and the Ensuing Implications

In 2014, Gifford observed that "the mobilization of a hard right wing Euroscepticism between 2010–13 represents one of the most profound challenges to a government's European policy that has been witnessed in the UK" (Gifford 2014). Indeed, the emergence and success of MFGs is impossible to ignore. "Far-right movements and groups are becoming more diverse, flexible, and are increasingly working beyond country borders to achieve their goals" (Ramalingam 2012). Such international alliances and working relationships are evidenced across Europe in multiple forms. The achievements of these non-traditional, often far from center, and sometimes extremist groups, denote the rise of a new form of fascism, a more palatable form of fascism far removed from Stalin or Hitler. The extreme nature of fascism in its purest most primal form belongs to another era, another generation; MF is at once distinctive and reborn from strains of traditional fascism, a unique manifestation reflecting the issues of the twenty-first century. Its unprecedented rise necessitates deeper study into and understanding of how and why. The impact of MF has unarguably led to a dramatically altered political landscape, an altered socio-cultural perspective and norm, destabilization of EU governments, and national, regional, and international political uncertainty.

The rise, threat, and impact of MF was evidenced in spectacular form with "Brexit" in June 2016. *Britain's exit (Brexit)* from the EU led to Prime Minister David Cameron's resignation the day following the historic referendum, and a worldwide audience anxious to determine the economic and political effects. UKIP, an MFG, has led the charge to leave the EU for years. Among the arguments made by the "Vote Leave" campaign was the belief that "Britain was being held back by the EU, which they said imposed too many rules" and the desire for "Britain to take back full control of its borders and reduce the number of people coming here to live and/or work. … The Leave campaign also objected to the idea of 'ever closer union' between EU member states and what they see as moves towards the creation of a 'United States of Europe'" (Wheeler and Hunt 2016). Nigel Farage, a founding member of UKIP and widely considered racist and xenophobic, served as the party's leader until July 2016—long enough to see his vision of a sovereign Britain become a reality. CNN's Bianca Britton (7/4/2016) recalled Farage had "long campaigned against Britain's open immigration policy with the EU, saying it has led to an influx of people who have damaged cohesion and created divisions within society." Britton noted that "Farage caused a stir when his party unveiled a poster before the referendum with the words 'Breaking Point. The EU has failed us all,' showing an image of migrants entering Europe" (Britton 2016).

Though the long-term effects are still unknown, the economy has proven more resilient than some believed. Though the pound remained at a 30-year low in August 2016, "share prices have recovered from a dramatic slump in value, with both the FTSE 100 and the broader FTSE 250 index, which includes more British-based businesses, trading higher than before the referendum" (Wheeler and Hunt, 2016). The social and political effects of Brexit remain largely unknown. What is abundantly clear is that Great Britain is entering unchartered territory with their historic move and setting the stage for a widespread political, social, and economic transformation. Indeed, according to the Pew Research Center (Stokes 2016), "EU favorability is down in five of the six nations surveyed in both 2015 and 2016. There has been a double-digit drop in France (down 17 percentage points) and Spain (16 points), and single-digit declines in Germany (8 points), the United Kingdom (7 points) and Italy (6 points)." In fact, the decline in support for the EU has increased most in older individuals:

> The drop-off in overall EU support in key countries in the past year has been driven by a fall in favorability among older people in particular. In France, EU backing among those ages 50 and older fell 19 points. In Spain it declined 16 points and in Germany 11 points. In each case this was larger than the decline in support among those ages 18 to 34. (Stokes 2016)

Brexit most certainly served as a rude awakening, but perhaps even more concerning is the influence and enmeshment of Russia, particularly in light of the growing possibility of an EU-Russia partnership. In 2016, Yakovenko commented on the significant advantages of an EU-Russia collaboration: "Europe's geographical closeness to Russia offers huge economic benefits, thus more cooperation with Russia would be a natural choice." He noted the potential impact of a Eurasian alliance and the benefits that could be reaped by an EU closer to Russia, Central Asia, and China economically. Further, such an alliance "would also lead to a greater security for Europe and might become an important contribution to a peace in 21st century" (Yakovenko 2016).

There is already support for Russia in European Parliament. Kreko et al. (2015) reported that "up to 20 percent of all MEPs currently vote at times in the interests of Putin's Russia." A 2015 study of far-right MEPs who now comprise part of the ENF in European Parliament (EP), found evidence of support for Putin's Russia before the new caucus had formed (Kreko, et al. 2015). Kreko, et al. (2015) also found that "in 93 percent of cases the pre-ENF members voted 'no' in Russia-related decisions, which essentially suited Russian interests."

In 2014, Front National's Marine Le Pen acknowledged: "I have a certain admiration for Vladimir Putin because he doesn't allow decisions to be forced upon him by other countries. I think he focuses first and foremost on what is good for Russia and the Russians" (Spiegel 2014). In fact, Kreko (2014) reported that "through what Putin calls the 'active means' of his 'Eurasian Doctrine,' Russia provides political and organizational support to 'friendly' organizations." Indeed, Le Pen has confirmed that, in November 2014, a Kremlin-linked bank lent her party €9M to help her finance Front National's campaign for the 2014 EP (Kreko, et al. 2015). Lichfield (2015) added that the loan "is expected to be the first tranche of a series of Russian payments which will fund the cash-strapped far right party up to the French presidential election in 2017."

As Lichfield (2014) observed, "this is part of a growing pattern of connections between Vladimir Putin's Russia and far-right and Europhobic parties in the European Union." Here are only a few examples of eyebrow-raising associations:

- A new policy, supported by the Finns Party, is being tested in municipalities close to the Russian border, where instead of mandatory Swedish, Finnish pupils will have mandatory lessons in Russian instead (Sundberg 2015);
- Fifteen out of 25 major European far-right parties are vocal and open supporters of Russia and Russian interests (Kreko 2014);
- In its 2014 Defense Policies, the British National Party lists as an objective: "Engage constructively with Russia as a natural ally and trading partner" (BNP 2014);
- In 2014, several European far-right groups were invited to attend the Russian National Forum (hosted by the Intelligent Design Bureau) with an objective of developing a new national doctrine for Russia and Europe with the far-right parties. Among those invited: Jobbik, Austrian Freedom Party, Swiss People's Party, Golden Dawn, National Front (Laruelle 2015);

- The crisis in Ukraine has revealed the close bonding of European far-right parties with Russia. Far-right parties sent "independent observers" to the Crimean referendum and their representatives in the EP have joined forces with far-left parties to reject a resolution condemning the Crimean annexation and the "destabilization of eastern Ukraine" (Kreko 2014);
- Jobbik's MP, Márton Gyöngyösi, has stated that "Hungary should welcome Russia gaining ground against the West, as a new balance of power will probably be advantageous for Hungarian national interests" (Klapsis 2015); and
- Vlaams Belang leadership has stated for the record "I think we can be a good partner for Russia in the European Parliament. And Russia sees us as a potential partner" (Kreko 2014).

Though perhaps not surprising, collectively these items are certainly alarming, particularly in terms of international relations and political affairs. The landscape has changed, and continues to change, throughout Europe with effects felt worldwide. An article in the May 31, 2014 *Economist* echoes this concern:

> The global repercussions may be more worrying. The new European Parliament will probably be more sceptical of free markets and less favourable to free trade, particularly the ambitious Transatlantic Trade and Investment Partnership with America. One of Ms Le Pen's demands is the immediate suspension of these negotiations. Moreover, anti-EU parties are often markedly pro-Russian. Internationally, the loser of these elections could be America—and the winner, Russia.

In a 2015 story on the increasing ties between European parties and Russia, CNBC reported that Russia appeared to be capitalizing on widespread disenchantment: "As for Russia's motivation, destabilizing the European Union at one of the most vulnerable points—and when east-west relationships have soured—is key." Neil Barnett, the founder of risk consultancy and CEE specialist Istok Associates, told CNBC: "This is part of a broad spread of measures designed to confuse and demoralize the opposition. This part is opportunistic, taking advantage of disillusionment with the existing political order in Europe" (CNBC 2015).

Adding to the level of concern is recognition that many countries and parties believe they need Russia to succeed. Hungarian prime minister Viktor Orban commented that "without co-operation with the Russians we cannot achieve our goals" (CNBC 2015). In fact, CNBC (2015) noted no less than 11 established and highly concerning party connections with Russia.

An area of growing concern is the United States. The 2016 US presidential election seemed almost a B-movie remake of Brexit, with surprisingly similar themes of immigration, rights, employment, and benefits serving as a common denominator. Once again, a nation was divided. An atmosphere of hostility and contention coupled with renewed nationalism and populism served to provide a nearly identical backdrop on both sides of the Atlantic. Vicious and divisive campaigns unfolded—not only between the parties themselves, but among the citizens fervently supporting them. President-elect Donald Trump, in fact, openly supported Brexit and called himself "Mr Brexit." Above all, the presidential campaign precipitated a rebirth of nationalism. It reinvigorated the entire country, engaging, inciting, and charming even the casual observer into political action and discourse. The increased public involvement sparked hope of greater engagement and interest from broader and long-silent segments of society.

Yet the unity each campaign sought would ironically morph into an "Us vs. Them" mentality, creating divisions that would extend far beyond the focus of the campaign. The open hostility toward people whose only crime was a vote different from their own is deeply troubling, not only because of its intensity and often baseless origin but because of the belief that such attacks are acceptable, warranted, and justified. Europe, the United States, and a host of nations around the world, have found themselves in a space and time when the citizenry is questioning its government, its leaders, its goals. In this age of instant access to information, civil rights, accountability, and an increased sense of entitlement, the public is demonstrating with increased frequency and ferocity their sense of empowerment and newly found voice to criticize and question authority and process.

The year 2017 revealed not only a changed political landscape but an eerie sense of foreboding. The foundational cracks in the political system have created an atmosphere that has not only served to empower and motivate those who before stood silent, it has provided the rationale for those seeking to justify their actions.

The common threads between fascism and euroscepticism can no longer be ignored: nations in social and political turmoil, a rebirth of nationalism, group formation and rise, and a new generation in a state of revolt. MF is the manifestation of groups borne from the unique synthesis of traditional traits and end-of-the-twentieth-century social and political change. As Klapsis (2015) keenly observed: "Russia is not a threat but rather an asset to peace and stability in Europe. For the Kremlin, the growing success of far-right parties (with the backing of Russia, where necessary) is clearly an advantage since it is thought that this will destabilise EU governments and the EU itself." Indeed, though countries see Russia as their aide in the struggle, the opposite is also true: by offering support to other countries (often strategically located) Russia gains influence and the potential for regional hegemony.

The relationships Russia has cultivated with successful and ascending Eurosceptic groups offer indisputable, viable, and alarming evidence of an underlying master plan in which foes become allies, acquaintances are dissociated, and compatriots serve both wittingly and unwittingly as strategic pawns. A deeper understanding of the causal conditions that have allowed MFGs to emerge and rise could allow for preemptive networking and building of relationships. Engaging in dialogue to gain a mutual understanding of needs and motivations can have far-reaching benefit. As the saying goes, it is far better to build bridges than tear them down.

In 2011, Langenbacher observed that "the important thing is to understand how the radical right arose as a phenomenon, and particularly the current success of right-wing populist parties in Europe in terms of its social origins, before we can develop meaningful counter-strategies" (Langenbacher 2011).

The threat from the left and right throughout Europe which I call Millennial Fascism, is indicative of a new reality and new political landscape and must be viewed with a sense of urgency. Examining the groups that have emerged will provide insight into the elements which can serve as agents of change as well as methods to counter their rise.

Statistics clearly indicate an increase in the number MFGs corresponding with the FOTW. The resultant cultural shift provided an environment hospitable to their development. But not every group that formed after the FOTW was successful. This study offered insight into potential causal conditions and was able to pinpoint variables that lead to an MFG's success.

A goal of the OO model was to pinpoint specific variables rather than provide an open-ended framework. This goal was accomplished. The variables of consistent leadership, consistent ideology, public outreach, and marketing presence were found to lead MFGs to success in two separate combinations. Likewise, nationalism, euroscepticism, number of members, and freedom from corruption also lead to success in various combinations, though to a lesser degree. This look into MFGs demonstrated that it is the power of several variables in the presence of each other that leads to success.

One of the main goals of this research was a desire to identify specific variables that led to a MFG's success in order to better isolate and understand causal conditions. The identification of opportunity created externally by a trigger event and the subsequent culture shift, and internal organizational capacity resulting from consistency in leadership and ideology, marketing efforts, and public involvement, provides researchers with the ability to examine one dynamic that has allowed for MFGs to achieve success.

The use of the phrase "one dynamic" was intentional. This study is not contending that the variables identified here as causal conditions leading to MFG success are the only such conditions than can result in that outcome. There may be others. However, this research does claim that the variables identified in this study as causal conditions that do lead to success, bear a need for deeper study and analysis. It is believed that the components of these causal conditions can be narrowed down even further to identify variables with the strongest relationship to success. Such minimization will lead to stronger, clearer paths to success.

A goal of social science study is identifying the predictors that lead to a certain outcome. Understanding the trajectory of MFGs is of critical importance, particularly in light of the implications noted above. The ability to identify groups that possess the identified elements leading to success provides political bodies, intelligence agencies, and scholars the opportunity to be a step ahead and proactively strategize methods and means for interception, cooperation, or any level in between. This research offers political scientists, analysts, and sociologists enhanced insight into the tools that can be used to analyze, predict, and perhaps even preempt, potential sources of development, strife, or concern.

The insight it provides offers the potential for a better understanding of the underlying dynamics within changing cultures, as well as improvement in international, interregional, and interlocal relationships. The implications and benefits of this additional insight are many, but perhaps most importantly seek to contribute to the fortitude of the "3Ds" of US national security: diplomacy, development, and defense.

Maurice Bardéche wrote that "fascism is, by its essence, nationalist, and while it originates as the reaction to a crisis, all fascist reaction is resurrection" (Griffin 1991). His comments, though made in 1961, remain relevant nearly a half century later in the new millennium. Not only is this statement prescient, it underscores three main points of this dissertation: the emergence and success of the non-traditional parties christened MFGs was a reaction to a trigger event; nationalism is a fundamental element of MFGs; and, that the emergence and ascension of MFGs has served as a rebirth of traditional values. In a realm of could be, maybe, and possibly, one thing is certain: MFGs have been able to achieve levels of success never before imagined and have forever changed the face of politics in Europe.

Bibliography

Al Jazeera. Far-right parties sweep EU polls; May 26, 2014. Accessed March 28, 2015. http://www.aljazeera.com/news/europe/2014/05/far-right-parties-sweep-eu-polls-20145261436233584.html

Albert, Michel. *Capitalisme contre Capitalisme*; Paris: Seuil; 1992.

All About Turkey. Political parties in Turkey; All About Turkey.com; 2015. http://www.allaboutturkey.com/parti.htm#chp

Allievi, Stefano. Conflicts, Cultures and Religions: Islam in Europe as a Sign and Symbol of Change in European Societies; *Yearbook on Sociology of Islam*, pp.18–27; 2005.

Almeida, Dimitri. Towards a Post-radical Front National? Patterns of Ideological Change and dédiabolisation on the French Radical Right, *Nottingham French Studies*; 52(2): 167–176; 2013.

Almeida, Paul. Cycles of Protest; Oxford Bibliographies; 2014. Accessed June 21, 2014. http://www.oxfordbibliographies.com/view/document/obo-9780199756223/obo-9780199756223–0086.xml#

Amenta, E., Carruthers B. G. and Zylan Y. A Hero for the Aged: The Townsend Movement, the Political Mediation Model, and United-States Old-age Policy, 1934–1950, *American Journal of Sociology*; 98(2): 308–339; 1992.

Anderson, C. Economics, Politics and Foreigners: Populist Party Support in Denmark and Norway, *Electoral Studies*; 15: 497–511; 1996.

Anthias, F. and Yuval-Davis, N. The Concept of 'Race' and the Racialization of Social Divisions. In *Racialized Boundaries*, 1–20, London: Routledge; 1992.

Anti-Defamation League; Joerg Haider: The Rise of an Austrian Extreme Rightist; March 9, 2004. Accessed June 16, 2015. http://archive.adl.org/backgrounders/joerg_haider.html#.VfjCZJeqm_k

Appelrouth, Scott and Edles, Laura Desfor. *Sociological Theory in the Contemporary Era: Text and Readings*; Thousand Oaks, CA: Pine Forge Press; November 29, 2010.

Arendt, Hannah. *Origins of Totalitarianism*; revised edition. New York: Harcourt, Brace and World; 1966.

Arslan, Deniz. AK Party's anti-Semitic, anti-Western rhetoric a dangerous trend; *Today's Zaman*; March 16, 2014. http://www.todayszaman.com/diplomacy_ak-partys-anti-semitic-anti-western-rhetoric-a-dangerous-trend_342054.html

Arzheimer, Kai. Contextual Factors and the Extreme Right Vote in Western Europe, *American Journal of Political Science*; 53(2): 259–275; 2009.

Ayres, Jeffrey M. Political Process and Popular Protest: The Mobilization against Free Trade in Canada, *American Journal of Economics and Sociology*; 55(4): 473–488; October 1996.

BBC. Greek elections: Main parties from SYRIZA to Golden Dawn explained; *BBC News*; January 26, 2015. http://www.bbc.com/news/world-europe-30913028

BBC. Netherlands Islam Freedom: Profile of Geert Wilders; Interview excerpts from October 2009; 2009. http://www.bbc.com/news/world-europe-11443211

BBC. 'New UKIP' will take votes from Labour, says Nigel Farage; March 16, 2014. http://www.bbc.com/news/uk-politics-26602101

BBC. Profile: Far-right Sweden Democrats; September 15, 2014. http://www.bbc.com/news/world-europe-29202793

BBC. Profile: Ukraine's ultra-nationalist Right Sector; April 28, 2014; http://www.bbc.com/news/world-europe-27173857

BBC. Ukraine's revolution and the far right; *BBC News*; March 7, 2014. http://www.bbc.com/news/world-europe-26468720

BBC. UKIP: The story of the UK Independence Party's rise; By Alex Hunt Politics; November 21, 2014. http://www.bbc.com/news/uk-politics-21614073

BBC. What is a fascist? BBC Magazine; October 20, 2009. http://news.bbc.co.uk/2/hi/uk_news/magazine/8316271.stm

BBC News. Fifty sentenced for Birmingham EDL protest violence; BBC; January 9, 2015. http://www.bbc.com/news/uk-england-birmingham-30751692

BBC News. Profile: Greece's far-right Golden Dawn party; October 1, 2013. http://www.bbc.com/news/world-europe-24346993

BBC News. World News. July 21, 2015. http://www.bbc.com/news/world-europe-33593500

Bahceli, Yoruk. Wilders tells Dutch parliament refugee crisis is "Islamic invasion;" *Reuters*; September 10, 2015.

Baker, David. The Political Economy of Fascism: Myth or Reality, or Myth and Reality? *New Political Economy*; 11(2): 227–50; June 2006.

Bartlett, Jamie, Littler, Mark, McDonnell, Duncan, Froio, Caterina. New political actors in Europe: Beppe Grillo and the M5S; *DEMOS*; 2013.

Bell, Bethany. Austria's Freedom Party sees vote rise. *BBC News*; May 26, 2014. http://www.bbc.com/news/blogs-eu-27572494

Benford, Robert D. and Snow, David A. Framing Processes and Social Movements: An Overview and Assessment, *Annual Review of Sociology*; 26: 611–39; 2000.

Bengtsson, Mattias. The Sweden Democrats: A not so Swedish party; *Al Jazeera*; Dec 17, 2014. http://www.aljazeera.com/indepth/opinion/2014/12/sweden-democrats-not-so-swedis-20141217735195335 78.html

Berg-Schlosser, Dirk and Quenter, Sven. Macro-Quantitative vs. Macro-Qualitative Methods in Political Science – Advantages and Disadvantages of Comparative

Procedures using the Welfare-State Theory as an Example. *Historical Social Research*; 21: 3–25; 1996.

Bernburg, Jon Gunnar. Anomie, Social Change and Crime, *British Journal of Criminology*; 42(4): 729–742; 2002.

Berntson, Marit A. *Fascism*; Oxford Bibliographies; Oxford University Press; 2013. http://www.oxfordbibliographies.com/view/document/obo-9780199756384/obo-9780199756384–0082.xml

Bertoncini, Yves and Koenig, Nicole. Euroscepticism or Europhobia: Voice vs. Exit? Notre Europe Jacques Delors Institute, Policy Paper 121; November 27, 2014.

Black, Tim. Labour's loss has been UKIP's gain; *Spiked*; Last Modified May 11, 2015. http://www.spiked-online.com/newsite/article/labours-loss-has-been-ukips-gain/16962#.VVSwtJO5LVI

Bollier, Sam. A guide to Greece's political parties: As many as ten parties look set to win seats in the Hellenic Parliament in elections this Sunday; *Al Jazeera*, May 1, 2012. Accessed January 8, 2016. http://www.aljazeera.com/indepth/features/2012/05/20125120322955327.html

Bomsdorf, Clemens. Danish Right-Wing Party Wins Largest Share of Votes in EU Election. *Wall Street Journal*; May 25, 2014.

Borrud, Gabriel. Talk of banning far-right party heats up in Germany, after Tröglitz refugee home attack; *Deutsche Welle*; June 4, 2015. http://www.dw.com/en/talk-of-banning-far-right-party-heats-up-in-germany-after-tr%C3%B6glitz-refugee-home-attack/a-18363656

Brack, Nathalie and Startin, Nicolas. Introduction: Euroscepticism, from the Margins to the Mainstream, *International Political Science Review*; 36(3): 239–249; 2015.

Brambilla, Michelle. Italy's Northern League: Eurosceptics with their own pan-European project; *The Guardian*; January 26, 2012. http://www.theguardian.com/world/2012/jan/26/italy-northern-league-european-project

Brand, K. W. Historical antecedents of new social movements; Prepared for Joint Seminar on New Social Movements, Florida State University, Tallahassee; 1987.

Briggs, Billy. The Schweiger File: Nazi hunter criticises Austrian government; The Ferret; August 17, 2015.

Britton, Bianca. Farage to resign as UKIP leader in wake of 'Brexit' vote; *CNN*. July 4, 2016. www.cnn.com/2016/07/04/europe/farage-resign-ukip-brexit/

Brown, Archie. Tracing the rise of EU anti-establishment politics; *BBC News*; Last modified February 13, 2015. http://www.bbc.com/news/uk-politics-31426488

Bruneau, Nicholas. New European Parliament, New Strategy; 3 Communications; Last modified May 26, 2014. http://3communications.com/new-european-parliament/

Bulgarian Helsinki Committee. Submission to the Human Rights Committee regarding the consideration of the third periodic report of Bulgaria; 102nd session (July 11–29, 2011); Geneva; 2011. http://www2.ohchr.org/english/bodies/hrc/docs/ngo/BHC_Bulgaria_HRC102.pdf

Bundeswahlleiter. Bundestag Election; The Federal Electoral Committee, Federal Returning Officer. Accessed September 30, 2015. http://www.bundeswahlleiter.de

Burleigh, Michael and Wipperman, Wolfgang. *The Racial State: Germany 1933–1945*; Cambridge and New York: Cambridge University Press; 1991.

Burrin, Philippe. *La De´rive fasciste*; Paris: Le Seuil; 1986.

Business Insider. Hungary's Anti-Semitic Jobbik Party Is Spreading Across Eastern Europe; *Business Insider*; April 9, 2014. http://www.businessinsider.com/r-special-report-from-hungary-far-right-party-spreads-ideology-tactics-2014–09#ixzz3jCqoEbYu

Cammett, John M. Communist Theories of Fascism 1920–1935, *Science and Society*; 31(2): 149–163; 1967.

Caramani, Daniele and Mény, Yves. *Challenges to Consensual Politics: Democracy, Identity, and Populist Protest in the Alpine Region*; Brussels: PIE Peter Lang; 2005.

Caren, Neal. *Political Process Theory; Blackwell Encyclopedia of Sociology*; edited by George Ritzer; Blackwell Publishing, 2007. Accessed June 18, 2012. http://www.blackwellreference.com/subscriber/tocnode?id=g9781405124331_chunk_g978140512433122_ss1-41

Carey, Sean. Undivided Loyalties: Is National Identity an Obstacle to European Integration? *European Union Politics*; 3(4): 387–413; 2002.

Chambers, Madeline. Germany moves towards ban on far-right NPD party; *Reuters*; December 5, 2012. http://uk.reuters.com/article/2012/12/05/uk-germany-farright-idUKBRE8B40MA20121205

Chamorro-Premuzic, Tomas. The Dark Side of Charisma; *Harvard Business Review*; November 16, 2012. Accessed December 12, 2014. https://hbr.org/2012/11/the-dark-side-of-charisma

Channel 4 News. Far-right extremism: who are the EDL? Channel 4, UK; May 28, 2013. http://www.channel4.com/news/edl-far-right-extremism-woolwich-lee-rigby

Chossudovsky, Michel. 9/11 and America's "War on Terrorism," *Global Research*, 2015. Accessed November 28, 2015. http://www.globalresearch.ca/9–11-and-america-s-war-on-terrorism/24975

CHP-EU. What is this Merkez Türkiye Project? CHP EU Representation – Brussels website; May 25, 2015. http://chpbrussels.org/2015/05/25/what-is-this-merkez-turkiye-project/

Clavel, Geoffroy. Le Front national compte 83.000 adhérents, le plus haut niveau depuis sa foundation; *Huffington Post-France*; October 30, 2014. Accessed January 26, 2016. http://www.huffingtonpost.fr/2014/10/30/front-national-83000-adherents-plus-haut-fondation_n_6077574.html?utm_hp_ref=france

Clemens, Elisabeth. *The People's Lobby: Organizational Innovation and the Rise of Interest Group Politics in the United States, 1890–1925*; Chicago, IL: University of Chicago Press; 1997.

CNBC. Russia's European Party Relationships; *CNBC*; February 23, 2015. Accessed February 15, 2016. http://www.cnbc.com/2015/02/23/the-european-ties-russia-is-binding-closer.html

CNN. European stocks rise as elections wrap up; CNN; Last modified May 26, 2014. Accessed February 11, 2015. http://money.cnn.com/2014/05/26/news/economy/europe-ukraine-elections/

Coffé, Hilde. The Adaptation of the Extreme Right's Discourse: The Case of the Vlaams Blok; Ethical Perspectives, *Journal of The European Ethics Network*; 12(2): 205–230; 2005.

Connolly, Sean P. Review of Michèle H. Richman, Sacred Revolutions: Durkheim and the College of Sociology; *Bryn Mawr Review Of Comparative Literature*; 4(2): Cornell University, Spring 2004.

Cooper, Alice Holmes. *Paradoxes of Peace: German Peace Movements since 1945*; Ann Arbor, MI: University of Michigan; 1996.

Costain, Anne N. *Inviting Women's Rebellion; A Political Process Interpretation of the Women's Movement*; Baltimore: Johns Hopkins University Press; 1992.

Council on Europe. Study on Homophobia, Transphobia and Discrimination on Grounds of Sexual Orientation and Gender Identity; Danish Institute for Human Rights; no date. http://www.coe.int/t/Commissioner/Source/LGBT/SwitzerlandSociological_E.pdf

Counterpoint. Counterpoint's Guide to Populism at the 2014 European Elections, Counterpoint, UK. May 6, 2014. http://counterpoint.uk.com/counterpoints-guide-to-populism-at-the-2014-european-elections/

Cragun, Ryan and Deborah, Cragun, et al. *Introduction to Sociology*, Edition 1. Wikibooks, Blacksleet River. 2006.

Cress, Daniel and Snow, David A. The Outcomes of Homeless Mobilization: The Influence of Organization, Disruption, Political Mediation, and Framing, *American Journal of Sociology;* 105(4): 1063–1104; January 2000.

Crouch, Colin, and Streeck, Wolfgang (eds). *Political Economy of Modern Capitalism: Mapping Convergence and Diversity*; Thousand Oaks, CA: Sage; 1997.

Cunningham, Matthew. Australian Fascism? A Revisionist Analysis of the Ideology of the New Guard, *Politics, Religion & Ideology*; 13(3): 375–393; September 2012.

CVCE. Historical events in the European integration process (1945–2009): European Political Groups; Last modified 2015. http://www.cvce.eu/en/collections/unit-content/-/unit/02bb76df-d066–4c08-a58a-d4686a3e68ff/a5fa9b56–55e1–4d7a-b191–34739fbb6799

Cyclopaedia.net. Secretary of the Fascism and Freedom Movement; 2013. http://zh.cyclopaedia.asia/wiki/Secretary_of_the_Fascism_and_Freedom_Movement

Dabilis, Andy. New Democracy Says SYRIZA Incites Violence; *The Greek Reporter*; January 23, 2013. http://greece.greekreporter.com/2013/01/23/new-democracy-says-SYRIZA-incites-violence/#sthash.LAw0yhRb.dpuf

Daily Sabah. Turkey Condemns Violence; *Daily Sabah*; October 10, 2014. http://www.dailysabah.com/nation/2014/10/10/turkey-condemns-violence

Dandolov, Philip. The sinking fortunes of Euroscepticism in Bulgaria; Portal on Central Eastern and Balkan Europe, 2014. Accessed January 31, 2015. http://www.pecob.eu/sinking-fortunes-Euroscepticism-Bulgaria

Davies, Lizzy. "Italian senator says black minister has 'features of orangutan;'" *The Guardian*, July 14, 2013. Accessed August 6, 2015. http://www.theguardian.com/world/2013/jul/14/italian-senator-roberto-calderoli-cecile-kyenge

De Felice, Renzo. *Interpretations of Fascism*; Cambridge, MA and London; 1977.

de Jong, Alex. Pro-gay and anti-Islam: Rise of the Dutch far-Right; RoarMag.org; February 8, 2015.

de La Baume, Maïa. Le Pen denied front-row seat in Parliament; *Politico*; July 2, 2015. http://www.politico.eu/article/le-pen-denied-front-row-seat-in-parliament/

de Vreese, Claes H. A Spiral of Euroscepticism: The Media's Fault? *Acta Politica*, 42: 271–286; 2007.

Della Porta, Donatella and Tarrow, Sidney. Unwanted Children - Political Violence and the Cycle of Protest in Italy, 1966–1973, *European Journal of Political Research*; 14(5–6): 607–632; November 1986.

Democratic Society. Congress of the New Right; *Democratic Society*; May 13, 2014. http://www.demsoc.org/2014/05/13/congress-of-the-new-right-knp/

Democratic Society. Lega Nord; UK; April 22, 2014. Accessed December 10, 2015. http://www.demsoc.org/2014/04/22/lega-nord/

Democratic Society. Slovak National Party; UK; May 19, 2014. Accessed October 6, 2015. http://www.demsoc.org/2014/05/19/slovak-national-party-sns/

Dewinter, Filip. Vlaams Belang approves Holocaust resolution in Flemish parliament; Flemish Parliament; 2005. http://gatesofvienna.blogspot.com/2007/10/vlaams-belang-on-holocaust.html

DF (DPP). Danskfolkeparti.dk Official website, 2015. Accessed November 18, 2015. http://www.danskfolkeparti.dk/The_Party_Program_of_the_Danish_Peoples_Party

Dodd, Vikram and Taylor, Matthew. Muslims criticise Scotland Yard for telling them to engage with EDL; *The Guardian*, September 2, 2011.

Duarte, Esteban and Tadeo, Maria. Popular Podemos Party; *Bloomberg Business*; March 8, 2015. http://www.bloomberg.com/news/articles/2015–03–08/spain-s-post-franco-elite-under-attack-from-podemos-rise

Duijvelaar, Christy. Beyond Borders; Department of Sociology, Wageningen Agricultural University, The Netherlands; May 1996. Accessed April 12, 2015. http://archive.rec.org/REC/Publications/BeyondBorders/cover.html

Durkheim, Emile. *The Elementary Forms of the Religious Life, A Study in Religious Sociology*; George Allen and Unwin Ltd; London; (1912); Revised Edition Oxford University Press; 1965.

Durkheim, Emile. *The Division of Labor in Society; 1893*; [Excerpt from Robert Alun Jones. Emile Durkheim: An Introduction to Four Major Works], 24–59, Beverly Hills, CA: Sage Publications, Inc., 1986.

Dutch News. Anti-gay, anti-women Polish party links up with Wilders in Europe; *DutchNews*.nl; June 16, 2014. http://www.dutchnews.nl/news/archives/2014/06/anti-gay_anti-women_polish_par/

Dvorin, Tova. German Politician Dismissed Over Anti-Semitic 'Simpsons' Post; *Israel National News*, September 30, 2014. http://www.israelnationalnews.com/News/News.aspx/185629#.VgwCcpeqm_k

Dzhambazova, Boryana. Religious minorities suffer violent attacks from Bulgarian nationalists; *Global Post*; Jun 11, 2011. http://www.globalpost.com/dispatch/news/regions/europe/110609/bulgaria-muslims-nationalists

Eatwell, Roger. Community Cohesion and Cumulative Extremism in Contemporary Britain, *The Political Quarterly*; 77(7): 204–16; 2006.

Eatwell, Roger. *Fascism: A History*; New York: Allen Lane; 1996b.

Eatwell, Roger. On defining the "Fascist Minimum": The Centrality of Ideology, *Journal of Political Ideologies*; 1(3): 303–319; October 1996. DOI: 10.1080/13569319608420743.

Eatwell, Roger. Reflections on Fascism and Religion, *Totalitarian Movements and Political Religions*; 4(3): 145–166; 2003.

Eco, Umberto. *UR-FASCISM*; The New York Review of Books; Last modified June 22, 1995. http://www.nybooks.com/articles/1856

Economist. The Eurosceptic Union: The impact of the rise of anti-establishment parties, in Europe and abroad; *The Economist*; May 31, 2014.

Economist. SYRIZA wins; *The Economist*; January 25, 2015. Accessed October 9, 2015. http://www.economist.com/blogs/graphicdetail/2015/01/greeces-election

ECRR. ECRI 5th Report on Italy. Information Provided by the European Roma Rights Centre (ERRC); 2015. Accessed December 3, 2015. http://tbinternet.ohchr.org/Treaties/CESCR/Shared%20Documents/ITA/INT_CESCR_CSS_ITA_21312_E.pdf

Eisinger, Peter K. The Conditions of Protest Behavior in American Cities, *American Political Science Review*; 81: 11–28; 1973.

Elgot, Jessica. Fears over 'antisemitism' in New Greek coalition government; *The Jewish Chronicle*; November 14, 2011. Accessed October 16, 2015. http://www.thejc.com/news/world-news/58265/fears-over-antisemitism-new-greek-coalition-government

Ellinas, Antonis A. *The Media and the Far Right in Western Europe: Playing the Nationalist Card*; Cambridge, UK: Cambridge University Press; 2010.

Ellingson, Ter. *The Myth of the Noble Savage*; Berkeley, CA: University of California Press; 2001.

Elliott, Thomas. Fuzzy Set Qualitative Comparative Analysis Part 2; Presentation to the Statistics Group, UCI; February 27, 2013.

Encyclopaedia Britannica. Fascism: Politics- Austria; 2015. Accessed October 6, 2015. http://www.britannica.com/topic/fascism/Varieties-of-fascism#ref742243

English Defence League. Official Website; 2015. Accessed October 6, 2015. http://www.englishdefenceleague.org/?page_id=9

Epstein, Jessica. Daniel Duerr, Lane Kenworthy, and Charles Ragin. Comparative Employment Performance: A Fuzzy-Set Analysis. In Kenworthy, L. (ed), *Method and Substance in Macrocomparative Analysis* (Research Methods Series) 2008th Edition. A. Hicks; Palgrave and MacMillan; 2008.

Erickson, Liam and Murphy, D. *A History of Anthropological Theory*; Toronto, Canada: University of Toronto Press, Higher Education Division; 3rd Edition; 2008.

Erk, Jan. From Vlaams Blok to Vlaams Belang: The Belgian Far-Right Renames Itself, *West European Politics*; 28(3): 493–502; May 2005.

EU Business. Far-right party becomes Finland's second-largest: Poll; *EU Business*. March 17, 2011.

EurActiv.com. Euroscepticism: More than a British phenomenon; EurActiv - EU News & policy debates; Last modified January 2013. http://www.euractiv.com/sections/eu-elections-2014/euroscepticism-more-british-phenomenon-286609

EurActiv.com. 22% of Bulgarians want to join Russia's 'Eurasian Union'; May 15, 2014. http://www.euractiv.com/sections/eu-elections-2014/22-bulgarians-want-join-russias-eurasian-union-302163

Europe by Numbers. Europe in the 'right' direction: Extremism; August 7, 2014. https://europebynumbers.wordpress.com/

European Communities. Building Parliament: 50 Years if European Parliament History; European University Institute; 2009.

European Commission. The Transformation of Political Mobilisation and Communication in European Public Spheres; *EuroPub*; 2005.

European Conservatives and Reformists Group (ECR). Official Website; Accessed May 25, 2015. http://ecrgroup.eu/about-us/the-ecr-in-the-european-parliament/

European Election and Referendum Database. 2015. Accessed October 4, 2015. http://www.nsd.uib.no/european_election_database/country/italy/parties.html

European Parliament. Official Website. 2016. http://www.europarl.europa.eu

European Parliament. Factsheet 2015; Accessed May 15, 2015. http://www.europarl.europa.eu/ftu/pdf/en/FTU_1.3.1.pdf

Europhobia. UKIP's new Europe of Freedom and Democracy group; July 2, 2009. http://www.jcm.org.uk/blog/2009/07/ukips-new-europe-of-freedom-and-democracy-group/

Evans, Geoffrey and Butt, Sarah. Explaining Change in British Public Opinion on the European Union: Top Down or Bottom Up? *Acta Politica*; 42: 173–190; 2007.

Evola, Julius. *Fascism Viewed from the Right*; Budapest, Hungary: Arktos Media; Ltd; 1974/2013.

Faiola, Anthony. Europe's new Energizer Bunnies of hate; *Washington Post*; May 27, 2014. https://www.washingtonpost.com/news/worldviews/wp/2014/05/27/europes-new-energizer-bunnies-of-hate/

Fallon, Kathleen. Euroscepticism and Neofascism: Should we be scared? Last modified July 1, 2014. http://www.standnow.org/blog/euroscepticism-and-neofascism-should-we-be-scared

Fascism and Freedom Party. Official Website; 2015. Accessed September 8, 2015. http://www.fascismoeliberta.info

Feffer, John. Bulgaria's Ataka Party: An Unlikely Blend of Left and Right; *Foreign Policy in Focus*; August 15, 2013. http://fpif.org/bulgarias-ataka-party-an-unlikely-blend-of-left-and-right-2/

Finland Department of Ministry. True Finns Party; 2015. http://finland.fi/life-society/whats-up-with-the-true-finns-party/

Fischer, Teresa. German parties see membership fall as political activism goes online; *DPA International*; December 28, 2015.

Flood, Chris and Usherwood, Simon. Ideological Factors in Party Alignments on the EU: A comparison of three cases; EUSA tenth biennial international conference, Montreal, May 17–19, 2007.

Foght, Thomas. DF kaprer medlemmer som aldrig før: Tredjestørst i Danmark; MetroXpress; June 6, 14. Accessed January 26, 16: http://www.mx.dk/nyheder/danmark/story/21593829

Fontaine, Pascal. *Voyage to the Heart of Europe 1953–2009*; Belgium: Lannoo Publishers; 2010.

Foot, John. Why ignorant racists still flourish in multicultural Italy; *The Guardian*; July 15, 2013. http://www.theguardian.com/commentisfree/2013/jul/15/ignorant-racists-italy-cecile-kyenge

Foreign Policy. How a Former Neo-Nazi Party Became Sweden's Third-Largest; *Foreign Policy;* September 16, 2014. http://foreignpolicy.com/2014/09/16/how-a-former-neo-nazi-party-became-swedens-third-largest/

Fossum, John E. and Trenz, Hans-Jörg. The EU's Fledgling Society: From Deafening Silence to Critical Voice in European Constitution-Making, *Journal of Civil Society*; 2(1): 57–77; 2006.

Frank, Andre Gunder and Fuentes, Marta. On Studying the Cycles in Social Movements; Conference on "Movimientos Cyclicos y Recurrencias en Politica y Economia" sponsored by Fundacion Pablo Iglesias, Madrid May 18–21, 1992.

Frayer, Lauren. Spain's new left-wing Podemos party stirring up elections; *LA Times*; May 17, 2015. http://www.latimes.com/world/europe/la-fg-spain-podemos-20150517-story.html

Freebase. Fascism and Freedom Movement; Google Freebase: A community-curated database; 2015. http://www.freebase.com/m/09smvx

Freedom House. Freedom in the World- Austria; 2013. Accessed November 14, 2015. https://freedomhouse.org/report/freedom-world/2013/austria

Freedom House. Freedom in the World- Austria; 2015a. Accessed November 14, 2015. https://freedomhouse.org/report/freedom-world/2013/austria

Freedom House. Freedom in the World- France; 2015b. Accessed November 14, 2015. https://freedomhouse.org/report/freedom-world/2015/france

Freedom House. Freedom in the World- Hungary; 2015c. Accessed October 29, 2015. https://freedomhouse.org/report/freedom-world/2015/hungary

Front National. "Marine Le Pen's statement about the 2011 Norway attacks;" Front National (in French). July 24, 2011. http://www.frontnational.com/2013/08/les-personnes-agees-meprisees-par-leur-ministre-michele-delaunay/

Gabel, Matthew. *Interests and Integration: Market Liberalization, Public Opinion, and European Union*; Ann Arbor: University of Michigan Press; 1998.

Gabel, Matthew. Economic Integration and Mass Politics: Market Liberalization and Public Attitudes in the European Union, *American Journal of Political Science*; 42(3): 936–53; 1998b.

Gamson, William A. *The Strategy of Social Protest*; Homewood, IL; Dorsey Press and Wadsworth; 1990.

Garrod, Joel Z. A Brave Old World: An Analysis of Scientific Racism and BiDil, *McGill Journal of Medicine*; 9(1): 54–60; January 2006.

Garcia, Gustavo. "Podemos ya tiene más 'militantes' que el PSOE;" *El Boletin*; October 28, 2014.

Geertz, Clifford. Thick Description: Toward an Interpretive Theory of Culture. In *The Interpretation of Cultures*, 3–30, New York: Basic Books, 1973.

Gentile, Emilio. Fascism and The Italian Road To Totalitarianism; 19th Internation Congress of Historical Sciences, Oslo; August 6–13, 2000; Specialised Themes Nr.12 "Forms Of Totalitarianism And Dictatorship;" 2000. Accessed March 3, 2015. http://www.oslo2000.uio.no/program/papers/s12/s12-gentile.pdf

Gentile, Emilio. Fascism as Political Religion, *Journal of Contemporary History*; 25(2/3): 229–251; June, 1990.

Gentile, Emilio. *Il culto del littorio: la sacralizzazione della politica nell'Italia fascista*. (The cult of the fasces: the Sacralization of Politics in Fascist Italy); Bari: Laterza; 1993.

Gentile, Emilio. *The Sacralization of Politics in Fascist Italy*, translated by Keith Botsford; Cambridge, MA: Harvard University Press, 1996.

Gentile, Giovanni. Fascismo e cultura, 58, Milan, 1928; idem, *Che cos'e ilfascismo*, 145; Florence, 1925.

George, Alexander and Bennett, Andrew. *Case Studies and Theory Development in the Social Sciences*; Cambridge, MA: MIT Press; 2005.

Giddens, Anthony. *Capitalism and Modern Social Theory: An Analysis of the Writings of Marx, Durkheim and Max Weber*; Cambridge: Cambridge University Press; 1971.

Gifford, Chris. The People against Europe: The Eurosceptic Challenge to the UK's Coalition Government, *Journal of Common Market Studies*; 52(3): 512–528; 2014.

Gingrich, Paul. Power, Domination, Legitimation, and Authority (lecture), University of Regina, SK, Canada; 1999. Accessed June 1, 2015. http://uregina.ca/~gingrich/o12f99.htm

Givens, Terri. The role of socio-economic variables in the success of radical right parties. Unpublished paper, University of California, Los Angeles, Department of Political Science; 2000.

Golden Dawn. Διαβάστε περισσότερα: Official Website; Accessed August 17, 2015. http://www.xryshaygh.com/en/information#ixzz3j6MDSMGm

Golder, Matt. Explaining Variation in the Success of Extreme Right Parties in Western Europe, *Comparative Political Studies*; 36(4): 432–466; May 2003.

Goodwin, Matthew. The Roots of Extremism: The English Defence League and the Counter-Jihad Challenge; *Chatham House Open Briefing*; Europe; March 2013. http://www.openbriefing.org/docs/rootsofextremism.pdf

Gordon, Jerry. Austria Launches Hate Speech Investigation of Wilders while his Freedom Party leads Dutch Polls; *New English Review*; July 28, 2015. http://www.newenglishreview.org/blog_direct_link.cfm/blog_id/61976/Austria-Launches-Hate-Speech-Investigation-of-Wilders-while-his-Freedom-Party-leads-Dutch-Polls

Govan, Fiona. Greece's Golden Dawn to enter EU Parliament for first time; *The Telegraph*; May 25, 2014. http://www.telegraph.co.uk/news/worldnews/europe/greece/10855840/Greeces-far-right-Golden-Dawn-set-to-join-European-Parliament.html

Graham-Harrison, Emma. Nigel Farage's new friend in Europe: 'When women say no, they don't always mean it;' *The Guardian*; November 8, 2014. http://www.theguardian.com/politics/2014/nov/08/nigel-farage-ukip-europe-janusz-korwin-mikke

Griffin, L. J., Botsko, C., Wahl, A. M. and Isaac, L. W. Theoretical Generality, Case Particularity: Qualitative Comparative Analysis of Trade-union Growth and Decline, *International Journal of Comparative Sociology*; 32(1–2): 110–136; 1991.

Griffin, Roger D. "Fascism." Democracy Digest. Conference of Young Nigerian Democrats, Young Democrats of Nigeria, November 2013. Accessed August 30, 2015. https://conferenceofyoungnigeriandemocrats.files.wordpress.com/2013/11/fascism.pdf

Griffin, Roger. *Fascism*; London: Oxford University Press; 1995.

Griffin, Roger. *International Fascism: Theories, Causes and the New Consensus*; London: Bloomsbury USA, 1998.

Griffin, Roger. Interregnum or Endgame? Radical Right Thought in the "Post-fascist" Era, *The Journal of Political Ideologies*; 5(2): 163–78; 2000.

Griffin, Roger. Introduction: God's Counterfeiters? Investigating the Triad of Fascism, Totalitarianism and (Political) Religion, *Totalitarian Movements and Political Religions*; 5(3); 2004.

Griffin, Roger. *The Nature of Fascism*; London, UK: Pinters Publisher Limited; 1991.

Griffin, Roger. *The Palingenetic Core of Fascism*; *Che cos'è il fascismo?* Chapter in A. Campi (ed.), *Che cos'è il fascismo? Interpretazioni e prospecttive di richerche* (pp. 97–122). Ideazione Editrice, Rome, 2003. Accessed May 13, 2015. https://www.libraryofsocialscience.com/ideologies/docs/the-palingenetic-core-of-generic-fascist-ideology/index.html

Griffin, Roger. Studying Fascism in a Postfascist Age. From New Consensus to New Wave? *Journal of Comparative Fascist Studies*; *Fascism* 1: 1–17; 2012.

Guardian. What's the difference between BNP and Ukip voters? *The Guardian*; April 14, 2014. http://www.theguardian.com/commentisfree/2014/apr/14/bnp-ukip-voters-politics-immigration

Hague. Politics in the Netherands; ProDemos –House for Democracy and the Rule of Law; Netherlands: The Hague; 2013.

Hakhverdian, Armen and van Elsas, Erika, van der Brug, Wouter and Kuhn, Theresa. Euroscepticism and education: A longitudinal study of twelve EU member states, 1973–2010; GINI Discussion Paper 92; August 2013.

Halikiopoulou, Daphne, Nanou, Kyriaki and Vasilopoulou, Sofia. The Paradox of Nationalism: The Common Denominator of Radical Right and Radical Left Euroscepticism, *European Journal of Political Research*; 51(4): 504–39; 2012.

Halla, Martin, Wagner, Alexander F. and Zweimuller, Josef. Immigration and Voting for the Extreme Right; Working Papers 083, Department of Economics - University of Zurich; November 12, 2014.

Hallett, Nick. Marine Le Pen Would Win French Presidential Election if it Were Held Today, Poll Says; *Breitbart;* Last modified August 1, 2014. http://www.breitbart.com/london/2014/08/01/marine-le-pen-would-win-french-presidential-election-if-it-were-held-today-poll-says/

Harmsen, R. and Spiering, M. Introduction: Euroscepticism and the Evolution of European Political Debate. In R. Harmsen and M. Spiering (eds), *Euroscepticism: Party Politics, National Identity and European Integration*, 16, Amsterdam: Rodopi, 2004.

Heine, Friederike. Hard knocks for anti-euro party; *Spiegel*; August 14, 2013. Friederikehttp://www.spiegel.de/international/germany/anti-euro-party-alternative-for-germany-faces-violent-threats-from-left-wing-activists-a-916531.html

Heinisch, Reinhard and Landsberger, Christa. Salience Matters - An Innovative Approach to Capturing the Effects of Eurosceptical Attitudes in Parties and Publics; University of Salzburg; Paper prepared for Presentation at the "Tag der öste rreichischen Politikwissenschaft," University of Salzburg, December 2, 2011.

Helsinki Times. Soini condemns hate speech and political violence; *Helsinki Times*; August 10, 2015. http://www.helsinkitimes.fi/finland/finland-news/politics/13486-soini-condemns-hate-speech-and-political-violence.html

Heneghan, Tom. Europe far right courts Israel in anti-Islam drive; *Reuters*; December 20, 2010.

Herzog, Alexander and Tucker, Joshua. The Dynamics of Support: The Winners –losers Gap in Attitudes toward EU Membership in Post-communist Countries, *European Political Science Review*; 2(2): 235–267; 2009.

Hill, Jenny. What next for Germany's Eurosceptic AfD party? *BBC News*; July 21, 2015. Accessed August 12, 2015. http://www.bbc.com/news/world-europe-33593500

Hofstede, Geert. Gert Jan Hofstede, Michael Minkov. *Cultures and Organizations: Software of the Mind*. Revised and Expanded 3rd Edition. New York: McGraw-Hill USA; 2010.

Holmqvist, Anette and Röstlund, Lisa. "Medlemsström till partierna i krisen". Aftonbladet (in Swedish); December 8, 2014.

Hood, Stuart and Jansz, Litza. *Fascism: A Graphic Guide*; London: Icon Books; 2013.

Hooghe, Liesbet and Marks, Gary. A Postfunctionalist Theory of European Integration: From Permissive Consensus to Constraining Dissensus, *British Journal of Political Science*; 39(1): 1–3; 2009.

Hooghe, Liesbet and Marks, Gary. Calculation, Community, and Cues: Public Opinion on European Integration, *European Union Politics*; 6(4): 419–43; 2005.

Hooghe, Liesbet and Marks, Gary. Making of a Polity. The Struggle over European Integration. In Herbert Kitschelt, Gary Marks, Peter Lange and John Stephens (eds), *Continuity and Change in Contemporary Capitalism*, 70–97, Cambridge: Cambridge University Press, 1999.

Hooghe, Liesbet and Marks, Gary. Sid in Movement: Becoming A Transnational Scholar; Special paper for Sidney Tarrow's Retirement; Ithaca: Cornell University; June 2–4, 2011.

Hooghe, Liesbet and Marks, Gary (eds). Understanding Euroscepticism. Special issue of *Acta Politica*; 42(2–3); 119–27; 2007.

Hooghe, Liesbet (ed). What drives Euroskepticism? Special issue of *European Union Politics*; 8(1); 2007.

Hooghe, Liesbet, Huo, Jingjing and Marks, Gary. Does Occupation Shape Attitudes on Europe? Benchmarking Operationalizations, *Acta Politica*; 42: 329–351; 2007.

Hope, Christopher. Ukip is a Racist Party; *The Telegraph*; October 2, 2013. Accessed November 14, 2015. http://www.telegraph.co.uk/news/politics/ukip/10351499/Ukip-is-a-racist-party-says-Heseltine.html

Hosi Wien. *Hosi Wien: No Coalition with Racism; Homosexuelle Initiative*; Accessed September 13, 2015. http://www.hosiwien.at/haider/

Hudson, John and Kühner, Stefan. Qualitative Comparative Analysis and Applied Public Policy Analysis: New Applications of Innovative Methods, *Policy and Society*; 32(4): 279–87; 2013.

Huysseune, Michel. A Eurosceptic Vision in a Europhile Country: The Case of the Lega Nord, *Modern Italy*; 15(1): 63–75; 2010.

Iglesias, Pablo. Alexis Tsipras; *Time Magazine*; April 16, 2015. Accessed January 12, 2016. http://time.com/3823031/alexis-tsipras-2015-time-100/

Iglesias, Pablo. Understanding Podemos; New Masses, New Media – 8; *New Left Review*; 93; May-June 2015.

Imig, Doug and Tarrow, Sidney. Political Contention in a Europeanising Polity, *West European Politics*; 23(4): 73–93; 2000.

Index of Economic Freedom. The Heritage Foundation; Index of Economic Freedom 2015. Accessed October 13, 2015. http://www.heritage.org

Inglehart, Ronald and Baker, Wayne E. Modernization, Culture Change, and the Persistence of Traditional Values, *American Sociological Review*; 65: 19–51; February, 2000.

Institute for European Policy. Slovak National Party. National Identity in Central-eastern Europe; 2013. Accessed September 9, 2015. http://www.ceeidentity.eu/database/manifestoescoun/slovak-national

International Business Times. Migrant crisis: Who is EU refugees quota rebel Slovakian PM Robert Fico; *International Business Times*; September 23, 2015.

International Business Times. Right Sector Ultra-Nationalists Back Odessa Jews over Holocaust Memorial Nazi Defacement; *International Business Times*; April 10, 2014. http://www.ibtimes.co.uk/right-sector-ultra-nationalists-back-odessa-jews-over-holocaust-memorial-nazi-defacement-1444276

Iordachi, Constantin. *Comparative Fascist Studies: New Perspectives*; London: Routledge; 2009.

Ishchenko, Volodymyr. Ukraine has ignored the far right for too long – it must wake up to the danger; *The Guardian*; November 13, 2014. http://www.theguardian.com/commentisfree/2014/nov/13/ukraine-far-right-fascism-mps

Ivaldi, Giles. The Front National at 40: The evolution of Europe's radical right; October 4, 2012. http://www.policy-network.net/pno_detail.aspx?ID=4265&title=The-Front-National-at-40-The-evolution-of-Europes-radical-right

Ivarsflaten, Elisabeth. What Unites Right-Wing Populists in Western Europe? Re-Examining Grievance Mobilization Models in Seven Successful Case, *Comparative Political Studies*; 41: 3–23; 2008.

Jackman, R. and Volpert, K. Conditions Favoring Parties of the Extreme Right in Western Europe, *British Journal of Political Science*; 26: 501–521; 1996.

JamesinTurkey. The Republican People's Party; 2015. http://www.jamesinturkey.com/roundups/political-parties/republican-peoples-party-chp/

Jensen, Jarl Niclas Bojesen. The rise and rise of the Danish People's Party, *The Local-*Denmark, June 3, 2015. Accessed June 21, 15. http://www.thelocal.dk/20150603/the-rise-and-rise-of-the-danish-peoples-party

Jobbik.com. Official website for the Jobbik Movement for a Better Hungary. Accessed September, 2015. http://jobbik.com/short_summary_about_jobbik

Johnson, Simon. Swedish leader condemns violence linked to far right; *Reuters*; March 10, 2014. http://www.reuters.com/article/2014/03/10/us-sweden-farright-idUSBREA291OE20140310

Jolly, Seth, and Oktay, Sibel. "Explaining Turkish Party and Public Support for the EU;" The Biennial Meeting of the European Union Studies Association; Boston, 2011.

JTA (Jewish Telegraphic Agency). From the Archive: Laos, LAOS and anti-Semitism; May 16, 2014. http://www.jta.org/2014/05/16/news-opinion/the-telegraph/from-the-archive-laos-laos-and-anti-semitism

Kallis, Aristotle A. To Expand or Not to Expand? Territory, Generic Fascism and the Quest for an 'Ideal Fatherland', *Journal of Contemporary History*; 38(2): 237–260; April 2003.

Karstedt-Henke, Sabine. Theorien zur Erklärung terroristischer Bewegungen. In Erhard Blankenberg (ed), *Politik der inneren Sicherheit*, 198–234, Frankfurt: Suhrkamp, 1980.

Kassam, Ashifa. 'Yes he can!' How Spanish indignado Pablo Iglesias aims to use a wave of protest to build 'a decent country;' *The Guardian*; July 5, 2014. http://www.theguardian.com/world/2014/jul/06/pablo-iglesias-indignado-podemos-spain

Kaymak, Erol. *Neo-Populist Party Appeal and Realignment: The Emergence of a New Politics Cleavage*; Lubbock, TX: Texas Tech University; 1999.

Keck, Margaret and Sikkink, Kathryn. *Activists Beyond Borders: Advocacy Networks in International Politics*. Ithaca, NY: Cornell University Press; 1998.

Kedourie, E. *Nationalism*. London: Hutchinson; 1960.

Kietz, Daniela and Von Ondarza, Nicolai. Eurosceptics in the European Parliament- Isolated and Divided in Brussels but Driving National Debates; Stiftung Wissenschaft und Politik, German Institute for International and Security Affairs; February 2014.

Kitschelt, Herbert P. Political Opportunity Structures and Political Protest: Anti-nuclear Movements in Four Democracies, *British Journal of Political Science*; 16: 57–85; 1986.

Kitsikis, Dimitri. *Ἡ τρίτη ἰδεολογία καὶ ἡ Ὀρθοδοξία*, Athens: Hestia Books; 1998.

Klapsis, Antonis. *An Unholy Alliance: The European Far-Right and Putin's Russia*; Brussels, Belgium: The Wilfried Martens Centre for European Studies; 2015.

Knigge, Pia. The Ecological Correlates of Right-wing Extremism in Western Europe, *European Journal of Political Research*; 34: 249–279; 1998.

Knight, Ben. PEGIDA aims to launch political party; *Deutsche Welle*; July 7, 2015. http://www.dw.com/en/pegida-aims-to-launch-political-party/a-18567063

Knight, Ben and Goebel, Nicole. German AfD tries to shake off 'Tea Party' tag; *Deutsche Welle*; May 21, 2014. http://www.dw.com/en/german-afd-tries-to-shake-off-tea-party-tag/a-17506323

KNP Programme. Congress of the New Right election Program 2014 (Program wyborczy do PE 2014); http://www.nowaprawicajkm.pl/info/program-wyborczy/program-wyborczy

Koopmans, Ruud. New Social Movements and Changes in Political Participation in Western Europe, *Western European Politics*; 19: 28–50; 1996.

Koopmans, Ruud. Protest in Time and Space. The Evolution of Waves of Contention. In David A. Snow, Sarah A. Soule, and Hanspeter Kriesi (eds), *The Blackwell Companion to Social Movements*, 19–46, Oxford: Blackwell, 2004.

Koopmans, Ruud and Kriesi, Hanspeter. Institutional Structures and Prevailing Strategies. In Hanspeter Kriesi, Ruud Koopmans, Jan Willem Duyvendak, and Marco G. Giugni (eds), *New Social Movements in Western Europe: A Comparative Analysis*, 26–52, Minneapolis: University of Minnesota Press, 1995.

Kopecký, Petr and Mudde, Cas. The Two Sides of Euroscepticism. Party Positions in European Integration in East Central Europe, *European Union Politics*; 3(3): 300; 2002.

Kreko, Peter. How big will Russia's political footprint be in Europe? *UB* Post, Mongolia; June 2014. Accessed August 12, 2014. http://ubpost.mongolnews.mn/?p=9527

Kreko, Peter, Macaulay, Marie, Molnár, Csaba and Győri. Lóránt. Political Capital Institute (Hungary). Europe's New Pro-Putin Coalition: the Parties of 'No;' Institute of Modern Russia; August 3, 2015. Accessed February 14, 2016. http://imrussia.org/en/analysis/world/2368-europes-new-pro-putin-coalition-the-parties-of-no

Kriesi, Hanspeter, Edgar Grande, Romain Lachat, Martin Dolezal, Simon Bornschier, Timotheos Frey. Globalization and the Transformation of the National Political Space: Six European Countries Compared, *European Journal of Political Research,* 45(6): 921–56; 2006.

Kriesi, Hanspeter, Edgar Grande, Romain Lachat, Martin Dolezal, Simon Bornschier, Timotheos Frey. *West European Politics in the Age of Globalization*; Cambridge: Cambridge University Press; 2008.

Kropczynski, Jessica N. Examination of the Use of Online and Offline Networks by Housing Social Movement Organizations; Theses and Dissertations—Sociology, University of Kentucky; Paper 11, 2013.

Krouwel, André and Abts, Koen. The Structure of Political Discontent: A Typology of Eurorejectionism, *Acta Politica*; 42(2/3): 252–270; 2007.

Kulaoğlu, Hüseyin. CHP ve HDP'den homo'lara destek" ("Support for Homos by the CHP and the HDP"); *Yeni Akit*, May 27, 2015.

Kuper, Adam and Kuper, Jessica (eds). *Racism; The Social Science Encyclopedia*, 716: 1996.

Langenbacher, Nora. *Is Europe on the "right" path? Right--wing extremism and right-wing populism in Europe*; Washington, DC: Friedrich-Ebert-Stiftung; 2011.

Lansford, Tom. *Political Handbook of the World 2015*; Thousand Oaks, CA: CQ Press, an imprint of Sage Publications, Inc.; 2015.

LAOS. Popular Orthodox Rally. http://www.laos.gr

Laqueuer, Walter. *Fascism: Past, Present, Future*; Oxford, UK: Oxford University Press; 1997.

Laruelle, Marlene. *Eurasianism and the European Far Right: Reshaping the Europe–Russia Relationship*; Lexington Books, July 1, 2015.

Lee, Martin A. Former Left-Wing, German Extremist Horst Mahler Switches to Neo-Nazi National Democratic Party; Southern Poverty Law Center, 2015. https://www.splcenter.org/fighting-hate/intelligence-report/2015/former-left-wing-german-extremist-horst-mahler-switches-neo-nazi-national-democratic-party

Lega Nord. http://www.leganord.org/

Legewie, Nicolas. An Introduction to Applied Data Analysis with Qualitative Comparative Analysis (QCA), *Qualitative Social Research*; 14(3), Art. 15 – September, 2013.

Leonard, Mark, Torreblanco, José Ignacio, Francescon, Silvia, Kundnani, Hans, Buras, Piotr, Guérot, Ulrike and Klau, Thomas. "The Continent-wide Rise of Euroscepticism;" European Council on Foreign Relations, Policy Memo No. 79, 2013. http://www.theguardian.com/commentisfree/2013/apr/24/continental-euroscepticism-rise (Accessed ay 13, 2015).

Lesniak, Peter. A Guide to Far-Right and Far-Left of the New European Parliament; *Huffington Post*; July 26, 2014. http://www.huffingtonpost.co.uk/peter-lesniak/european-parliament_b_5392502.html

Leviev-Sawyer, Clive. Bulgarian Parliament rejects far-right Ataka's anti-gay; *Independent Balkan News Agency/ Sofia Globe*; January 30, 2014. http://www.balkaneu.com/bulgarian-parliament-rejects-far-right-atakas-anti-gay-law/

Lewis-Beck, M., and Stegmaier, M. Economic Determinants of Electoral Outcomes, *Annual Review of Political Science*, 3: 183–219; 2000.

Lichfield, John. €40m of Russian cash will allow Marine Le Pen's Front National to take advantage of rivals' woes in upcoming regional and presidential elections; *The Independent*; November 27, 2014.

Lichfield, John. Marine Le Pen battered by controversy as details emerge of hacked Kremlin text messages and holocaust-minimising from her father; *The Independent;* April 3, 2015.

Liphshiz, Cnaan. France's National Front gaining among Jews with tough stance on Arab anti-Semitism; *Jewish Telegraphic Agency*; September 23, 2014. http://www.jta.org/2014/09/23/news-opinion/world/frances-national-front-gaining-among-jews-with-tough-stance-on-arab-anti-semitism-1

Lochocki, Timo. The unstoppable far right: How established parties' communication and media reporting of European affairs affect the electoral advances of right-populist parties; The German Marshall Fund of the United States; April 2014.

Lochocki, Timo. Germany's Divided Right-Wing Nationalists; The German Marshall Fund of the United States; February 10, 2015. Accessed July 13, 2015. http://www.gmfus.org/blog/2015/02/10/germany%E2%80%99s-divided-right-wing-nationalists

Loveless, M. and Rohrschneider, R. Public Perceptions of the EU as a System of Governance, *Living Reviews in European Governance*; 3(1); 2008.

Lowen, Mark. Greece's Golden Dawn: 'Don't say a word or I'll burn you alive'; *BBC News*, Athens; October 2, 2013. http://www.bbc.com/news/world-europe-24363776

Lubbers, M. and Jaspers, E. A Longitudinal Study of Euroscepticism in the Netherlands: 2008 versus 1990, *European Union Politics*; 12(1): 21–40; 2011.

Lynch, P. and Whitaker, R. Where there is Discord, Can They Bring Harmony? Managing Intra-party Dissent on European Integration in the Conservative Party, *The British Journal of Politics & International Relations*; 4(3): 399–428; 2012.

Mahçupyan, Etyen. The era of soft neo-nationalism at the CHP; *Today's Zaman*; July 26, 2012.

Malone, Jack. Examining the Rise of Right Wing Populist Parties in Western Europe; Honors Thesis, St. John's University; 2014.

Mann, Michael. *Fascists*; Cambridge, UK: Cambridge University Press; 2004.

Mansheim, Michael. Euroscepticism and Neofascism: should we be scared? STAND, July 1, 2014. Accessed June 1, 2015. http://standnow.org/2014/07/01/euroscepticism-and-neofascism-should-we-be-scared/

Marks, Gary and Steenbergen, M. (eds). *European Integration and Political Conflict*, Cambridge: Cambridge University Press; 2004.

Marks, Gary, and McAdam, Doug. On the Relationship of Political Opportunities to the Form of Collective Action: The Case of the European Union. In Donatella della Porta, Hanspieter Kriesi and Dieter Rucht (eds), *Social Movements in a Globalizing World*, 97–111, New York: St. Martin's Press, 1999.

Marks, Gary, and McAdam, Doug. Social Movements and the Changing Structure of Political Opportunity in the European Community, *West European Politics*; 19(2): 249–78; 1996.

Marks, Gary, Hooghe, Liesbet, Nelson, Moira and Edwards, Erica. Party Competition and European Integration in the East and West: Different Structure, Same Causality, *Comparative Political Studies*; 39(2): 155–175; March, 2006.

Martin, P. *Le vote Le Pen: L'électorat du Front National* [The Le Pen vote: The electorate of the National Front] (Notes de la Fondation Saint-Simon, No. 84). Paris: Saint-Simon; 1996.

Marx, Karl and Engels, Frederick. *Manifesto of the Communist Party; Marx/Engels Selected Works, Vol. One*; Progress Publishers, Moscow, pp. 98–137 (February 1848) 1969.

Mason, Paul. Greece: Trying to understand SYRIZA; *BBC News*; May 14, 2012. http://www.bbc.com/news/world-europe-18056677

Maximilian Popp and Andreas Wassermann. Prying into Pegida: Where Did Germany's Islamophobes Come From? *Spiegel*; January 12, 2015. http://www.spiegel.de/international/germany/origins-of-german-anti-muslim-group-pegida-a-1012522.html

Mayer, N. and Perrineau, P. (eds). *Le front national à découvert [The national front uncovered]*. Paris: Presses de la Fondation Nationale des Sciences Politiques; 1989.

McAdam, Doug. *Political Process and the Development of Black Insurgency, 1930–1970*; Chicago, IL: University of Chicago Press; 1982.

McAdam, Doug, Tarrow, Sidney G. and Tilly, Charles. *Dynamics of Contention; Cambridge Studies in Contentious Politics*; Cambridge, UK: Cambridge University Press; 2001.

McCarthy, John D. and Zald, Mayer N. Resource Mobilization and Social Movements: A Partial Theory, *The American Journal of Sociology*; 82(6): 1212–1241; May, 1977.

McCarthy, John D. and Zald, Mayer N. *The Trend of Social Movements in America: Professionalization and Resource Mobilization*; Morristown, NJ: General Learning Press; 1973.

McDonald-Gibson, Charlotte. Fall of the Dutch far-right: How a racist speech too far cost the flamboyant Geert Wilders his chance at the EU; *The Independent*; April 3, 2014. http://www.independent.co.uk/news/world/europe/fall-of-the-dutch-farright-how-a-racist-speech-too-far-cost-the-flamboyant-geert-wilders-his-chance-at-the-eu-9236348.html

McHugh, Jess. European Anti-Austerity 2015: Podemos, Spain's Protest Party, Looks To An Uncertain Future After Tsipras Resignation, Dips In The Polls; *International Business Times;* September 2, 2015. http://www.ibtimes.com/european-anti-austerity-2015-podemos-spains-protest-party-looks-uncertain-future-2079500

McHugh, Jess. How The EU Migrant Crisis Is Fueling Right-Wing Politicians And Refugee Policies In Europe; *International Business Times*; August 27, 2015. Accessed September 15, 2015: http://www.ibtimes.com/how-eu-migrant-crisis-fueling-right-wing-politicians-refugee-policies-europe-2071326

McLaren, Lauren M. Public Support for the European Union: Cost/benefit Analysis or Perceived Cultural Threat? *The Journal of Politics*; 64: 551–566; 2002.

Melissaris, Emmanuel. Golden Dawn: Organising, encouraging, sustained by violence; May 31, 2015. https://www.opendemocracy.net/can-europe-make-it/golden-dawn-organising-encouraging-sustained-by-violence

Meret, Susi. *The Danish People's Party, the Italian Northern League and the Austrian Freedom Party in a Comparative Perspective: Party Ideology and Electoral Support*; Aalborg: Institut for Historie, Internationale Studier og Samfundsforhold, Aalborg Universitet. (SPIRIT PhD Series; No. 25); 2010. http://vbn.aau.dk/files/20049801/spirit_phd_series_25.pdf

Merrick, Jane. Eurosceptic claims 200 Tory MPs now favour a British exit from EU; *The Independent*, November 30, 2014. Accessed January 13, 2015. http://www.independent.co.uk/news/uk/politics/eurosceptic-claims-200-tory-mps-now-favour-british-exit-from-eu-9893245.html

Mesežnikov, Grigorij. National and Right Wing Radicalism in the New Democracies: Slovakia; Paper for the workshop of the Friedrich Ebert Foundation on Right-wing extremism and its impact on young democracies in the CEE countries; 2009.

Meyer, David S. Protest Cycles and Political Process: American Peace Movements in the Nuclear Age, *Political Research Quarterly*; 46: 451–79; 1993.

Meyer, David S. Protest and Political Opportunities, *Annual Review of Sociology*; 30: 125–45; 2004.

Meyer, David S. *A Winter of Discontent: The Nuclear Freeze and American Politics*; Santa Barbara, CA: Praeger; 1990.

Meyer, David S. and Minkoff, Debra C. Conceptualizing Political Opportunity, *Social Forces*; 82(4): 1457–1492; June, 2004.

Meyer, David S. and Whittier, Nancy. Social Movement Spillover, *Social Problems*; 41(2): 277–98; May, 1994.

Michaletos, Iannis. Left-wing Terrorist Attacks and Organized Violence in Greece, 2008–2012. Balkanalysis.com. Accessed November 11, 2015. http://www.balkanalysis.com/greece/2013/02/14/left-wing-terrorist-attacks-and-organized-violence-in-greece-2008–2012/

Milesi, Patrizia, et al. *Extreme Right Activists in Europe*; Chapter 6: Italy: Routledge; 2006. http://www.researchgate.net/profile/Patrizia_Catellani/publication/249009788_Italy_The_offspring_of_fascism/links/00b7d51e299540e209000000.pdf

Mills, C. Wright. *The Power Elite*; Oxford, UK: Oxford University Press; 1956.

Milza, Pierre. *Fascisme français: passét présent*; Paris: Groupe Flammarion; 1987.

Minkenberg, Michael. *Transforming the Transformation? The East European Radical Right in the Political Process*; New York: Routledge; 2015.

Mionis, Sabby. Greek Economic Tragedy Brings Neo-Nazis and Racists in the Political Mainstream, *Huffington Post*; 2012. http://www.huffingtonpost.com/sabby-mionis/greece-chrysi-avgi_b_1377137.html

MIT. Reading Global Clients' Signals; *MIT Sloane Management Review and Report*; April 3, 2014.

Morris, Marley, Mölzer, Andreas, Obermayr, Franz, Lunacek, Ulrike, and Kolarska-Bobińska, Lena. Populist snapshots: Austrian Freedom Party (FPÖ) in the European Parliament; Open Democracy.com; June 11, 2014. https://www.opendemocracy.net/can-europe-make-it/marley-morris-and-colleagues/populist-snapshots-austria

Mosse, George L. *The Fascist Revolution: Toward a General Theory of Fascism*; New York: Howard Fertig Publisher; 1999.

Mudde, Cas. *Populist Radical Right Parties in Europe*; Cambridge: Cambridge University Press; 2007.

Mudde, Cas. "Sussex v. North Carolina: The Comparative Study of Party-Based Euroscepticism" *Sussex European Institute* Working Paper No. 121 (EPERN Working Paper No. 23); 2011.

Mussolini, Benito. *Luoghi comuni? Destra e sinistra; en Il Popolo d'Italia*; July 29, 1922.

Mussolini, Benito. *What is Fascism*, (with Giovanni Gentile) Italian Encyclopedia; 1932.

Nairn, Tom. The modern Janus, *New Left Review*; 1(94): 3–29; 1975.

Nardelli, Alberto. Party membership in UK is Tiny; *The Guardian*; September 29, 2014. Accessed January 25, 2016. http://www.theguardian.com/news/datablog/2014/sep/29/labour-conservatvies-uk-party-membership-is-tiny

Nelis, Jan. Italian Fascism and Culture: Some Notes on Investigation; *HAOL*, No. 9, 141–151; Invierno, 2006.

Neocleous, Mark. *Fascism*; Buckingham: Open University Press; 1997.

New Observer. Europe of Nations and Freedoms; *The New Observer Online*. January 27, 2016. Accessed February 19, 2016. http://newobserveronline.com/europe-of-nations-and-freedoms-holds-first-meeting/

Nicholas, Anna. Spain's Podemos party says it can win, but can it? *The Telegraph*; November 22, 2014. Accessed November 13, 2015. http://my.telegraph.co.uk/expat/tag/podemos/

Nolte, Ernst. *Three Faces of Fascism*; New York: Holt, Rinehart, and Winston; 1966.

Novaković, Igor. The rise of political extremism in Bulgaria - The political party "Ataka;" MIREES Interdisciplinary Master's East European Research and Studies Alma Mater Studiorum; University of Bologna; 2008.

NPD. Official website. Accessed October 4, 2015. http://www.npd-sh.de

NPD Party Program. Das Parteiprogramm der Nationaldemokratischen Partei Deutschlands (NPD); Beschlossen auf dem Bundesparteitag Am; 4./5.6.2010 in Bamberg. http://medien.npd.de/dokumente/parteiprogramm.pdf

Oberschall, Anthony. *Social Conflict and Social Movements*. Englewood Cliffs: Prentice-Hall, Inc.; 1973.

Olson, Mancur. *The Logic of Collective Action*; Cambridge, MA: Harvard University Press; 1965.

Olszański, Tadeusz A. Svoboda Party – The New Phenomenon on the Ukrainian Right-Wing Scene; Centre for Eastern Studies (OSW); July 4, 2011. http://mercury.ethz.ch/serviceengine/Files/ISN/137051/ipublicationdocument_singledocument/fd513b79–1b42–403d-bde8–3d3d3a6a6f32/en/commentary_56.pdf

Open Europe. Meet the man who wants to blow up the European parliament; Open Europe; May 9, 2014. http://openeuropeblog.blogspot.com/2014/05/meet-man-who-wants-to-blow-up-european.html

Orange, Richard. Anti-immigrant Sweden Democrats now the biggest party, according to poll, *The Telegraph*; August 20, 2015. http://www.telegraph.co.uk/news/

worldnews/europe/sweden/11814498/Anti-immigrant-Sweden-Democrats-now-the-biggest-party-according-to-poll.html

Orwell, George. "As I Please;" column in *Tribune* magazine and reprinted in *The Collected Essays, Journalism, and Letters of George Orwell, Vol. 3, As I Please*, 1943–1945, ed. Sonia Orwell and Ian Angus (New York: Harcourt, Brace and World, 1968); 24 March 1944. Accessed December 12, 2015. http://www.orwell.ru/library/articles/As_I_Please/english/efasc

Osborn, Andrew and Faulconbridge, Guy. UK's Eurosceptic UKIP party storms to victory in Europe vote; *Reuters*; May 26, 2014. Accessed November 18, 2014. http://www.reuters.com/article/2014/05/26/us-eu-elections-britain-idUSBREA4O0EM20140526

Oudenampsen, Merlin. Explaining the Swing to the Right: The Dutch Debate on the Rise of Right-Wing Populism. In Ruth Wodak, Majid Khosravinik, Brigitte Mral (eds), *Right-Wing Populism in Europe: Politics and Discourse*, 191, Bloomsbury, London: A&C Black; 2013.

Paelinck, Gianni. Open VLD heeft de meeste leden en steekt CD&V voorbij; *deredactie.be;* October 30, 2014.

Papadogiannis, Nikolaos. Power to Our People: Syriza and the History of Greek Left-Wing Nationalism; *Foreign Affairs*; September 21, 2015. https://www.foreignaffairs.com/articles/greece/2015–09–21/power-our-people

Passmore, Kevin. *Fascism: A Very Short Introduction*; Oxford, UK: Oxford University Press; 2002.

Paxton, Robert O. *The Anatomy of Fascism*; New York: Knopf Publishing Group; 2005.

Paxton, Robert O. The Five Stages of Fascism, *The Journal of Modern History*; 70(1): 1–23; March, 1998.

Paxton, Robert O. *What is Fascism*? New York: Random House; 2004.

Payne, Stanley. *A History of Fascism 1914–45*; London: University College London Press; 1995.

Payne, Stanley. *Fascism: Comparison and Definition*; Madison, WI: University of Wisconsin Press; p. 7; 1980.

Peters, Andrea. Right Sector threatens violence throughout Ukraine; *The World Socialist*. July 18, 2015.

Pew Research Center. Political Polarization in the American Public: Section 1: Growing Ideological Consistency, June 12, 2014. Accessed December 4, 2015. http://www.people-press.org/2014/06/12/section-1-growing-ideological-consistency/?beta=true&utm_expid=53098246–2.Lly4CFSVQG2lphsg-KopIg.1&utm_referrer=https%3A%2F%2Fwww.google.com

Pezard, Stephanie. *The Front National and the Future of French Foreign Policy*; The Rand Blog; Rand Corporation; Last modified March 2015. http://www.rand.org/blog/2015/03/the-front-national-and-the-future-of-french-foreign.html

Pfisterer, Sophia. Denmark – (not) an oasis in Europe; *EMAJ Magazine*; May 25, 2011. http://emajmagazine.com/2011/05/25/denmark-%E2%80%93-not-an-oasis-in-europe/

Piano, Aili. *Freedom in the World 2005: The Annual Survey of Political Rights and Civil Liberties*, Freedom House, UK: Rowman and Littlefield Publishers; 2005.

Pinto, António Costa. *Rethinking the Nature of Fascism: Comparative Perspectives*; Basingstoke, UK: Palgrave; 2011.

Pipes, Daniel. Sweden's Populist Surge; *Washington Times*; August 25, 2015. http://www.washingtontimes.com/news/2015/aug/25/daniel-pipes-swedens-populist-surge/

Pirie, Ian. Social Movements Theory, Lecture Notes. 2007. Accessed January 12, 2015. http://imagining-other.net/socialmovementstheory.htm

Piven, Frances Fox and Cloward, Richard A. Normalizing Collective Protest. In Aldon D. Morris and Carol McClurg Mueller (eds), *Frontiers in Social Movement Theory*; New Haven, CT: Yale University; 1992.

Piven, Frances Fox and Cloward, Richard A. *Poor People's Movements: Why They Succeed, How They Fail;* New York: Vintage Books; 1977.

Podemos.info. Official Podemos Website. Accessed October 9, 2015. http://podemos.info

Poli, Eleonara and Rosselli, Chiara. The Eurosceptic revolution: much ado about nothing? Open Democracy; Last modified September 26, 2014. https://www.opendemocracy.net/can-europe-make-it/eleonora-poli-chiara-rosselli/eurosceptic-revolution-much-ado-about-nothing

Politikka. Vihreiden ja perussuomalaisten jäsenmäärät vahvassa nousussa; March 31, 2013. Accessed January 26, 2016. http://www.hs.fi/politiikka/a1364692661448

PoliticsForum.org. The Swedish Far-right isn't dumb; *Politics Forum*; 23 July 2015. Accessed October 4, 2015. http://www.politicsforum.org/forum/viewtopic.php?f=28&t=162383

Pop, Valentina. German anti-euro party broadens its platform to left and right; *EU Observer*; March 26, 2014. https://euobserver.com/eu-elections/123618

Πρίφτη, Κατερίνα. The History of SYRIZA: How A Small Party Came to Power; *Huffington Post*, Greece; January 27, 2015. http://www.huffingtonpost.com/2015/01/26/greece-SYRIZA-history_n_6547798.html

Prodhan, Georgina. Right wing strong on Europe fears ahead of Austria poll; *Reuters*; September 25, 2013.

Project Gutenberg. Popular Orthodox Rally; World Public Library; 2015. http://www.self.gutenberg.org/articles/popular_orthodox_rally

Pugliese, Stanislao G. *Fascism, Anti-fascism, and the Resistance in Italy: 1919 to the Present*; Oxford, England, UK: Rowman & Littlefield Publishers, Inc., 2004.

Putnam, Robert D. *Making Democracy Work: Civic Traditions in Modern Italy*; Princeton, NJ: Princeton University Press; 1993.

Quine, Maria Sop. *Population Politics in Twentieth Century Europe: Fascist Dictatorships and Liberal Democracies*; Abingdon, UK: Routledge, 46–47; 1995.

Radio Sweden. The Sweden Democrats – Sverigedemokraterna, 8 Augusti 2014. http://sverigesradio.se/sida/artikel.aspx?artikel=5933075

Ragin, Charles C. *Fuzzy-Set Social Science*; Chicago: University of Chicago Press; 2000.

Ragin, Charles C. *Redesigning Social Inquiry: Fuzzy Sets and Beyond*; Chicago: University of Chicago Press; 2008.

Ragin, Charles C. *The Comparative Method: Moving beyond Qualitative and Quantitative Strategies*; Berkeley: University of California Press; 1987.

Ragin, Charles C. and Rubinson, Claude. Fuzzy Set Qualitative Comparative Analysis; University of Arizona. Accessed December 4, 2015. http://www.u.arizona.edu/~cragin/fsQCA/index.shtml

Ramalingam, Vidhya. Far-Right Extremism: Trends and Methods for Response And Prevention; Policy Briefing-Institute for Strategic Dialogue, December 2012.

Ramswell, Prebble Q. Interest in the Far Right, Google Trends Data Visualization; November 7, 2015.

Rawlinson, Kevin. English Defence League prepares to storm local elections; *UK Independent;* November 25, 2011. http://www.independent.co.uk/news/uk/politics/english-defence-league-prepares-to-storm-local-elections-6267740.html

Ray, Leonard. Measuring Party Orientation towards European Integration: Results from an Expert Study, *European Journal of Political Research*; 36(2): 283–306; 1999.

Ray, Leonard. When Parties Matter: The Conditional Influence of Party Positions on Voter Opinions about European Integration, *Journal of Politics*; 65 (4): 978–994; 2003.

Religion of Peace. Race, Racism (and Islam); Religion of Peace; Accessed October 10, 2015. http://www.thereligionofpeace.com/pages/racism-trop.htm

Renton, Dave. *Fascism: Theory and Practice*; London: Pluto Press; 1999.

Renton, Dave. *Toward a Marxist Theory of Fascism*; 1997. Accessed August 23, 2014. http://www.dkrenton.co.uk/old/old3.html

Reuters. Fico favorite as Slovakia sets June 12 poll; *Reuters*; February 1, 2010. Accessed April 17, 2015. http://www.reuters.com/article/2010/02/01/us-slovakia-politics-idUSTRE6104OC20100201

Rhodes, Martin, and van Apeldoorn, Bastiaan. *Capitalism versus Capitalism in Western Developments in West European Politics*; edited by Martin Rhodes, Paul Heywood, and Vincent Wright. New York: St. Martin's Press, 171–189; 1997.

Richman, Michèle H. *Sacred Revolutions: Durkheim and the College of Sociology*; Minneapolis: University of Minnesota Press; 2002.

Right Sector. Official Website; Accessed August 18, 2015. http://pravyysektor.info/

Rihoux, Benoit and Ragin, Charles S. *Configurational Comparative Methods: Qualitative Comparative Analysis (QCA) and Related Techniques (Applied Social Research Methods*); Washington, DC: Library of Congress; 2009.

Ritzer, George. *Sociological Theory*; Third edition; New York: McGraw-Hill; 2008.

Robins-Early, Nick. A Field Guide to Europe's Radical Right Political Parties; *The Huffington Post*; February 12, 2015. http://www.huffingtonpost.com/2015/02/12/europe-far-right_n_6511022.html

Rolfe, Brett. Building an Electronic Repertoire of Contention, *Social Movement Studies*; 4(1): 65–74; May, 2005.

Rootes, Chris. A. Political Opportunity Structures: Promise, Problems and Prospects, *La Lettre de la maison Française d'Oxford*; 10: 75–97; 1999.

Roushas, Roxani. *Understanding the electoral breakthrough of Golden Dawn in Greece: A demand and supply perspective*; International Migration Institute (IMI), Oxford University Department of International Development; 2013.

Routedge. *Theories of Race*; Abingdon, UK: Routledge Encyclopedia of Philosophy: Questions to Sociobiology; 18; 1998.

Rovny, Jan. Conceptualising Party-based Euroscepticism: Magnitude and Motivations, *Collegium*; 29: 31–47; 2004.

Rt.com. Swiss anti-immigration party remains most popular – poll; June 25, 2015. http://www.rt.com/news/269737-swiss-support-anti-immigration/

Rucht, Dieter. The Impact of National Contexts on Social Movement Structures: A Cross-Movement and Cross-National Perspective. In Doug McAdam, John D. McCarthy, and Mayer Zald (eds), *Comparative Perspectives on Social Movements*, 185–204; Cambridge, UK: Cambridge University Press; 1996.

Rucht, Dieter and Friedhelm Neidhardt. The Analysis of Social Movements: the State of the Art and Some Perspectives for Further Research. In D. Rucht (ed), *Research on Social Movements: the State of the Art in Western Europe and the USA*, 443, Boulder, CO: Westview Press, 1991.

Rydgren, Jens. Explaining the Emergence of Radical Right-Wing Populist Parties: The Case of Denmark, *West European Politics*; 27(3); 474–502; 2004.

Sabin, Lamiat. Nigel Farage defends outspoken Polish MEP as 'saving' Ukip; *The Independent*, October 22, 2014.

Sagener, Nicole. Dario Sarmadi, Erika Körner. Germany's right-wing populists join hands with anti-Islamist Pegida; *EurActiv*. January 9, 2015.

Sakai, J. Confronting Fascism: Discussion Documents for a Militant Movement, Kersplebedeb and Anti-Racist Action Chicago; 2002. Accessed May 21, 2015. http://www.kersplebedeb.com/mystuff/books/fascism/shock.html

Sangsari, Marcel. Digital innovation propels political success story in Spain; *The Globe and Mail*; March 19, 2015. Accessed January 1, 2016. http://www.theglobeandmail.com/news/world/digital-innovation-propels-political-success-story-in-spain/article23542220/

Scally, Derek. German anti-Islam group Pegida presents six-point plan on immigration rules; *Irish Times*; January 12, 2015. http://www.irishtimes.com/news/world/europe/german-anti-islam-group-pegida-presents-six-point-plan-on-immigration-rules-1.2063543

Scarrow, Susan. *Multispeed membership parties.* Paper prepared for "Contemporary Meanings of Party Membership", ECPR Joint Sessions of Workshops, Salamanca, Spain; April 10–15, 2014.

Schulman, Moritz Josef. Pegida Spokesman: We are no Nazis; *YNet Magazine News*; January 24, 2015. http://www.ynetnews.com/articles/0,7340,L-4618182,00.html

Schulze, Ingo. Pegida: Germany's useful idiots; *The Guardian*; February 1, 2015. http://www.theguardian.com/world/2015/feb/01/pegida-germanys-useful-idiots

Schwab, Sabine and Joyner, Alfred. From Pegida to Syriza: The rise of radical Europe; *International Business Times;* Accessed February 6, 2015. http://www.ibtimes.co.uk/pegida-syriza-rise-radical-europe-1486915

Schneider, Carsten Q. and Wagemann, Claudius. Standards of Good Practice in Qualitative Comparative Analysis (QCA) and Fuzzy-Sets, *Comparative Sociology*; 9: 1–22; 2010.

Serricchio, Fabio, Myrto Tsakatika and Lucia Quaglia. Euroscepticism and the Global Financial Crisis, *Journal of Common Market Studies*; 51(1): 51–64; 2013.

Sheppard, Charlotte. Online news consumption in Europe; PageSuite; 08 June 2015. Accessed December 28, 2015. http://www.pagesuite.com/blog/blog_story.aspx?storyID=2051

Shuster, Simon. Meet the German Activist Leading the Movement Against 'Islamization;' *Time Magazine*; January 15, 2015. http://time.com/3668889/pegida-germany-islamization/

Siddi, Marco. Rising Euroscepticism and the dominance of national interests, EU-28 Watch- Issue 10*; Institut für Europäische Politik*, Berlin; 2014. Accessed July 7, 2015. http://eu-28watch.org/issues/issue-no-10/rising-euroscepticism-and-the-dominance-of-national-interests/

Skenderovic, Damir. The SVP: A success story of right-wing populism; Policy Network; January 21, 2013. http://www.policy-network.net/pno_detail.aspx?ID=4317&title=The-SVP-A-success-story-of-right-wing-populism

Skocpol, Theda. Bringing the State Back In: Strategies of Analysis in Current Research. In Peter B. Evans, Dietrich Rueschemeyer, and Theda Skocpol (eds), *Bringing the State Back In*, 3–37, Cambridge: Cambridge University Press, 1985.

Sliwinski, Michael. "Right-Wing Groups in Europe: A Rising Force?;" Law Street Media. Last Modified January 2015. Accessed January 2, 2016. http://lawstreetmedia.com/issues/world/declining-europe-leads-rise-right-wing-groups/

Smelser, Neil J. *Theory of Collective Behavior*; New York: Free Press; 1963.

Smith, Dr. Evan. "Defining fascism: some notes on the Marxist interpretation." From his blog: Hatful of History. December 14, 2012. Accessed October 18, 2014. https://hatfulofhistory.wordpress.com/2012/12/14/defining-fascism-some-notes-on-the-marxist-interpretation/

Smith, Helena. Greece's Golden Dawn party describes Hitler as 'great personality;' *The Guardian*; April 16, 2014. http://www.theguardian.com/world/2014/apr/16/greece-golden-dawn-hitler

Smith, Philip. Durkheim and Criminology: Reconstructing the Legacy, *Australian & New Zealand Journal of Criminology* (Australian Academic Press); 41(3): 333–344; 2008.

Smythe, S. A. Italy Is Not Just Racist, It's Anti-Black; *Okay Africa*, August 1, 2013. http://www.okayafrica.com/news/italy-racism-anti-black-cecile-kyenge/

Snow, David A., Soule, Sarah A. and Kriesi, Hanspeter (eds). *The Blackwell Companion to Social Movements*; Hoboken, NJ: Blackwell Publishing; 2004.

Solsten, Eric (ed). *Austria: A Country Study*; Washington: GPO for the Library of Congress, 1994.

Sorenson, Catharina. "Love me, love me not…A typology of public euroscepticism;" Sussex European Institute, Working Paper 101; January 2008.

Speigel. Interview with Marine Le Pen: 'I Don't Want this European Soviet Union;' *Speigel* Online International; Interview Conducted by Mathieu von Rohr; June 3, 2014. http://www.spiegel.de/international/europe/interview-with-french-front-national-leader-marine-le-pen-a-972925.html

Speigel.de. Anti-Semitism in Parliament: Hungary's Far-Right Rhetoric Reaches New Dimension; By Keno Verseck; November 28, 2012. Accessed February

4, 2014. http://www.spiegel.de/international/europe/far-right-rhetoric-in-hungary-reaches-new-dimension-a-869826.html

Spiegel, Peter. Alexis Tsipras: Greece's radical or realist? *Financial Times*; January 23, 2015. http://www.ft.com/intl/cms/s/0/301636be-a2e6–11e4–9c06–00144feab7de.html#axzz3npD6botJ

Squires, Nick. 'Independence for northern Italy and an end to euro, says Northern League leader;' *The Telegraph*, Dec 16, 2013. http://www.telegraph.co.uk/news/worldnews/europe/italy/10520482/Independence-for-northern-Italy-and-an-end-to-euro-says-Northern-League-leader.html

Squires, Nick. What is the Golden Dawn trial about? *The Telegraph*, April 20, 2015. http://www.telegraph.co.uk/news/worldnews/europe/greece/11548387/What-is-the-Golden-Dawn-trial-about.html

Stanley, Tim. English Defence League leader endorses Ukip. This is a nightmare for Nigel Farage; *The Telegraph*; April 4, 2013. http://blogs.telegraph.co.uk/news/timstanley/100210451/english-defence-league-leader-endorses-ukip-this-is-a-nightmare-for-nigel-farage/

Sternhell, Zeev. *The Birth of Fascist Ideology: From Cultural Rebellion to Political Revolution*; Princeton, NJ: Princeton University Press; 1995.

Stockemer, Daniel. The Swiss Radical Right: Who are the New Voters of the Swiss Peoples` Party? *Representation*; 48(2): 197–208; 2012. http://blogs.lse.ac.uk/europpblog/2012/09/17/swiss-peoples-party-stockemer/

Stokes, Bruce. Euroskepticism Beyond Brexit. Pew Research Center. June 7, 2016. Accessed August 25, 2016. http://www.pewglobal.org/2016/06/07/euroskepticism-beyond-brexit

Stokes, Bruce. *Faith in European Project Reviving*: Chapter 4. The Rise of Nontraditional, Eurosceptic Parties; Pew Research Center; June 2, 2015.

Sundberg, Jan. Who are the nationalist Finns Party? *BBC News*; May 11, 2015. http://www.bbc.com/news/world-europe-32627013

Svoboda.org. Official Svoboda website; 2015. Accessed October 6, 2015. http://en.svoboda.org.ua/about/program/

SVP.ch. Swiss People's Party Official Website; Accessed August 18, 2015.

Swank, D. and Betz, H. G. "Right-wing populism in Western Europe: The impact of structural change, political institutions, and economic performance on party electoral fortunes in 16 nations;" Paper presented at the annual meeting of the American Political Science Association, Chicago; 1995.

Switzerland Business Law Handbook. Washington, DC: International Business Publications, USA; 2012.

Szczerbiak, Aleks and Taggart, Paul (eds). *Opposing Europe? The Comparative Party Politics of Euroscepticism. Vol. 1: Case Studies and Country Surveys*; Oxford: Oxford University Press; 2008a.

Szczerbiak, Aleks and Taggart, Paul (eds). *Opposing Europe? The Comparative Party Politics of Euroscepticism. Vol. 2: Comparative and Theoretical Perspectives*; Oxford: Oxford University Press; 2008b.

Taggart, Paul. A Touchstone of Dissent: Euroscepticism in Contemporary Western European Party Systems, *European Journal of Political Research*; 33(3): 363–388; 1998.

Taggart, Paul and Szczerbiak, Aleks. Contemporary Euroscepticism in the Systems of the European Union Candidate States of Central and Eastern Europe, *European Journal of Political Research*; 43(1): 1–27; January 2004.

Taggart, Paul and Szczerbiak, Aleks. "Parties, positions and Europe: Euroscepticism in the EU candidate states of Central and Eastern Europe;" Opposing Europe, Sussex European Institute, Working Paper, no. 461–38, 2001.

Taguieff, Pierre-André. Discussion or Inquisition: The Case of Alain de Benoist, *Telos*; 98–99: 54; Winter 1993–Spring 1994.

Tarrow, Sidney. Contentious Politics in a Composite Polity. Chapter Eleven in Doug Imig and Sidney Tarrow (eds). *Contentious Europeans: Protest and Politics in an Emerging Polity*. Rowman and Littlefield, 2001.

Tarrow, Sidney. Cycles of Collective Action: Between Movements of Madness and the Repertoire of Contention. In Mark Traugott (ed), *Repertoires and Cycles of Collective Action*, Durham and London: Duke University Press, 1995.

Tarrow, Sidney. *Democracy and Disorder: Protest and Politics in Italy*, 1965–1975; Oxford, UK: Clarendon Press; 1989.

Tarrow, Sidney. National Politics and Collective Action, Recent Theory and Research in Western Europe and the USA, *Annual Review of Sociology*; 14: 421–440; 1988.

Tarrow, Sidney G. *Power in Movement: Social Movements, Collective Action and Politics*; Cambridge, UK: Cambridge University Press; [1994] 1998.

Tarrow, Sidney G. *Struggle, Politics, and Reform: collective action, social movements, and cycles of protest*. Western Studies Program Occasional Paper No. 21; 2nd Edition; Ithaca, NY: Cornell University Center for International Studies; 1989, 1991.

Tarrow, Sidney. *The New Transnational Activism*; Cambridge, MA: Cambridge University Press; 2005.

Tavits, Margit. Organizing for Success: Party Organizational Strength and Electoral Performance in Postcommunist Europe, *The Journal of Politics*; 74(01): 83–97; January 2012.

Taylor, Matthew. English Defence League: Inside the violent world of Britain's new far right; *The Guardian*; May 28, 2010. Accessed May 5, 2015. www.theguardian.com/uk/2010/may/28/english-defence-league-guardian-investigation

Teitelbaum, Benjamin R. Sweden's Fraying Tolerance; *NY Times*. September 16, 2014. http://www.nytimes.com/2014/09/17/opinion/swedens-fraying-tolerance.html?_r=0

Terry, Chris. Party for Freedom (PVV); The Democratic Society-Europe; May 11, 2014. Accessed August 12, 2015. http://www.demsoc.org/deme/europe/blog/party-for-freedom-pvv/

The Encyclopedia of Marxism. Fascism; Last modified 2008. Accessed June 27, 2015. https://www.marxists.org/encyclopedia/terms/f/a.htm#fascism

The Flemish Republic. Newspaper published by the Flemish Independence Party Vlaams Belang; 2015. http://www.flemishrepublic.org/4/

The Flemish Republic. Police Violence: Vlaams Belang Vindicated; *Flemish Republic*; May 25, 2009. Accessed November 14, 2015. http://www.flemishrepublic.org/8/28

The Fondation Robert Schuman. Parliamentary Elections in Belgium; 25th May 2014. http://www.robert-schuman.eu/en/doc/oee/oee-1516-en.pdf

The Turkey Analyst. The CHP Congress, Leadership Cults, and Turkish Democracy; *The Turkey Analyst*; May 8, 2008. http://www.turkeyanalyst.org/publications/turkey-analyst-articles/item/122-the-chp-congress-leadership-cults-and-turkish-democracy.html

The United States Department of State. Country Reports on Human Rights Practices for 2011: Greece; Bureau of Democracy, Human Rights and Labor; 2011. http://www.state.gov/documents/organization/186569.pdf

Thiem, Alrik. Conditions of Intergovernmental Armaments Cooperation in Western Europe, 1996–2006, *European Political Science Review*; 3(1):1–33, 2011.

Thiem, Alrik and Dusa, Adrian. QCA: A Package for Qualitative Comparative Analysis, *The R Journal*; 5/1; June, 2013.

Thomas, James, O'Mara-Eves, Alison and Brunton, Ginny. *Using qualitative comparative analysis (QCA) in systematic reviews of complex interventions: a worked example*; National Center for Biotechnology Information, U.S. National Library of Medicine; June 20, 2014.

Thorlindsson, Thorolfur. Durkheim's Theory of Social Order and Deviance: a Multilevel Test, *European Sociological Review*; 20(4): 271–285; 2004.

Thran, Malte and Boehnke, Lukas. The Value-based Nationalism of Pegida, *Journal for Deradicalization*; 3; 2015.

Tilly, Charles. Contentious repertoires in Great Britain, 1758–1834, In M. Traugott (ed.), *Repertoires and Cycles of Collective Action*; Durham, NC: Duke University Press; 1995.

Tilly, Charles. *From Mobilization to Revolution*; New York: McGraw-Hill; 1978.

Tilly, Charles. *The Contentious French*; Cambridge, MA: Belknap Press; 1986.

Tomasino, Arthur P. Fuzzy-set Qualitative Comparative Analysis Summary. Working paper. Bentley University; 2015.

Tostes, Ana Paula. Explaining Intolerance in an Integrated Europe, *Dados – Revista de Ciências Sociais*; 52(2): 335–376; 2009.

Tremlett, Giles. The Podemos revolution: how a small group of radical academics changed European politics; *The Guardian*; March 31, 2015. http://www.theguardian.com/world/2015/mar/31/podemos-revolution-radical-academics-changed-european-politics

TRTWorld. Left-wing CHP asks Erdogan for right to form coalition govt; August 18, 2015. http://beta.trtworld.com/turkey/left-wing-chp-asks-erdogan-for-right-to-form-coalition-govt-6244, Accessed November 14, 2015.

The Turkey Analyst. The CHP Congress, Leadership Cults, and Turkish Democracy; *The Turkey Analyst*; May 8, 2008. http://www.turkeyanalyst.org/publications/turkey-analyst-articles/item/122-the-chp-congress-leadership-cults-and-turkish-democracy.html

Tzilivakis, Kathy. Heated reactions to far-right ministers; *IRED;* November 19, 2011.

Tzur, Nissan. EXCLUSIVE: Ukip's far-right Euro partner attacks 'Holocaust industry; *Jewish Chronicle* Online; October 21, 2014. http://www.thejc.com/news/uk-news/124483/exclusive-ukips-far-right-euro-partner-attacks-holocaust-industry

Udland, Myles. There's a new political risk looming in Europe; *Business Insider/Berenburg*; September 6, 2015. http://www.businessinsider.com/european-nationalism-risk-2015–9

US Department of State. Country Reports on Human Rights Practices for 2007; *Committee on Foreign Affairs*; August 2008.

Üstüntağ, Gülten. CHP strives to be central party by pursuing new policy direction; *Today's Zaman*; September 6, 2014. http://www.todayszaman.com/anasayfa_chp-strives-to-be-central-party-by-pursuing-new-policy-direction_357862.html

Uzun, Melih and Kaleagasi, Bartu. Erdogan's AKP loses majority government to progressive HDP; Turkish Election results; *Social Humanist*; June 7, 2015.

van Noort, Wim. *Bevlogen Bewegingen: Een vergelijking van de anti-kernenergie-kraak- en milieubeweging*; Amsterdam: SUA; 1988.

van Versendaal, Harry. The genealogy of violence; As Golden Dawn extremism grows, some critics blame chronic tolerance of left-wing radicalism; ΗΚΑΘΗΜΕΡΙΝΗ; July 1, 2013. Accessed July 7, 2015. http://www.ekathimerini.com/147443/article/ekathimerini/comment/the-genealogy-of-violence

Vasilopoulou, Sofia. European Integration and the Radical Right: Three Patterns of Opposition, *Government and Opposition*; 46(2): 223–244; 2011.

Vasilopoulou, Sofia and Halikiopoulou, Daphne. *Golden Dawn's 'nationalist solution': explaining the rise of the far-right in Greece*; London School of Economics and Political Science. Last modified May 12, 2015. http://blogs.lse.ac.uk/europpblog/2015/05/12/golden-dawns-nationalist-solution-explaining-the-rise-of-the-far-right-in-greece/

Vis, B. Governments and Unpopular Social Policy Reform: Biting the Bullet or Steering Clear? *European Journal of Political Research*; 48(1): 31–57; 2009.

Von Storch Interview. Interview with Beatrix von Storch, chairman of the Civil Coalition e. V.; 2011. http://www.swg-hamburg.de/Beitrage_aus_der_Rubrik_-_Kult/Die_Gesellschaft_kann_nicht_das_leisten.pdf

Wagner-Nagy, Thomas. "Far-Right Parties in the European Parliament;" University for Peace. January 5, 2015. Accessed August 12, 2015. http://www.monitor.upeace.org/innerpg.cfm?id_article=1074

Wagsty, Stefan. Europe's resurgent far-right seeks to capitalise on Paris terror; *Financial Times*; Accessed January 8, 2015. http://www.ft.com/cms/s/0/6d29ce92–974e-11e4–9636–00144feabdc0.html#slide0

Walsh, Jason. "Has Europe turned fascist, really?" *Vox Europe*; Last modified May 2014. http://www.voxeurop.eu/en/content/blog/4770241-has-europe-turned-fascist-really

Waterfield, Bruno. European Parliament to ban Eurosceptic groups; *The Telegraph*; May 27, 2008. Accessed October 12, 2014. http://www.telegraph.co.uk/news/politics/2038813/European-Parliament-to-ban-Eurosceptic-groups.html

Weber, Max. *Economy and Society: An Outline of Interpretive Sociology*; New York: Bedminster Press; 1968.

Weber, Max. *The Protestant Ethic and the Spirit of Capitalism*; New York: The Citadel Press, [1904] 1930.

Weber, Max. *The Religion of India: The Sociology of Hinduism unil Buddhism*; edited by H. H. Gerth and D. Martindale. New York: The Free Press; [1919] 1958.

Weber, Max. *The Theory of Social and Economic Organization*; Easford, CT: Martino Fine Books, [1964] 1982.

Weissman, George Lavan. *Leon Trotsky's FASCISM: What It Is and How to Fight It*; Pioneer Publishers; April 1969. Accessed March 20, 2015. https://www.marxists.org/archive/trotsky/works/1944/1944-fas.htm

Wellings, Ben. "English nationalism and Euroscepticism overlap and support each other in important ways;" London School of Economics; April, 2014. Accessed February 13, 2015. http://blogs.lse.ac.uk/politicsandpolicy/english-nationalism-and-euroscepticism/

Wessels, Bernhard. Roles and orientations of members of parliament in the EU context: Congruence or difference? Europeanisation or not? *The Journal of Legislative Studies*; 11(3): 446–65; 2005.

West, Ed. UKIP are not 'far Right'. There's nothing extremist about rejecting the 'benefits of diversity; *The Telegraph*; March, 12 2012. Accessed July 3, 2015. http://blogs.telegraph.co.uk/news/edwest/100143056/ukip-are-not-far-right-theres-nothing-extremist-about-rejecting-the-benefits-of-diversity/

Wheeler, Brian and Hunt, Alex. Brexit: All you need to know about the UK leaving the EU; *BBC News*; August 24, 2016. Accessed August 24, 2016. http://www.bbc.com/news/uk-politics-32810887

White, Jonathan. The Politicisation of the EU in Sociological Perspective; Workshop: 'Does European Integration Theory need Sociology? Towards a Research Agenda;' ECPR Joint Sessions, Rennes, 11th-16th April 2008. Accessed March 12, 2015. http://ecpr.eu/Filestore/PaperProposal/6e762d2d-0e77–4171–8783–342dc9dd1ea9.pdf

Wickham-Crowley, Timothy. P. A Qualitative Comparative Approach to Latin American Revolutions, *International Journal of Comparative Sociology*; 32(1–2): 82–109; 1991.

Wintour, Patrick and Watt, Nicholas. Ukip wins European elections with ease to set off political earthquake; *The Guardian*; May 25, 2014.

World Justice Project. WJP Open Government Index; Washington, DC; 2015. Accessed various 2014, 2015. http://worldjusticeproject.org/open-government-index

Yahoo News. "Ukrainian ultranationalist party Svoboda, a history of violence;" Yahoo News; August 31, 2015. http://news.yahoo.com/ukrainian-ultranationalist-party-svoboda-history-violence-211617262.html

Yakovenko, Alexander. Russia–EU relations: Between sanctions and broader European integration; *Russia Today* (RT), TV-Novosti. July 7, 2016. Accessed August 25, 2016. https://www.rt.com/op-edge/349896-russia-eu-relations-sanctions/

Yale University. *Nazi Conspiracy and Aggression Volume IV*; Lillian Goldman Law Library; Yale University, 2008. Accessed November 29, 2015. http://avalon.law.yale.edu/imt/1708-ps.asp

Yilmaz, F. Right-wing Hegemony and Immigration: How the Populist Far-right Achieved Hegemony through the Immigration Debate in Europe, *Current Sociology*; 60: 368–382; 2012.

Zabala, Santiago. Far-left Podemos has already changed Spain; *Al Jazeera*. May 18, 2015.

Zaslove, Andrej. *The Re-invention of the European Radical Right: Populism, Regionalism, and the Italian Lega Nord*; Kingston, Canada: McGill- Queen's University Press; 2011.

Zawadzki, Sabina, Hosenball, Mark and Grey, Stephen. In Ukraine, nationalists gain influence - and scrutiny; *Chicago Tribune/Reuters*; March 18, 2014. Accessed June 17, 2015. http://articles.chicagotribune.com/2014–03–18/news/sns-rt-us-ukraine-crisis-farright-insight-20140318_1

Zimmer, Oliver. *Nationalism in Europe, 1890–1940*, Chapter 4, pp. 80–107. London: Palgrave; 2003.

Index

9/11, 72, 92, 113–15

Alternative for Germany (AfD), 18, 39, 42, 43, 93, 105, 107, 108, 118, 119, 122, 123, 130, 131, 142, 148
anomie, 27, 98.
  See also Durkheim, Emile
anti-austerity, 73
anti-elitism, 20
anti-establishment parties, 17
anti-immigrant, 4, 18, 42, 56, 67, 69, 82–83, 92, 120
anti-Muslim, 44, 57
anti-Semitic, 37, 116;
  as a variable, 40–96
anti-Semitism, 35, 37
ATAKA, 39, 43–45, 94, 115
Austria, 4, 18, 39, 56–58, 66, 78, 93–94, 105, 107–8, 110, 112, 114, 120, 123, 126, 155.
  See also Freedom Party of Austria
authoritarian regime, 10, 33–34, 36, 61

Bachmann, Lutz, 71–72
Belgium, 5, 16–18, 40, 58, 91, 93–94, 105, 107, 110, 112, 118, 125, 128, 130;
  Flemish Block, 2;
  Flemish Interest, 91.
  See also Vlaams Belang
Berlin Wall, 29, 113–17.
  See also Fall of the Wall
Brexit, 153–54, 157
Britain. *See* United Kingdom
Bulgaria, 39, 43–45, 94, 114–15.
  See also ATAKA

causal conditions, 97–142, 143, 146, 148, 150, 158–59;
  analysis, 105–42;
  data compilation, 105–42
CHP. *See* Republican People's Party (Turkey)
clash of civilizations, 114, 116
cleavage theory, 20
coglbeur. *See* cognitive liberation, euroscepticism
coglibnat. *See* cognitive liberation, nationalism
cognitive liberation, 98, 101–2, 105–6, 109–10, 121, 133, 135–37, 140;
  attachment to country, 112;
  confidence in the EU, 111;
  data compilation, 109–13;
  euroscepticism, 110;
  how proud of nationality, 112;
  nationalism, 110–13;
  as PP causal condition, 109–13;

trust in the EU, 110.
See also Political Process Model (PP) components
collective action, 27, 99–100, 102, 118
collective effervescence, 21.
See also Durkheim, Emile
confidence in the EU, *110*–11
Congress of the New Right, 18, 39, 45, 94
Conservative Party of Romania, 18
considea. *See* consistent ideology
consistency, 103, 118
consistent ideology, 118–20, 133, 140, 146, 148, 150–51, 158.
See also Organizational/Opportunity Model (OO) components
consistent leadership, 118–20, 146–51, 158.
See also Organizational/Opportunity Model (OO) components
consldr. *See* consistent leadership
cultural change, 113–17, 153, 158;
cultural shift, 158;
following trigger event, 115–17;
as result of opportunity, 115.
See also Organizational/Opportunity Model (OO) components

Danish People's Party, 4, 18, 39, 47, 48, 93, 107, 108, 119, 126
Denmark, 1, 4, 18, 39, 47–48, 94, 105, 107, 110, 112, 122–23
Durkheim, Emile, 27, 98
Dutch Freedom Party (PVV), 18, 39, 48–50, 72, 93–94, 105, 107–9, 118, 120, 124, 127, 130–32

Eatwell, Roger, 8, 12, 32, 50
Eco, Umberto, 11
economic freedom, 106–7;
data compilation, 107
Eisinger, Peter, 99, 106.
See also political opportunity
England, 4, 13, 16, 19, 39, 40, 50, 51, 88, 105, 107, 118, 125, 127;
Conservative Party (England), 16;
English Defence League (EDL), 39, 50;
Englishness, 19
equifinality, 134
Euro-critical, 18, 43
Euroenthusiast, 22
Euro-nationalist, 91
European integration, 3, 16, 21, 22, 36, 41, 114, 117, 121
European Parliament, 1, 3–5, 15–23, 26–28, 30–31, 33, 37, 41, 43–50, 52, 54–55, 57–62, 64–65, 68, 70–82, 85, 87, 89–90, 98, 102, 109–11, 114–15, 118–21, 128, 134, 139, 153–57;
Christian Democrats, 49;
European Conservatives and Reformists, 18, 22, 37, 42, 48;
European Democrats, 18;
European Free Alliance, 19;
European People's Party, 18;
European United Left, 18, 19, 37, 74;
Europe of Freedom and Democracy, 17;
Europe of Nations, 18, 19, 29, 57, 64;
Europe of Nations and Freedom (ENF), 18–19;
The Greens, 19;
MEP, 4, 16, 18, 42–43, 46, 54, 118;
Nordic Green Left, 18, 19, 37, 74;
Party of European Socialists, 18
European Union (EU), 1, 16, 23, 39–94, 110, 155–56;
in determining euroscepticism, 39–94;
non-Inscrit, 16;
Treaty on European Union, 23;
Union for Europe of the Nations, 19.
See also euroscepticism; Eurosceptics
Europhobe, 22
Eurorealist, 22
Euroreject, 17, 22, 30

Eurosceptic, 2–4, 15–23, 28–30, 35, 37, 41, 43–48, 50, 52–53, 55–56, 58, 60, 62, 64–65, 68, 70, 72, 74, 76–77, 79, 81, 83, 85, 88, 90, 93, 98, 101, 106, 109, 120, 128, 158;
  defined, 3;
  as a qualifier for MF, 40–41
euroscepticism, 3, 15, 17, 19, 21–23, 31, 36, 97, 109, 110, 133;
  categorization, 15;
  definition, 3;
  degrees, 15;
  factors of, 22;
  historical shift to, 3;
  North Carolina School, 22;
  North Carolina/Sussex debate, 22;
  variety of causes for rise, 20
Eurozone, 22, 106
extreme right, 29, 59, 61, 64, 66, 69, 80, 114, 121.
  See also far-right

Fall of the Wall (FOTW), 113–17, 158;
  as oppportunity in OO model, 113.
  See also Berlin Wall
Farage, Nigel, 4, 18, 89, 90, 120, 154.
  See also United Kingdom Independence Party
far-right, 2, 4–5, 17–18, 20, 28, 30, 32, 44, 57–61, 71, 76, 91, 113, 155–57;
  interest in far right over time, *28*.
  See also extreme right; radical right
fascism, 1–15, 23, 25–29, 31–39, 52–54, 61, 97–98, 100–101, 105, 117, 153, 155, 157–59, 164;
  categorizing, 31;
  as described by Mussolini, 37;
  difficulty in defining, 7;
  fascist minimum, 10;
  five stages of fascism, 11;
  Marxist interpretation, 26;
  as Millennial Fascism, 25–37;
  modern lens, 12–14;
  negative connotation, 12, 25, 32, 36;
  new threat in new era, 1–7;
  revival of, 26;
  similarity to euroscepticism, 25–31;
  single definition, 32;
  Third Way, 32;
  traditional fascism, 25, 32–33;
  traditional lens, 8–12
Fascism and Freedom Movement, 39, 52–53, 94
Finland, 39, 54–56, 94, 105, 107, 110, 112, 114, 122
Finns Party, 39, 54–56, 93–94, 105, 107–8, 118–19, 123, 126, 130–31, 155
Five Star Movement, 45, 155
FN. *See* Front National
FOTW. *See* Fall of the Wall
FPÖ. *See* Freedom Party of Austria
France, 4, 9, 13, 16, 17, 18, 19, 30, 34, 39, 59, 60, 64, 105, 107, 110, 112, 122, 124, 126, 154;
  Socialist Party (France), 19.
  See also Front National; Le Pen, Marine
freedom from corruption, 106–7, 137, 158;
  data compilation, 107
  table, *107*
Freedom Party of Austria (FPÖ), 4, 18
Front National (FN), 4, 13, 18, 19, 29, 31, 39, 58, 59, 60, 93, 105, 107, 108, 118, 120, 124, 126, 131, 155.
  See also Le Pen, Marine
fsQCA, 105, 107–8, 118, 122, 131–36, 142, 150.
  See also QCA

gay marriage, 46, 53, 92
Gentile, Emilio, 8, 13, 34
Germany, 4, 8, 13, 16–18, 34, 36, 39–40, 42–43, 64, 69–72, 74, 88, 93, 94, 105, 107–8, 110, 113–14, 116, 119, 121–23, 130, 154.
  See also Alternative for Germany; National Democratic Party of Germany; Pegida
Goebbels, Josef, 56, 80, 121

Golden Dawn, 4, 18, 30, 32, 39, 61, 62, 65, 155
Great Britain. *See* United Kingdom
Greece, 20, 30, 32, 37, 39–40, 61, 64–65, 86, 88, 94, 105, 107, 110, 112, 118, 125, 127, 130.
  See also Golden Dawn; LAOS; Syriza
Griffin, Roger, 7, 8, 9, 10, 11, 12, 23, 25, 29, 32, 34, 36, 37, 108, 116, 117, 159
Grillo, Beppe, 18, 73.
  See also Five Star Movement

Haider, Jorg, 28, 56, 57.
  See also Freedom Party of Austria
hard euroscepticism, 21.
  See also euroscepticism
Hitler, Adolf, 5, 7–8, 12, 34, 46, 56, 62, 72, 114, 116, 121, 153
Holocaust industry, 46
homophobic ideology:
  homophobia, 48;
  as a qualifier for MF, 39–94
Hungary, 114, 156.
  See also Jobbik
Huntington, Samuel, 114, 116.
  See also clash of civilizations

ideological consistency. *See* Organizational/Opportunity (OO) Model components
ideology, 5, 7, 10–11, 13, 22, 26, 29–41, 44, 52–53, 57, 59, 61, 68, 75, 78, 81, 84, 93, 103, 118–21, 133, 140–41, 146, 148, 150–51, 158;
  as causal condition, 118–20.
  See also consistent ideology
Iglesias, Pablo, 73–74, 86.
  See also Podemos
immigration, 5, 19, 20, 21, 48, 49, 50, 52, 53, 55, 56, 57, 58, 59, 60, 61, 65, 66, 72, 73, 82, 83, 84, 85, 86, 90, 106, 119, 120, 154, 157
indigenous organizational strength, 98, 101, 105–6, 108, 133, 136, 143, 146, 148–51;
  data compilation, 108;
  description, 98–101;
  membership size, 108–9;
  as PP causal condition, 108–9
indorgst. See indigenous organizational strength
Islamic invasion, 13
Islamization, 58, 71–72
Islamophobia, 41
Italy, 8, 13, 16–17, 34, 39, 52–54, 66–69, 73, 94, 122, 128, 154;
  Fascism and Freedom Movement, 39, 52–53, 94;
  Five Star Movement, 18, 73;
  Grillo, Beppe, 18, 73;
  Italian fascism, 13

Jobbik, 4, 13, 18, 30, 39, 63, 64, 115, 155, 156

Kallis, Aristotle, 8, 29
Kitsikis, Dimitri, 9, 10, 33;
  list of fascist values, 9
Kjærsgaard, Pia, 47, 119.
  See also Danish People's Party
KNP. *See* Congress of the New Right
Korwin-Mikke, Janusz, 45–47.
  See also Congress of the New Right

LAOS, 66, 94
Laqueuer, Walter, 8, 23
left-wing, 34, 37–38, 61, 72, 75, 86, 88, 120
Lega Nord, 18, 39, 66–68
Le Pen, Marine, 14, 19, 28–29, 59, 60, 120–22, 155, 156.
  See also Front National

Maastricht Treaty, 16, 23, 88, 114
manifesto, 44, 55, 64, 66, 72, 78–79, 81–83, 86, 88, 90–92, 120, 129–31

marketing presence, 121–28, 133, 139–41, 146–48, 150–51, 158;
as causal condition, 121–28
markpres. *See* marketing presence
Marx, Karl, 25, 98
Marxist(m), 7, 8, 12, 26, 27, 29, 34, 98. *See also* Marx, Karl
McAdam, Doug, 109, 121, 143. *See also* Political Process Theory (PPT)
media mentions, 131–*32,* 142;
scoring, 131–32
Members of European Parliament (MEP), 4, 5, 16–18, 42–43, 45, 155;
as measure of organizational aptitude, 117–18
Merkel, Angela, 71, 74
Meyer, David, 99–100, 102. *See also* political opportunity
Millennial Fascism (MF), 5, 9, 23, 25, 31, 35, 37–39, 100–101, 105, 153–59;
causal conditions, 97–103;
characteristics, 35–38;
defining, 35–38;
description, 38;
elements for success, 158;
evidence for, 31–33;
genesis, 105;
global impact, 156;
impact on economy, 154;
impact on the United States, 157;
implications, 153–59;
new category of fascism, 31;
rise, 1–5;
Russian influence, 154–56;
traits, 36–38;
variables, 40–41
Millennial Fascist Group (MFG), 15, 23, 39–95, 118, 129, 130, 131, 132, 133, 135, 136, 143, 146, 148, 153, 158;
analysis of causal conditions, 105–43;
causal conditons for success, 97–103;
elements leading to rise, 143–51;
qualification, 39–95;
qualification results, *94*
qualified parties, 93;
Mudde, Cas, 21, 22, 114
multiculturalism, 21
Mussolini, Benito, 1, 5, 7–8, 13, 26, 37, 53
Mussolinism, 13

National Democratic Party of Germany (NPD), 39, 69–70, 94
nationalism, 2–3, 5, 27, 33–35, 39–94, 109–13, 133–51, 157–59;
analysis as causal condition, 134–39;
attachment to country, *112*;
as cognitive liberation, 109–13;
compatibility with right-wing, 31;
extremism, 31;
how proud of nationality, *112*–13;
irrational doctrine, 27;
neo-nationalism, 20;
as a qualifier for MF, 39–94
nationalist/reformist ideology:
as a qualifier for MF, 40–41. *See also* Organizational/Opportunity Model (OO) components
Nazi, 30, 34–36, 43, 56–58, 70, 77, 79, 82, 114, 121
Nazism. *See* Nazi
necessary conditions, 141, 143, 150
neo-fascist, 7, 13, 30, 34, 40, 53, 77
neo-Nazi, 4, 18, 33–35, 40, 53, 57, 62, 70, 81, 121
neo-Nazism, 33–35. *See also* Neo-Nazi
Netherlands, 16–17, 39, 48–50, 64, 94, 105, 107, 110, 112, 124. *See also* Dutch Freedom Party; Wilders, Geert
Nolte, Ernst, 8, 12;
three faces of fascism, 12

non anti-Semitic/racist/homophobic:
as a qualifier for MF, 40–41
non-racist, 60;
as a qualifier for MF, 40–41
non-violent, 2, 37, 40–94;
as a qualifier for MF, 40–41
Northern League, 66–68

occurring post-Cold War:
as a qualifier for MF, 40–41
online marketing presence, 121–28.
See also Organizational/Opportunity Model (OO) components
opportunity. *See* political opportunity
opposition to EU, 22;
six-point scale, 21
organizational aptitude, 117–18;
as MEP in OO model, 118.
See also Organizational/Opportunity Model (OO) components
Organizational/Opportunity Model (OO), 101–3, 105, 113–33, 139–43, 146–51.
See also testing and analysis of models
Organizational/Opportunity Model (OO) components:
consistent ideology, 118–20;
consistent leadership, 118–20;
cultural change, 115;
media mentions, 130–31;
online marketing presence, 121–28;
opportunity, 113;
organizational aptitude, 117–18;
public outreach, 128–32;
success as MEP, 118
Organizational/Opportunity Model (OO) theory, 101–3;
Structural Organizational Theory, 101
Orwell, George, 2, 7

palingenetic ultranationalism, 8, 11, 32, 116–17;
palingenesis, 11, 116.
See also Griffin, Roger
parsimonious result, 135, 140, 144–45, 148–50
Party of Professors, 42
Party of the Swedes, 40, 71, 94
Paxton, Robert, 1, 8–9, 11, 13–15, 17, 23, 66, 115–16;
five stages of fascism, 11;
three main components, 9
Payne, Stanley, 8–12, 29, 33;
typology of fascism, *10*
Pegida, 40, 71–72, 94
Perussuomalaiset. *See* Finns Party
Podemos, 40, 73–74, 93–94, 96, 105, 107–8, 118, 120, 124, 126, 128–31, 139, 142, 145, 148
Poland, 18, 39, 45–47, 94, 114
political opportunity, 31, 32, 98–108, 116, 133, 135, 136, 140, 143–48, 150–51;
freedom from corruption, 107;
openness of government, 106;
as result of trigger event, 22, 50, 99, 102–3, 113–17, 158–59.
See also Political Process Model (PP) components; Organizational/Opportunity Model (OO) components
Political Process Model (PP) components:
cognitive liberation, 109;
cognitive liberation, euroscepticism, 109–10;
cognitive liberation, nationalism, 110–13;
indigenous organizational strength, 108–9;
political opportunity, 106–7;
success as MEP, 118, 133.
See also testing and analysis of models
Political Process Theory (PPT), 98–102;
critiques, 102
polopp. *See* political opportunity
Popular Orthodox Rally. *See* LAOS

populism, 3, 5, 29, 31, 37, 38, 98, 157;
populist, 20–23, 29, 32, 35, 38;
populist agenda, 47, 50, 55, 61, 79, 84, 91, 119–20;
populist parties, 13, 17, 29, 79, 106, 114, 158;
rise in populist parties, 13, 31
protest cycles, 98, 100–101
public outreach, 128–32;
grassroots activism, 128–29.
See also Organizational/Opportunity Model (OO) components
pubout. *See* public outreach

QCA, 105, 113, 132, 150;
fuzzy set QCA, 105, 107–8, 110, 118, 122, 131, 133–36, 142, 150

racism(t), 12, 25, 34–35, 38, 41, 121–22;
as a disqualifier for MFG, 39–94;
scientific, 35, 37;
white supremacy, 81
radical right, 27–28, 38, 57, 59, 84, 106, 114–15, 158.
See also far-right
Ragin, Charles, 132, 134, 136, 146, 150.
See also QCA
rebirth, 11, 23, 32, 33, 98, 116, 157, 159
Renton, Dave, 8–12, 26–28, 31–32, 37
Republican People's Party (CHP) (Turkey), 40, 74–75, 94;
three transformations, 75
resource mobilization, 98–99, 101–2
Right Sector, 40, 76–77
Russia, 29, 30, 34, 72, 77, 97, 116, 154–58

Siderov, Volen, 43–45, 115–16.
See also ATAKA
Slovakia, 78–79, 94, 114
Slovak National Party, 40, 78–80, 94
social media, 121–22, 126–31, 141–42
social movements, 16, 25, 36, 87, 91, 98–101;
social movement theory, 91
soft euroscepticism, 15, 21, 37, 65, 74.
See also euroscepticism
Spain, 40, 73–74, 94, 105, 107, 110–12, 118, 122, 12, 126, 130, 154.
See also Podemos
Sternhell, Zeev, 8–9, 12
Strache, Heinz Christian, 57–58, 123.
See also Freedom Party of Austria
Svoboda, 81–82, 94
Sweden, 18, 40, 58, 71, 84, 94, 105, 107, 110, 112, 114
Swedish Democrats, 40, 82, 93–94, 105, 107, 109, 118, 120, 125, 127, 130–31
Swiss People's Party, 28, 40, 84–85, 93, 105, 107, 109–10, 118, 120, 127, 155
Syriza, 37, 40, 73, 86–88, 93–94, 105, 107, 109, 115, 118, 120, 125, 127, 130–32

Tarrow, Sidney, 25, 98, 99, 100, 101, 102, 117;
triangular structure of relations, 100.
See also protest cycles; Political Process Theory (PPT)
testing and analysis of models, 134–51;
analysis of necessary conditions, 136–37, 141;
coincidence, 137, 141–42;
comparison of causal paths, *151;*
conclusion, 150–51;
joint model summary, 149–50;
models tested jointly, 148–50;
of OO model, 139–42, 146–47;
OO model summary, 147–48;
of PP model, 134–39, 143–46;
PP model summary, 146;
truth table analysis, 134, *136*, 139–*40*, *149*;
visual representations, 137–39, 142
Treaty of Lisbon, 4, 64
Treaty of Versailles, 114
True Finns. *See* Finns Party

Tsipras, Alexis, 87–88, 120.
  See also Syriza
Turkey, 40, 74–76, 78, 94
Twitter, 122–29

Ukraine, 40, 76–77, 80–82, 94, 156.
  See also Right Sector; Svoboda
ultra-nationalist(m), 8, 29, 32
United Kingdom (UK), 17, 18, 19, 20, 42, 61, 79, 88, 89, 90, 106, 110, 129, 153;
  British National Party, 2.
  See also United Kingdom Independence Party
United Kingdom Independence Party (UKIP), 4, 13, 18–19, 30, 40, 52, 88–93, 105, 107, 109, 118, 120, 125, 127, 131, 153–54.
  See also Farage, Nigel
us vs. them, 114, 157

Vlaams Belang, 5, 18, 40, 58, 91–93, 105, 107, 109, 118, 120, 125, 128, 131, 139, 146, 148, 156
Von Storch, Beatrix, 42–43, 95.
  See also Alternative for Germany

Weber, Max, 12, 98
Wilders, Geert, 48–50, 120, 124, 127, 132.
  See also Dutch Freedom Party
World Values Survey, 110–12, 118

xenophobia(c), 17, 34, 41–42, 44, 62, 68, 70, 72, 74, 78–79, 81–82, 85, 116, 154

About the Author

Dr. Prebble Q. Ramswell is a political analyst who spent six years working in Counterterrorism for the Central Intelligence Agency. Upon moving to Florida in 2009, Ramswell embraced a new challenge: running for City Council in March 2014. Her successful bid for Councilwoman led to state appointments on the Growth Management and Economic Development Board and the International Relations Committee with the Florida League of Cities. In July 2014, Ramswell was appointed by Florida senate president Don Gaetz to serve on the Board of Directors of the Senate Committee *Florida is for Veterans* and, in 2016, was elected by the council to serve as mayor pro tem.

Ramswell earned Bachelor's in Political Science, Psychology, and Sociology from the University of Houston, a Masters in Liberal Arts/Social Science from Texas Christian University, and a PhD in Political Science/International Development from the University of Southern Mississippi. Ramswell's areas of research include terrorism, extremism, euroscepticism, fascism, nontraditional parties and social movement organizations, and sociopolitical dynamics. A Chickasaw Indian, Ramswell has also written on indigenous peoples and the disappearance of Native American language.

Ramswell and her husband, Tony, live in Destin, Florida, with their daughter, Briar.

CPSIA information can be obtained
at www.ICGtesting.com
Printed in the USA
BVOW08*0821141117
499901BV00002B/8/P

9 781498 546034